# The Thread of Life

*The William James Lectures, 1982*

Richard Wollheim

# THE THREAD OF LIFE

Harvard University Press
Cambridge, Massachusetts

Copyright © 1984 by Richard Wollheim
All rights reserved
Printed in the United States of America
10  9  8  7  6  5  4  3  2

**Library of Congress Cataloging in Publication Data**

Wollheim, Richard, 1923 –
    The thread of life.

    (The William James lectures; 1982)
    Includes indexes.
    1. Life — Addresses, essays, lectures.   I. Title.
II. Series.
BD431.W78   1984      128       84-3807
ISBN 0-674-88757-3 (cloth)
ISBN 0-674-88758-1 (paper)

*For*
*Lizbeth Hasse*
*and Joel Fineman*

# Contents

# Preface

This book is a considerably revised and greatly enlarged version of the William James lectures in philosophy, which I delivered at Harvard University in the early months of 1982, at the invitation of the Department of Philosophy.

I was deeply honoured by this invitation, which also caused me some trepidation. Trepidation only increased when I realized that, if I was to show my gratitude for the invitation, then I should meet the challenge that it presented by taking as the theme for my lectures whatever engaged my most fundamental interests as a philosopher. The topic of living, or what it is to lead the life of a person, very soon suggested itself, for it would allow me not only to treat of a number of questions with which I was deeply concerned but also to order and combine the answers in a new scheme, which, I was becoming convinced, the subject matter required. I have tried to explain all this in Lecture I, which is where I do most to relate my thinking to contemporary discussion. But, once I had decided on this topic, trepidation only transferred itself from the problem I had been facing to the solution I thought I had found for it. How could I possibly do justice to so enormous a topic? And, particularly, how could I even attempt to do so within the narrow confines of philosophy? Inside the kind of philosophy in which I had been originally instructed, I knew what the answer to this last question would be: I couldn't. But, I wondered, might there not be a way of treating this topic that would be faithful, if not to the letter, then at least to the spirit, of early analytical philosophy?

It was at this point, in trying to discharge one debt which I already owed to the Harvard Department of Philosophy, that I incurred a second. For the thought came to my rescue that much of the remarkable work that had come out of the department in the last thirty years or so, done by those whom I was soon to be privileged to think of as my colleagues, had been achieved through a lifting of the very constraint that was troubling me. *They* had not worried whether what they were doing would be counted as philosophy by the conventional norms of the day. They had done what they needed to do, they followed the argument where it led, and, if this is no longer so apparent as it once must have been, the reason is that, after the fact, philosophy formed itself, re-formed itself, around their work, so that this work now appears as the centre of the subject. This thought inspired me.

To these two debts, which were already contracted by the time I arrived at Harvard with my lectures far from prepared, my stay there added a third. The conversation and the criticism of students and colleagues and the presence of a lively and varied audience greatly encouraged me. As I struggled each week to compose my lecture for the coming Monday afternoon, I had the good fortune to get to know Warren Goldfarb, Martha Nussbaum, and Hilary Putnam, and to see more of both Ronald Dworkin, an old friend with whom I had many conversations, and Nelson Goodman, and, all the while, across the street from Emerson Hall, there was the constant delight of the great Ruysdael exhibition organized by Seymour Slive. From Ruysdael I learnt, through many visits, how juxtaposition is also a mode of composition.

Then, in the course of the next eighteen months or so, after I had left Harvard, and as I gradually rewrote the lectures that I had given, I came to realize two things, one of which gave me no pleasure, while the other surprised and intrigued me. The first was how meagre the lectures must have been in their delivered form. The second was that, as they gained in elaboration, as I tried to fill in the argument or to insert related topics, the lectures turned out to be something like a compendium, an anthology, of thoughts I had had over many years of practising philosophy. Ideas that I had once believed in and employed but that had, to all appearance, been forgotten or discarded returned to take up, silently, vociferously, the place in my thinking which, I now had to believe, they had never really vacated. It was a strange experience.

One consequence is that these lectures as they now stand must owe more than I can possibly acknowledge to numerous philosophers who have influenced my ideas in ways that I cannot precisely identify: either through their own work or through comments they have made on work of mine that they have read or heard. In this last respect I have benefited greatly from the hospitality of universities in Great Britain, North America, India, Australia, Scandinavia, and Holland, where I have taught, lectured, or read papers. I should also like to thank psychoanalytic institutes in Great Britain and the United States which have invited me to give papers. Indeed, without the encouragement given me by psychoanalysts who have taken my work seriously, certain lines of thought would never have been pursued. But clearly my greatest single indebtedness of a general kind, the size of which I am able to recognize but which it would be impossible for me to detail, is to the Department of Philosophy at University College London, of which I had the excellent fortune to be a member for thirty-four years. Colleagues, and all those years of students, constantly refreshed my sense of what philosophy is and how it should be pursued. Throughout the time I have known it the department has always exemplified to a high degree the values that happen to please me most: audacity, toleration, a concern for tradition, and a disregard for authority.

There are however more specific debts that I contracted in the period immediately surrounding the delivery of these lectures, and these I am able to acknowledge individually. I am keen to do so. Friends and colleagues who have helped me fall into three groups.

In the first place, there are those who read individual lectures, in whole or in part, and commented on them. I have tried to benefit from their comments, and I should like to thank the following for their generous help: with Lecture I, David Wiggins and Bernard Williams; with Lecture II, Malcolm Budd, Jane Howarth, and Colin McGinn; with Lecture III, Jane Howarth and Herbert Morris; with Lecture IV, W. D. Hart and Herbert Morris; with Lecture V, Herbert Morris, Hanna Segal, and Peter Winch; with Lecture VI, Patrick Gardiner, Colin McGinn, and Leslie Sohn; with Lecture VII, Sam Scheffler, Hanna Segal, David Wiggins, and Bernard Williams; and with Lecture VIII, Myles Burnyeat, John Deigh, Jonathan Lear, and Peter Winch. They at any rate will be able to identify the errors from which they have rescued me.

Secondly, during the preparation of these lectures, their delivery, or the writing of the text, I had prolonged conversations on the theme of the lectures with certain friends and colleagues, who gave their time unsparingly and who entered into the idiolect of my thought with remarkable empathy. I should like to thank Bruce Ackerman, Sylvain Bromberger, Myles Burnyeat, Ronald Dworkin, James Hopkins, Colin McGinn, Sam Scheffler, and David Wiggins.

Thirdly, there are identifiable points of philosophy or fact which I owe to discussion or conversation with the following: Rogers Albritton, A. J. Ayer, Robert Binkley, Keith Campbell, G. A. Cohen, Donald Davidson, Keith Donnellan, Gareth Evans, Jerry A. Fodor, Yair Guttmann, Lizbeth Hasse, Dieter Henrich, Charles Kahn, David Kaplan, Eva Marginter, Sidney Morgenbesser, Thomas Nagel, Martha Nussbaum, John Searle, Hans Sluga, Timothy Sprigge, Barry Stroud, Zev Trachtenberg, Hayden White, and Bernard Williams. Seminars on the philosophy of mind at University College London, the University of California Berkeley, and Columbia University, in the years 1980 – 1983, as well as the Harvard seminar that accompanied the lectures themselves, encouraged and corrected my thinking.

An early version of Lecture III was given to the Oberlin Colloquium in 1970, a later version was delivered as the Rabbi Levi lecture at Princeton in 1973, and the text appeared, first, as 'Imagination and Identification' in my *On Art and the Mind* (Allen Lane, 1973, and Harvard University Press, 1974), and then, rewritten with a change of emphasis that the change in title reflected, as 'Identification and Imagination' in *Freud: A Collection of Critical Essays,* which I edited (Doubleday, 1974). The latter part of Lecture VIII formed the substance of a paper given to the Oberlin Colloquium in 1983, when my commentator was John Deigh, for whose perceptive comments I am very grateful and to whose criticisms I have devoted one section of the lecture: a text of this paper appeared as 'Ourselves and Our Future' in *How Many Questions? Essays in Honor of Sidney Morgenbesser,* edited by Leigh S. Cauman, Isaac Levi, Charles Parsons, and Robert Schwartz (Hackett Publishing Company, 1983). Clearly *The Thread of Life* has a special dependence upon the Oberlin Colloquium, which offers a model of philosophical exchange: I am very grateful for the two invitations I have received. A somewhat shorter version of Lecture VII was delivered as the Fran Gramlich lecture at Dartmouth College in April 1982, and I should like to thank the Department of Philosophy for the invitation. Some of the material used in Lectures III and V appeared in 'Wish Fulfilment' in *Rational Action,* edited by Ross Harrison (Cambridge University Press, 1980), and in 'The Bodily Ego' in *Philosophical Essays on Freud,* edited by James Hopkins and myself (Cambridge University Press, 1982). The penultimate section of Lecture VII derives from 'John Stuart Mill and Isaiah Berlin: The Ends of Life and the Preliminaries of Morality' in *The Idea of Freedom: Essays in Honour of Isaiah Berlin,* edited by Alan Ryan (Oxford University Press, 1979).

I am aware that the present book has many defects, though I might very well disagree with at least the fiercest of my critics about where they are to be found. If I had more years than are at my disposal, I could, perhaps, go some way towards eliminating them. However I am also aware that for the likely readers of this book the value that it will have will be with the project it attempts and the various lines of inquiry that it proposes. It seemed to me, therefore, that any further revision of the text that ran the risk of obscuring the general structure or character of the work without offering any sure gain in precision was to be avoided. In settling for a final state of the text, I had to weigh one capacity or incapacity of mine against another.

Omission is another matter. One way of characterizing in broad terms the ideology of my lectures — I distinguish here between their ideology and their topic — would be to say that they aim at a philosophy of mind, or a philosophical anthropology, of a kind that psychoanalytic theory requires. Hilary Putnam characterized my lectures to me in this way, and, from this point of view, if the philosophy is to be fully adequate to the task, then there are issues on which more, and others on which something, should have been said. These include the formation of the unconscious; the relations between need and desire; pleasure; the essential embodiment of the process of living; sexuality and how it colours the mental states of persons; wit and humour; and the force, or, as Freud called it, the dictatorship, of reason. In a slightly different book it would have been appropriate to have said more about volition and action, more about the emotions, more about the role of language in the development of the person, and something about materialism and something about solipsism. It would have required a change of philosophical persuasion on my part for me to have wanted to discuss the issues of free will, of personal responsibility, or of the metaphysical self, so long, at any rate, as these issues are taken at their face-value. The omission that I regret — though I have no clear idea how I would have made it good, and it is, in turn, an omission bound up with the character of these lectures and the nature of the audience to which they were addressed — is that there is no discussion of philosophical method, of the varieties of necessity, or of several methodological notions which I employ such as analysis, intuition, and essence. By contrast, it is no chance feature of these lectures that in an examination of the person there should be so much space given to abnormality: within our psychology, normality is the name for a tortuously effected and ill-defined achievement. Indeed at one time I thought of expanding Lecture VII, on the psychology of morality, into a study of the other great illusions to which we seem susceptible and against which both philosophy and psychology should recruit themselves: religion, particularly in its monotheistic tendency, the consciousness of race, the justification of war, the rights of parents over the bodies of their children, and male dominance, in which men and women cooperate so effectively.

*The Thread of Life* departs from current practice in that it does not plot its course by reference to the work of other philosophers, either traditional or contemporary. In the present case there are various reasons for writing in this way, but for opening my eyes, many years ago, to its general virtues I should like to express my gratitude to a philosopher to whom, on almost every other point of method or doctrine, I have found myself opposed: Gilbert Ryle. It is a pleasure to thank someone whose freshness of approach and generosity of temperament made him so exemplary a figure. The philosopher of the tradition to whom my intellectual debt is deepest is David Hume: I hope that this is obvious.

Much of the writing and rewriting of this book was done in public places. I should like to express my gratitude to the Café Flore in San Francisco, the Roma in Berkeley, Riverside Studios

London, and the Caffé Bianco in New York City. For nomadic writers such places are the equivalent of the great libraries that scholars tell me about.

My wife, Mary Day, helped me at many points in the preparation of this book. And in carrying, giving birth to, and caring for, our daughter Emilia, which coincided with the delivery and rewriting of these lectures, she provided me with what the more profound thinkers have always recognized as one of the great exemplars of human creativity. I owe much to friends on whom I imposed myself at different moments in the composition of this book: Sylvia Guirey, Maro and Matthew Spender, Sandra Fisher and R. B. Kitaj, Maud Russell, whom I greatly miss, Emma Tennant, Lizbeth Hasse and Joel Fineman, Patricia and Bernard Williams, Susan and Patrick Gardiner, and Stuart Hampshire. To Katherine Backhouse, who typed many, many versions of this book, was forced to master new technology in the preparation of the final version, worked inhuman hours, and, at all times, gave me support, advice, and encouragement, I am, as she knows, more heavily indebted than I can ever say. Finally, I should like to thank the two friends to whom this book is dedicated, without whose love, friendship, and quizzical concern for the outcome of my labours, there would, I am sure, not have been one.

The Oxford University Press has kindly given me permission to reprint a passage from the *Journals of Soren Kierkegaard,* translated and edited by A. Dru (London, 1938); and Sigmund Freud Copyrights Ltd., The Institute of Psycho-Analysis, the Hogarth Press Ltd., and Basic Books Inc. have given permission to reprint two passages from the Standard Edition of the *Complete Psychological Works of Sigmund Freud* (London, 1953–1974).

# I Living

1. An entry in Kierkegaard's *Journal* for the year 1843 opens with these words:

It is perfectly true, as philosophers say, that life must be understood backwards. But they forget the other proposition, that it must be lived forwards.

Kierkegaard goes on:

And if one thinks over that proposition it becomes more and more evident that life can never really be understood in time simply because at no particular moment can I find the necessary resting-place from which to understand it—backwards.

2. What is this thing, this phenomenon, of which Kierkegaard speaks in this passage?

'Life' is his word, and life is what I want to talk about in these lectures.

But Kierkegaard in this *Journal* entry was not talking about, and I shall not be concerned with, just any form of life. Lots of things which aren't even living have lives, such as α-particles, or refrigerators, or the great city of Venice, and of those things which have lives and are living, many don't lead their lives, such as oak trees, or the saints in heaven, or domesticated animals. In these lectures my interest will be confined to lives that are led, and, more specifically, to the lives that we lead, or the lives of persons. I leave it an open question whether any lives except those of persons are led. So there are lives, lives that are led, and lives led by persons, and I shall be concerned only with the last.

Nor is what I have said quite accurate. For I shall not be concerned with the lives themselves, with the things that are led. I shall be concerned, rather, with the leading of them or in the way in which they are led. A life is that which someone in his youth may — at any rate, if he is that kind of person — want to plan, and which then, on his deathbed, he may look back over as all but closed, and my concern is not with that but with how such a thing comes about.

The simplest way of putting the matter, which is not to be taken as a metaphysical claim, is this: There are persons, they exist; persons lead lives, they live; and as a result, in consequence — in consequence, that is, of the way they do it — there are lives, of which those who lead them may, for instance, be proud, or feel ashamed. So there is a thing, and there is a process, and there is a product. The thing, which is a person, is extended in space, and it persists through time. Being spatial, it has spatial parts, but it does not have temporal parts. The product, which is a person's life, is extended in time, and it can be traced through space. Being temporal, it has temporal parts, but it does not have spatial parts. The process, which is the leading of a life, occurs in, though not necessarily inside, the person, and it issues in his life. The life is his life, uniquely his, but others are not excluded from it. Others, leading their lives, lives that are uniquely theirs, may nevertheless participate in his, just as he, unless he is an unsung autochthonous stylite, will participate in theirs. There are innumerable ways in which this can happen. They can think about each other, act upon each other, and make each other's lives better or worse, as well as cause them to be or not to be.

3. The central claim of these lectures is the fundamental status of the process. In order to understand the thing that is the person, or in order to understand the product that is the person's life, we need to understand the process that is the person's leading his life. I shall however illustrate this claim rather than try to establish it, and the content of the claim, or precisely how we are to demarcate the process and to determine just what is and just what isn't the leading of a life, is something upon which I shall not attempt a frontal assault. My hope is that in the course of these lectures the content of the claim will clarify itself.

I shall begin with familiar attempts to answer the questions, What is a person? and What is a person's life? and I shall try to show how in each case difficulties that they run into compel us to take up the issue of what it is to lead the life of a person.

4. Let us start with the question, What is a person?

We are persons, and we know persons. We have friends, lovers, enemies, acquaintances, who are persons. All of us, all of them, have something in common, which is membership of a particular biological species, and, since we also know no human beings who are incontestably not persons, it is easy to conclude that to be a person is to be a human being. They are one and the same thing.

Nowadays this view is under attack: and the attack comes in two forms, one more extreme, the other more moderate. If it is true that, as things stand, all and only human beings are persons, there is, the argument claims, no necessity to this, and then the two forms of the argument diverge in the way they construe the alternative.

In its more extreme form the argument holds that there is no need for a person to be, to be identical with, some one member of any biological species. Arguably, at any given moment there must be some member of a biological species, some creature, with which a person coincides — this is the requirement that a person must be embodied — but at different moments he can coincide with different creatures, which can be different members of the same species or members of different species. In other words, though a person must be embodied, it is not required that he should have the same body throughout his life. In at least certain versions the more extreme form of the argument amounts to the denial that there is, within the conception of a person, any place for what I have called a thing: a person is not a thing, though a person's life will be threaded through things. Such a view is found in certain traditional metaphysical doctrines, like the transmigration of souls, and it reappears in contemporary philosophical fictions of brain fission and brain fusion. I doubt its coherence.

In its more moderate form the argument holds that, for each person, there must be some one single creature or just one member of some biological species with which it is identical, but there is no necessity that this creature should be a member of the human species. The view that persons must be human is branded as one form of speciesism, and it is claimed that there are many thought-experiments whose findings strongly suggest that in our ordinary thinking we totally reject speciesism. (That is to say, not merely do we ordinarily reject the automatic denial of rights to members of species that are clearly non-person species, but we also reject the automatic denial of personhood to members of species that are clearly non-human species.) Certainly there are few suppositions that come more naturally to the human mind than that there could be members of non-human species—'animals' I shall call them from now onwards, imprecisely, but following popular usage—which talk and think and feel and behave, which in effect live, as we do. To the contemporary mind it has come to seem natural to extend such suppositions beyond the biological species to extra-terrestrial creatures. We tell such stories to ourselves, and we delight in having them told to us. In time we outgrow their appeal, but we are not led to think of them as offending against necessity.

5. A compendium of such stories in Ovid's *Metamorphoses,* and I shall ask what sort of antidote this most appealing of poems provides to speciesism about personhood. Do not the stories that Ovid tells show us that to imagine animals, non-human animals, who are persons flouts no necessary truth about persons?

At first sight it may seem strange that I should appeal to the *Metamorphoses* solely for support for the argument in its weaker form, for, insofar as it does lend support to the argument in this form, does it not presuppose the argument in its stronger form? For if Ovid makes credible that there should be members of non-human species who are persons, he does so by telling us stories of persons who were human and are now apparently non-human. If we are to take Ovid's word for it, and to find something credible just because he asks us to imagine it, then we have to recognize that what he asks us to imagine, or the characters of his poems, are persons only if the argument in its strong form is true. For they are not identical with members of any one species, though at different moments they coincide with, or their lives are threaded through, different members of different species.

This may be so. It may be that, if we are concerned with the intelligibility of Ovid's stories as they unfold from beginning to end, this is how we have to think of the characters of these stories, and then it becomes problematic whether we can. But this is irrelevant to my purposes. I am not interested in what Ovid tries to show us about the imaginability of persons' becoming animals having started off as humans: I am interested only in what he actually shows us about animals' being persons, however they became so. My concern is not at all with the first part but exclusively with the second part of each story that Ovid recounts, or with what happens after the metamorphosis. So I ask, Does Ovid in describing the metamorphosed human being describe something that is at once a person and an animal?

The short answer is, No. For my purposes, Ovid's stories fall into two broad categories, but within neither do we find descriptions of what are both persons and animals. But why this is so is instructive.

In one kind of story the metamorphosed human being is an animal, certainly, but isn't — isn't any longer, we should say if we found the metamorphosis intelligible — a person: he or she is a regular animal. Cadmus is a regular serpent, Galanthis is a regular weasel, Arachne is a regular spider. At best these characters retain some trait that once was theirs before the metamorphosis, or that they enjoyed when they were persons, and this trait is woven into the physiognomy of the species to which they belong, but in no case is it sufficient to make its possessor a person. But note that in saying that the metamorphosed human being isn't a person I am not relying on finding the metamorphosis itself unintelligible. My reason is solely to do with how Ovid describes the creature as it is: it has nothing to do with how he claims that it came to be as it is. If Cadmus, Galanthis, Arachne aren't persons, this is so because the same holds true for every serpent, every weasel, every spider. Or so the ages have found.

In the other kind of story, which is more arresting, the metamorphosed human being certainly isn't an animal, and is, but (if I may put it like this) barely is, a person: he or she is a person in the disguise of an animal. This disguise sometimes saves the creature's life, though it can also be its ruin, or its death, and is all but invariably its sorrow. One such case is the gentle Io, turned into a heifer by Jove to conceal her from the cruel fury of Juno, at last making herself known by using her hoof to stamp the two letters of her name in the dust. Or we read of Actaeon the hunter, who is changed into a stag by Diana and has his own hounds set upon him: as they surround him and are about to tear him to pieces, he struggles to cry out his name, at which, he knows, they would fall back, but not a word comes out: *verba animo desunt.* Both Io and Actaeon assume the appearance of an animal, but not the property of being one.

This second kind of story no more settles the imaginability or otherwise of animals who are persons than the first kind, but it throws some light, if obliquely, on just what it is that this asks us to imagine. Io and Actaeon have something to tell us, which Cadmus and Galanthis and Arachne do not, about what it would be for an animal, a non-human animal, to be a person. To extract the moral from the fable we must look again at their predicament.

To begin with, their status as persons is under pressure: they are, as I found myself putting it, barely persons. One place where this shows itself is in the various things which they cannot do but which we would expect of persons. For instance, they cannot say who they are. And that they cannot do these things is because of the disguise they are forced to wear, because of the heavy fashion in which the appearance of an animal sits on them. But, it might be argued, the expectations they disappoint are not expectations that we have necessarily of persons. They are merely expectations that we have of human beings: so that in clinging to these expectations, we betray the very speciesism that appeal to the *Metamorphoses* is intended to test. In order to see whether it is true that Io and Actaeon are barely persons, let us turn from things which they cannot do to various things which they still can do, but only just. For these things bring out more clearly just what it is that their disguise does to them. What they can bring about is a mere simulation of what persons do, and this we register in the trouble we have in understanding it. So, for instance, when we read of Io stamping her name in the dust so that she might be recognized, or of Actaeon defiantly standing at bay against his pack of hounds, we have no difficulty in visualising the hoof furrowing the earth or the great antlered stag stretched to its full height, we have no difficulty in imagining the loneliness of the young tormented girl or the terror that overcomes the huntsman as he faces certain and painful death: but what in each case we cannot grasp is how the outer and the inner fit together. The disguise interposes itself to the detriment of our understanding. What Ovid presents as though it were a single coherent action has become decomposed into, on the one hand, not so much a desire as a wish, and, on the other hand, not so much a piece of behaviour as a mere innervation of limbs. How does one animate the other? And this dislocation spreads outwards across the creature, so that whole areas that we can make sense of only when they are the province of spontaneity become, we have now to believe, regulated by trial and error: facial and bodily expression, the acquisition of perceptual beliefs, the formation and execution of intention. If Io and Actaeon can still do some things that persons can do, they certainly can no longer do them in the way persons do them. Barely doing them, they are barely persons.

Now a consideration of these gross hindrances which Io and Actaeon have to endure uncovers an important fact. For it is not simply that their status as persons is under pressure for reasons connected with the disguise imposed on them, but why we think of these creatures as in disguise, why for us they are not animals but only disguised as animals, is because of what we know that their animal appearance does to them: how little it does for them, and how close it comes to preventing their being persons. Animalhood is for them a disability which strikes them at their core. The matter can be put counterfactually: If it were the case that Io and Actaeon were at once persons (which they barely are) and animals (which they aren't at all), then they would be persons *despite* being animals, and that is impossible. Animalhood — and this is true of non-human animalhood and of human animalhood — cannot run counter, nor can it be indifferent, to personhood.

The central moral to be drawn from Ovid's *Metamorphoses* is that, if it is imaginable that there are animals, non-human animals, that are persons, then they have to be — that is, they have to be imagined to be — persons through, or in virtue of being, animals. The rest of what the *Metamorphoses* has to teach us is by way of amplification of this one lesson.

How are we to take the phrase 'through being an animal'? There are three ways to take it. A creature could be a person just because it is an animal; or because it is the sort of animal it is; or because it is the particular animal that it is.

The first and third interpretations seem wrong, and on two related counts. Both counts concern how the interpretations grant entry into the extension of the concept person. First, there is the scale of the entry, which neither interpretation gets right. The first interpretation offers entry on a scale that is clearly too generous, in that it accepts the whole animal kingdom. The third interpretation offers entry on a scale that is certainly too restrictive, in that it admits animals one by one. But in each case the scale of entry is what it is because of, secondly, the criterion of entry, which again both these interpretations get wrong. For merely being an animal is manifestly an insufficient qualification for being a person. But equally it is hard to see how personhood could depend upon whatever is distinctive of a particular animal.

That the first interpretation is unacceptable is obvious, but the third interpretation may be worth a little more attention. The objection to thinking that animals could be recruited to personhood one by one lies in the fact that only small differences would separate successful candidates from closely related animals: differences that were minor and local. However it doesn't look as though what separates an animal that is a person from an animal that isn't a person could be a difference or differences of this nature. Perhaps the difference could be minor in itself, but its repercussions would have to be felt throughout the animal: the upshot would have to be structural rather than just local.

If at this point we turn to the second interpretation, or that animals that are persons are so through being the sort of animal they are, this seems acceptable on the two counts on which the others prove deficient. For the scale on which it offers entry into the extension of the concept person promises to be reasonable, and the criterion that it invokes for granting entry has just the right character. The interpretation recruits animals to personhood species by species on account of the structure shared by all members of the same species.

The second interpretation certainly fits in with our ordinary thought and speech, and it also serves to explain a certain awkwardness of phrase into which I have been forced. For not only do we in our considered thought think that an animal can be a person only if it belongs to a species that is a person-species, but in our speech we say that it is a person if it belongs to a person-species, however abnormal or degraded it might be. It is a person, even though, if normal or characteristic members of the species were like it, we would not think of that species as a person-species. Just as we do not recruit animals to personhood one by one, so we do not ignominiously discharge them one by one, and it is this fact, which is basically a fact of discourse, though it may also attest to the real character of species, that has led me into the awkwardness of saying that Io disguised as a heifer or Actaeon disguised as a stag are barely persons. They are persons because they are human beings, but, if human beings were characteristically like metamorphosed Io or metamorphosed Actaeon, then the human species would not be a person-species. Since that is not how things are, the human species, in claiming them for itself, continues to claim them for personhood, even *in extremis:* just as, when the time comes, it will claim us, even if senility has by then overtaken us.

Amplified thus far, the moral of Ovid's *Metamorphoses* runs: If a non-human animal is, or is to be, a person, then it must be so through, or in virtue of, being a member of that species to which it belongs. Its species provides it with its credentials, and much of the poignancy that attaches to the stories that Ovid tells arises because of the way in which their characters are required or encouraged to breach this principle.

However the question that remains is how a certain species comes to be selected as a person-species. A species is selected on the basis of its normal and characteristic members and what they are like — but what they are like in what respect? In some respect, we know, that depends on structural features of the creature: in some respect in which Io and Actaeon fall short of what might be expected of them, or in which no such expectations could ever have been formed of, say, the flies that tormented Io or the hounds that tore Actaeon apart.

The answer that it seems hard to postpone any longer is that species are selected as person-species, either in reality or in fiction, on the basis of how their members live, or how they lead their lives: of how they live in virtue of being members of that species.

It is at this point that we are taken back from the question, What is a person? to the question, What is it to lead the life of a person? Whether personhood attaches to a certain species, or to members of that species, depends on whether characteristic members of the species are thereby enabled to live in some appropriate way. What this appropriate way is is something still to be seen — it is the topic of these lectures — but arguments and thought-experiments alike that do not invoke how creatures live under the aegis of their species have, in consequence, nothing to tell us about how person-hood is distributed, and that is the most important single lesson that we can learn from Ovid's great poem.

6. I turn from the question, What is a person? to the question, What is a person's life? in the conviction that, if we do so, the course of our inquiry will be the same. Again, we shall be led back to the question, What is it to lead the life of a person? We can no more establish the nature of the product than we can the nature of the thing without invoking the nature of the process.

One, perhaps the prevailing, way of answering the question, What is a person's life? observes a common form. It proceeds in two stages. First, we deconstruct a person's life into parts. These parts will be, as we have seen, temporal parts, and, conversely, anything that decomposes into temporal rather than spatial parts must be, rather than a person, a person's life. The temporal parts into which a person's life decomposes are appropriately thought of as events: they are events of the kind that make up a person's life. Then the second thing is to try to find a relation that holds be-tween any two such events just in case they are parts of the same life. Thus the question, What is a person's life? is attempted by looking for a unity-relation for a life. A unity-relation is not the relation that any one life has to itself, it is not the relation of identity, but it is the relation that holds between any two parts of the same life. And from the start it must be conceded that any such relation is likely to be highly complex. It will be disjunctive in form, and it will include a number of strange relations that are the ancestrals of more familiar but non-transitive relations. In other words, it will state that the different events in a person's life will be related by this relation *or* by that relation *or* by the other relation: and in stating what these relations are it will replace such intransi-tive relations as 'is, or contains, a memory of' with the transitive 'is the last member of a sequence of events each of which is connected with its immediate predecessor in the sequence by being, or containing, a memory of it and of which the first member is'.

Distinctively, then, prevailing theories of a person's life are relational theories. If we ask why this is so, the answer is that, in adopting this form, the inquiry into a person's life reflects the aim with which it is currently conducted or the specific interest that it sets out to satisfy. Philosophical curiosity about a person's life tends to confine itself to a single issue — the identity of a person's life — and the guiding thought is that the identity-conditions for a life are to be sought not in some enduring property that the life has but in the way or ways in which its parts interrelate. So the identity-conditions get expressed as a unity-relation. It is because of the identity concern that prevailing theories of a person's life are invariably relational theories.

But if we now ask, Why have contemporary theorists of a person's life concentrated on the identity concern? the answer is that the view has prevailed that it is through the identity of a person's life that the identity of a person — a pressing concern — can be explained. Indeed, many philosophers have been so preoccupied that they haven't always noticed whether they were talking about a person and his identity or about a person's life and its identity. They reveal this when they take what they have convinced themselves is a perfectly satisfactory unity-relation for a person's life and re-employ it, without adjustment, as the criterion of identity for a person, and thus finish up with a view of a person as a collection of events spread over time, which cannot be right.

But I mention this so as to put what I have to say in perspective. For I want to consider the different theories of a person's life as though they set out to tell us what we might reasonably expect of them: that is, something, broadly, about the nature of a person's life, what it is. I take them to be metaphysical in inspiration. In consequence I take it that, if a relational theory is true, a person's life is essentially relational, or its nature lies in the way in which its parts are interrelated. Furthermore, since each relational theory is identified by the unity-relation it proposes, once we know which theory is true, we know which relation gives the essence of a person's life or where its nature lies. Unity-relations, it must be emphasised, can be advanced both inside and outside relational theories, but inside relational theories they propose the essence or nature of a person's life.

There is a bewildering variety of such theories, each with its own candidate unity-relation, but some order can be brought to the matter by subsuming the various theories under two very broad and not particularly well-defined cross-classifications. There are psychological theories as against corporeal theories, and there are constructionist theories as against non-constructionist theories.

First, then, psychological versus corporeal theories.

This is generally treated as the fundamental distinction, but we should be prepared to find that, once we stop looking at these theories solely in the light of the identity concern, and see what they can tell us broadly about a life, this way of classifying them may well turn out to be neither so significant nor, for that matter, so straightforward. I explain.

The natural way of taking the classification is this: A psychological theory is a theory that claims that the events of a single life are interrelated by a psychological relation, and then goes on to say what the specific relation is. A corporeal theory is a theory that claims that the events of a single life are interrelated by a corporeal relation, and then goes on to say what the specific relation is. Psychological and corporeal relations are not distinguished by the nature of the terms they relate: for instance, if materialism is right, psychological relations relate corporeal terms. Psychological and corporeal relations are then distinguished by certain properties of the terms they relate. They are distinguished by the properties that their terms must have to be related by them. An example of a psychological relation would be 'is, or contains, a memory of': and an example of a corporeal relation would be 'is spatio-temporally continuous with'. So an example of a psychological theory would be one that held that two events are events in the same person's life if and only if they belong to a sequence of events of which any pair of neighbouring events is such that the later one is or contains a memory of the earlier one. And an example of a corporeal theory would be one that held that two events are events in the same person's life if and only if they belong to a sequence of events of which any pair of neighbouring events are spatio-temporally continuous. However most candidate unity-relations, and in consequence, most candidate theories of a life, will far exceed these examples in complexity.

Now this, the natural, way of understanding the classification is all right, but only if it is understood with this reservation: that it classifies theories of a life according to the primary relation that they assert to hold between the events in a single life, where the primary relation is that which is supposed to give the criterion of identity for a life.

But theories of a person's life don't have to confine themselves to the assertion of a primary relation: they might also assert a secondary relation. They might say something about other ways in which events in a person's life must be related: other ways, interesting ways. Let us first take psychological theories. *Ex hypothesi* any such theory will put forward a psychological relation which — is its claim — pairs events of the sort that make up a life just in case they are events in one and the same life. But such a theory might well go on to specify a corporeal relation which will also hold between any pair of events that belong to the same life. This corporeal relation will, of course, be required to coincide with the relation that the theory asserts as primary. I call this relation the 'secondary relation' of the theory, and I call this development of the theory 'secondary elaboration.' And a precisely similar development can be envisaged for a corporeal theory. In each case, additional metaphysical principles may be required in order to move from the primary relation of the theory to the secondary relation.

Let me illustrate secondary elaboration by recycling the same crude theories of a life with which I illustrated the psychological/corporeal distinction.

So: We have a psychological theory which puts forward as primary the psychological relation 'is, or contains, a memory of'. Now such a theory might then go on to put forward as secondary the corporeal relation 'contains a memory-trace of'. This relation is corporeal, for, if it holds, it holds in virtue of some bodily facts about the terms it relates, and the theory would put it forward in the belief that any pair of events that satisfies the psychological relation must also be such that a memory-trace links the two of them. Or take a corporeal theory which puts forward as primary the corporeal relation 'is spatio-temporally continuous with'. Now such a theory might then go on to put forward as secondary the psychological relation 'is a matter of profound concern to or is profoundly concerned over'. This relation is psychological, for, if it holds, it holds in virtue of some psychological facts about the terms it relates, and the theory would put it forward in the belief that any pair of events that satisfies the corporeal relation must also be such that they will be linked, in a forward-looking or in a backward-looking way, by a special kind of concern.

Secondary elaboration might seem a strange thing, and that would be because it is highly unusual. It is not the way in which, within the philosophy of mind, theories of a life are formulated. They are not formulated in this way because of the narrow concern that such theories are constructed to satisfy: that is, a concern with identity-conditions. For identity-conditions are already given when the primary relation is given: secondary elaboration would be supererogatory. But if theories of a life are animated by a more generous interest in a person's life — for instance, an interest in what kind of thing it is — then secondary elaboration will come to seem appropriate. Just because the psychological interrelations or just because the corporeal interrelations (as the case may be) contain the identity-conditions for a life could not be a good reason to suppose that the complementary set of interrelations have nothing to tell us about the nature of a person's life. How could one possibly think that? — at least so long as one continued to think that the interrelations between the parts of a life hold the key to the nature of a life.

If it by now seems arbitrary to divide a theory of a person's life into two distinct parts, one of which is held to be the core and to contain the identity-conditions, the other of which is thought of as elaboration, this is to overlook such methodological commitments as the theory might have. The theory might insist on isolating as identity-conditions conditions that can be expressed in physical terms, or conditions that are self-evident, or conditions that can be appealed to in resolving practical disputes about the sameness or difference of objects: it might give pride of place to conditions that possess bare sufficiency for identity. The theory, then, might retain a preference for one kind of unity-relation over another: but it should not allow preference to turn to exclusiveness.

There is a natural cunning to the way in which relational theories of a life, psychological or corporeal, deny themselves secondary elaboration. For in the case of most theories that come to mind, the secondary relations they are likely to propose could only expose them to embarrassment: at that point, at any rate, they would lose the support they had found. But then that in turn, I would maintain, is the consequence of their having been developed in the way they have: with a myopic concentration upon the identity concern, reinforced by the conviction that this is to be satisfied by a unity-relation, and with too little thought given to the overall picture they offer of what kind of thing a person's life is.

But is is no aim of mine to pursue the varied difficulties into which relational theories of a life, psychological and corporeal, are likely to run or the parallel tactics that they can employ to get themselves out of these difficulties. I have introduced secondary elaboration and distinguished between the primary and the secondary relations that such a theory of a life might advance just so as to be able to make this claim: that any such theory, any relational theory of a life, must at some point put forward a psychological relation that holds just between the events of a single life, but it does not have, for this reason, to be a psychological theory. For it could be a corporeal theory, putting forward the psychological relation as secondary. But it must put forward a psychological relation because it is only by doing so that it allows itself to be tested against such intuitions as we have of what a person's life is. Told that a certain event, related to me here and now in a certain way, would therefore be part of my life, I could judge this assertion in a number of ways: but the only possible way in which I could judge such an assertion against my intuition is by trying to work out how I would stand psychologically to that event and the person to whom it would belong, and conversely how that person might be expected to stand psychologically to me here and now — though we shall later see that further assurance is needed before even that appeal returns any kind of answer. It is indeed to be noted that most persuasive presentations of a corporeal theory recognize this, in that they implicitly invoke the concern that a person must feel for future states of his present body: it is only when they do this that they have any chance of getting us to agree to their claim that a person goes where his body goes. Psychological relations, then, are crucial, but this doesn't mean that they are primary.

Now I pass to the other classification of theories of a life: constructionist versus non-constructionist theories.

By a constructionist theory I mean a theory — it can be a psychological theory or a corporeal theory — that holds that everything that needs to be said about the events that make up the life of a person — about, that is, such events taken singly — can be said without introducing a person who has them. On a constructionist theory a person arrives on the scene only when there is a set of suitably interrelated events, and then the person is or is identical with that set. The person appears *deus ex machina,* and the *machina* is the unity-relation. On such a theory to say of a single event that it is an event in some person's life is just to say that it is a member of an appropriately interrelated set of events of the kind that make up a life.

By contrast, a non-constructionist theory is a theory that maintains that no event in a person's life, even taken singly, can be adequately described without introducing the person who has it. There is always some person who integrally enters into any event that is of the kind that makes up the life of a person.

It seems to me beyond doubt that only a non-constructionist theory could possibly do justice to the facts of the case. Let me give two considerations that weigh with me, and mention a third.

First, a constructionist theory, not qualified by further metaphysical assumptions enjoying an independent authority, must allow that there could be events of the kind that normally make up a person's life but that turn out to belong to no one's life. They turn out to belong to no one's life because, though they are adequately formed, they are poorly related. So they float, outside lives. This consequence, which, it must be emphasised, it not merely compatible with constructionism but is, *ceteris paribus,* predicted by it, seems unacceptable. Secondly, a constructionist theory seems unable to account for a distinction that we make between two different ways in which we might imagine someone's standing to a certain experience. The distinction is this: We might imagine a certain experience to be someone's, or we might imagine that experience to be in someone. Looking down at a sleeping friend, I could imagine her to wake up and, in doing so, to feel a pain: alternatively I could imagine her to wake up and, as she does so, me to feel a pain in her. These are two distinct things that I could imagine, and that the latter is imaginable is not disproved by its probably being metaphysically impossible. Now the point I wish to make against constructionism is that in either case I am able to imagine the relevant eventuality without having to imagine events to flank it and *a fortiori* without having to imagine it related to flanking events. And this is something that the constructionist must deny. I am not sure precisely how the constructionist would account for each of the two imaginative projects, but he would attempt to do so through invoking differentiating ways in which the experience would be related, in the one case, to events in my friend's life and, in the other case, to events in my life. But the distinction I have in mind seems anterior to such relations, and this is fatal to constructionism.

A third consideration against constructionist theories depends on a deeper issue, of which I must postpone discussion until the next lecture. This consideration is the dependence of mental states on underlying mental dispositions and the further fact that these dispositions must be housed somewhere—and where else could they be housed but in a person?

I must, parenthetically, make it clear that my present objections are objections to constructionism about the person. They are not, and are not intended to be, objections to constructionism in general—though I might also have such objections.

If however it is true that a constructionist account of the events that constitute a person's life is unacceptable, so also must be, by extension, any theory of a life that confines itself wholly to the relations between such events. For what makes the description of any one such event incomplete unless it includes some reference to the person who enters into it surely also makes any description of a life incomplete if it refers only to the relations between the events that constitute it and makes no reference to the person who enters into each such event. If there are two events that belong to the same life and a person necessarily enters into each of these events, a theory of a life cannot confine its attention to the two events: it must also say something about the persons who necessarily enter into the events. It might say something about how one of these persons is related to the other, or it might say something about how what is true of one constrains or determines what is true of the other. Either way round, the original relational theory, defined by the unity-relation that it proposes, is supplemented.

A highly imperfect analogy may help to clarify this last point. Let us suppose there to have been a small alpine village which contained its own school of painters marked by a strong artistic tradition. Each painter painted the same general subject: that is, the life of the local saint broken down into a very large number of consecutive scenes. At the same time, despite the striking stylistic similarities between their work, each painter set great store — as indeed did the village as a whole — on authorship, and he would have thought his work to be traduced if it were confused with another's. Then a landslide destroyed the village and brought the activity of its painters to an end, and it was a few hundred years before scholars started to study the body of work that survived. When they began to do so, they early on appreciated that individual paintings belonged in series, and they set about reconstructing a number of such series by first carefully analysing the different scenes that the paintings represented — the changing costume, the age of the saint, the successive mutilations he underwent — and then ordering the paintings so that each series told a complete story of the saint's life narrated according to some one of the many slightly differing legends. What these early scholars did not allow for was that different painters never worked co-operatively on the same series: each series was the work of just one artist eager for personal fame. Once scholarship recognized this, then the principles by which the paintings were ordered into series radically changed. Scholars still continued to look at the content of each painting to make certain that one took up the story where its predecessor left off, but they now supplemented this method by insisting on first establishing the authorship of each painting, and then seeing that there was common authorship throughout any one series. From now onwards there were two criteria employed for inclusion in a series: sameness of authorship, and narrative continuity. Those art historians who continued to appeal uniquely to narrative considerations were regarded as primitive.

I hope that this analogy illustrates the point that, once it is recognized that persons necessarily enter into the events that make up the lives of persons, a purely relational theory of a life will not do. For, in addition to the relation that holds between different events in the same life, some supplementary requirement must be laid on who enters into these events. But if the analogy illustrates this point, it does more: it makes a very strong recommendation about what this requirement should be. What should be required is that one and the same person enters into each and every event that belongs to the same life. Interrelatedness of event is supplemented by identity of person.

The proposal is obvious, but it is exposed to an obvious difficulty. But, first, I must make the point that, if a relational theory is supplemented in this way, so that both interrelatedness and identity have to be satisfied for events to be events in one and the same life, the overall theory cannot continue to be thought of as a properly relational theory. It would not, for instance, follow from the theory being true that a person's life is essentially relational. I say this not for the dubious reason that identity is not a relation. My reason is that, within the supplemented theory, the terms between which the identity-relation is required to hold are not parts of a person's life: it is the person himself who provides the terms to the identity-relation. And this is not the right kind of relation for a relational theory: identity is not and could not be a unity-relation.

I turn to the obvious difficulty to which, I said, the new proposal is exposed. A relational theory supplemented — let us call it that — finds the essence of a person's life in two conditions. They are interrelatedness of event and identity of person. How do these two conditions hold together?

A standard way of putting such an objection would be to ask, What guarantee do we have that the two conditions will not come apart? Could we not have one and the same person entering into events that are not themselves appropriately interrelated? Or could we not have events that are appropriately interrelated but into which different persons enter? And if either of these eventualities came about, what would the theory then rule?

Now such an objection could be raised against any theory of a person's life that required multiple conditions of satisfaction. It could, for instance, be an objection to any strictly relational theory that involved itself in secondary elaboration. My objection, then, is more specific, more substantive. It asks how the two conditions fit together into a theory. And if this raises the question of what happens if the two conditions fall apart, what it also asks is, if they are both satisfied, what separate weight do the two conditions pull, or how they conjointly contribute to the picture of a person's life.

It is at this stage that, I suggest, we are led back from the question, What is a person's life? to the question, What is it to lead the life of a person? A return from the product to the process can afford us a view of the matter which places the two conditions in some unified perspective. In a picture dominated by the living of a life, each condition begins to assume its own distinctive place. The picture realigns itself in two stages.

The first stage is that interrelatedness of event will come to seem derivative. It will come to seem that such interrelatedness as is to be found between the events that make up a single life is something that comes about through the way in which persons lead their lives. This reduces at once the importance of the unity-relation and the importance of discovering the unity-relation. It ceases to seem important whether we can identify a relation that holds between events of the appropriate kind and gives a necessary and a sufficient condition for their being events in the same life, once we think of this relation as only the effect of what is really important.

So if we couldn't find the relation, we might become increasingly willing to ascribe this to a failure of our descriptive powers. The relation we might feel is too difficult to make explicit, and we might cease to worry about our failure so long as we could find something to say about the underlying process which imprints this pattern upon the lives that it produces. Or, again, if we appeared to discover such a relation and then found that it or some rough copy of it got stamped across different lives, this wouldn't worry us if it could be shown that this simulation came about not as a result of the process of living but through, say, a use or misuse of technology. If interrelatedness of what promised to be the appropriate kind occurs in some synthesized fashion, which itself transcends our comprehension, it is irrelevant.

If all this is true, then it looks as though there is a fundamental error in all relational theories of a life, an error which goes beyond mistakes of detail in the construction or formulation of the unity-relation. It is that they take a symptom for an essence. That which a person's life derives from the way in which it comes about they treat as itself constitutive of such a life.

The second stage in the transformation brought about by adopting the perspective of the process is that the identity of the person comes to seem less derivative than interrelatedness of event. For, given that the process must be embodied, questions such as whether the process can, once under way in a given person, be transferred from the body of that person to that of another, whether it can or cannot outlive the original body, whether it can or cannot be outlived by that body, must bear directly on the nature of the process, which interrelatedness does not. But it must be emphasized that what the correct answers to these questions are is a matter of inquiry: an inquiry, though, which cannot be conducted until we have a clear idea of what we are asking them about, or what the process is.

7. I have now returned twice to the question, What is it to lead the life of a person: once from the question, What is a person? once from the question, What is a person's life? In both cases I did so in support of a claim made at the beginning of the lecture that, whether we start with the thing or the product, inquiry returns us to something intermediate between the two, or to the process, which takes place in the thing and results in the product. I hope that by now I have said enough about this claim to make its character, if not its content, clear.

However I am not ready to leave the second part of the claim. For if what prompted the return from the nature of a person's life to what it is to lead the life of a person was the failure of relational theories to give an adequate account of what a life is, I want to consider the complement of this failure, for such theories also fail to give us an adequate account of death.

This second failure reveals itself in the following way: Let us suppose that there is a unity-relation, or a relation that holds between any two events that make up the same life. If this is so, then, when a person dies, there will be no future event that is related to the present and past events in his life as each of them is related to every other one. But it cannot be the case that, of these two facts, the second, or the absence of appropriate interrelatedness between events, explains the first, or death. It must be either that the first fact explains the second, or that there is a common explanation for the two. Yet a relational theorist, who sees in the unity-relation the essence of a person's life, must think that, when a life comes to an end, it does so not only when but because this relation ceases to hold. Relational theory, in other words, commits him to a relational account of death as well as to a relational account of life — and whatever are the implausibilities of the latter, those of the former are glaring.

This commitment is seldom explicitly acknowledged, but it is implicitly invoked in a form of argument that relational theorists tend to favour for settling differences between themselves or testing candidate unity-relations. For one way in which such differences might have been argued over is inductively, or by examining a large number of varied cases of lives and seeing what relation holds, or what relations don't hold, between any two events in the same life. But relational theorists prefer to argue by employing a special type of thought-experiment. One reason is that it is more economical to do so, but another reason is that, whenever such a thought-experiment is run and yields a decisive result, then, even if this result is negative or refutes a particular relational theory, it confirms relational theory as such. Any decisive result confirms relational theory because the way in which the result is reached, or the design of the thought-experiment, presupposes relational theory. And in presupposing relational theory, the design of the experiment assumes the relational account of death as well as the relational account of life: it draws on both.

The thought-experiments have, then, a common design, and each one falls into two parts. In the first part, the subject is asked to imagine a situation of some variable degree of complexity. Central to this situation is a sequence, or more than one sequence, of events of the kind that make up lives, and one of these sequences, or the one sequence (if there is only one), exemplifies the candidate unity-relation. Probably various bizarre circumstances surround the central situation. Then, in the second part of the thought-experiment, the subject is asked, either directly or obliquely, whether the sequence of events exemplifying the candidate relation is a person's life. He is expected to answer this question solely on the basis of what he has been told about the central situation, and the bizarre circumstances have been introduced, like certain erotic sculpture in Indian temples, to concentrate the mind even more strenuously on the central situation. The question is put to the subject directly when the sequence exemplifying the candidate-relation is singled out, and he is then asked, Does this sequence amount to a person's life? The question is put obliquely when, the sequence with the candidate-relation once again having been singled out, the subject is then asked something like, Should each event in this sequence be a matter of personal concern to whoever it is to whom any earlier event in the sequence belongs? Framed either way, but always by getting the subject to match what he is inclined to say against what he has been asked to imagine, the experiment sets out to tap certain deeply entrenched views that persons are supposed to have about the nature or the essential course of their lives. The subject is not, of course, asked for these views, which, it is conceded, it might not be in his power to give, but the questions he is asked are designed to engage with them.

To make the design of these thought-experiments fully explicit, we may credit them with a set of assumptions and a rule. The assumptions are assumptions that they make about the subject, the rule is a rule that they impose on him, and the imposition of the rule is held justified by the truth of the assumptions. The rule and the assumptions are closely connected, and jointly account for the favour in which these thought-experiments are held by relational theorists.

The assumptions are that we—'we', for each one of us is a potential subject for such a thought-experiment—having imagined what we have been told to, shall respond readily and unambiguously to the questions asked of us: that the responses we give will prove to be consistent, both over time and with one another: and that we are prepared to attach weight to these responses. And behind these assumptions is another, to the effect that we have intuitions that, brought to bear exclusively on the relations holding between events of the kind that make up lives, will be able to pronounce decisively whether a given sequence of such events belongs to one life, or to more than one life, and, if so, to how many. The rule, which completes the design of the thought-experiments, is that the subject must respond to the questions put to him solely on the basis of these intuitions: he must not seek out or make use of anything other than relational—that is, unity-relational—information.

Now insofar as any thought-experiment conforming to this design yields a decisive result, even if only of a negative kind, it confirms relational theory. It confirms the view that whether a certain sequence of events is a person's life or not is just a matter of how the events are interrelated, and it does so equally when it confirms and when it refutes some specific view about what this interrelation is. That it does so follows from the decisiveness of the result plus the way in which the result was reached. For it was reached by the subject first considering solely how the events in a certain sequence are interrelated, then bringing his intuitions to bear on these relational facts, and then deciding on the basis of them whether the sequence is a person's life. But an answer reached this way could be decisive only if, in turn, relations were essential or relational theory was true. Hence the thought-experiment presupposes relational theory.

But sometimes, because of the bizarre circumstances that these thought-experiments tend to introduce, the subject will find himself having to decide not just whether the experimental situation confronts him with only one life or with two simultaneous lives, but whether it confronts him with two consecutive lives: in other words, he will sometimes have to decide whether death has intervened. And since this is something that he has to decide as part, or in the course, of giving a decisive answer about the candidate relation, the design of the thought-experiment will insist that he decide it in just the same way, on just the same information, as he decides that issue: that is to say, by—solely by—bringing his intuitions to bear on the relational facts. The rule of the thought-experiment tells him that he must do this, and the assumptions assure him that he can. In other words, the assumptions tell him that the relational account of death is true, and the rule tells him to invoke it. Hence the design of the thought-experiment reveals the generally concealed commitment of relational theory.

My claim is that we do not have intuitions of the kind that these thought-experiments require of us: that is to say, intuitions about death based purely on relational facts. Since I have previously contended that the relational account of death is deeply implausible, this claim will be no surprise. But the two points are different, and to see that they are, to illustrate my present claim and to consider a powerful retort, I want to examine the issue in a concrete situation. For these purposes I select a pair of thought-experiments which, because of their extreme skill and ingenuity, have come to play an important part in disputes between relational theorists, whatever may have been their original aim. We owe these thought-experiments to Bernard Williams. I shall set them out only in as much detail as is necessary for my purposes.

Each thought-experiment requires the subject to imagine a certain situation. The first experiment requires him to imagine a situation that unfolds thus:

A and B, two persons, are told that an operation will be performed on each of them. In the course of the operation each person's memories and such like things will be extracted from him and placed in the body of the other. This means that, the operation over, there will be an A-body person (with B's memories and so on) and a B-body person (with A's memories and so on). Then one of these will be tortured and the other rewarded. Before the operation each person is asked how he would want, on strictly selfish grounds, the torture and the reward to be distributed between the two body-persons. And after the operation and the distribution of torture and reward, each body-person is asked whether he got what he wanted.

So much for the situation. Then, in the second part of the thought-experiment, the subject is asked to settle, in the light of his intuitions, two separate things: first, what distribution of torture and reward each person should ask for before the operation, and secondly, after the operation, under what actual distribution of torture and reward each body-person should say that he had got what he had previously asked for. The subject is in effect expected to do this by saying what he would say in the different positions.

For the second thought-experiment the situation changes, and it unfolds thus:

There is only A. A is told that he will undergo an operation, in the course of which his memories and such like things will be removed and beliefs about a past other than those beliefs he now has will replace them. 'Then' he is told, 'you will be tortured'.

And in the second part of this thought-experiment the subject is asked to settle, again in the light of his intuitions, just one thing: whether A should be frightened by what he has been told, or whether A should simply feel sorry for the A-body person to whom all this will happen. Again, the subject is in effect expected to do this by saying what he would say in A's position.

I suggest that, if we imagine ourselves as subjects in these thought-experiments, a question that we are likely to ask ourselves is whether, in the first situation, A and B survive their operation, and whether, in the second situation, A survives his operation, or whether in either case, death intervenes. We shall feel that, be-cause of the bizarre circumstances, we need to know this before we can bring to bear on the two central situations such intuitions as we have. In the second situation A, it is true, is told that he will survive his operation: but we aren't told this, we are told only that he is told this, so we want to know whether what he is told is correct.

Now the design of the thought-experiment will reject our re-quest out of hand. The rule will tell us that we may not make use of anything except relational information such as *ex hypothesi* we already have, and the assumptions will assure us that such infor-mation suffices. Furthermore, rule and assumptions will combine to tell us that we are misguided in trying to split the task set us into two. We do not need first to have information about the death or survival of the participants before we then go on to bring our intuitions to bear on the relational facts so as to settle such residual questions as where, or in what corporeal guise, the participants are to be found. The two lots of questions are to be answered in one.

But as a potential subject in the thought-experiment, I now

reply that this is unconvincing, and must seem so to anyone unless he has been convinced on general — that is, non-thought-experimental — grounds of the truth of relational theory. (And it might seem unconvincing even then.) I cannot, solely on the basis of relational information, settle issues of survival. I have no sure way of matching what I say to what I imagine. For instance, no matter what rupture of interrelatedness I imagine in a sequence of events, I could always imagine life going on through it: I could always imagine its being survived.

But, it will be countered, there are many persons who, enlisted as subjects in these thought-experiments, have no difficulty in settling, decisively, the issues of death or survival that come up. They have no difficulty in saying whether, in the first situation, A and B survive, or whether, in the second situation, A survives. And they don't ask for special information: they just answer the questions they are asked on the basis of what they have been told. Why should their performance carry less weight than mine?

Now I do not deny that there may be subjects in thought-experiments like these who can answer questions about death or survival without difficulty. My only claim is that they cannot do so by observing the rule of the thought-experiments. They must employ some other way of doing so, and I can think of two possibilities.

One way is that the subject might simply assume an answer to the questions that I claim he has no means of answering out of the materials supplied to him. Not having been told whether death intervenes, he takes it for granted that it has not, and that all the participants in the imagined situations survive. He would, we may assume, concede this if he could recognize that this is what he had done — which he might not be able to do. Thought-experiments like those under consideration do not make good faith easy to practise.

The other way the subject could employ is subtler, and it meets one requirement of the thought-experiment which the first breaches: it does not split what the subject is asked to decide into two. There is, with this way, no question of the subject first determining, on one kind of information, whether, say, A and B survive their operation, and then determining, on another kind of information, where or in what corporeal guise they do so. Nevertheless the rule of the thought-experiment is not observed.

The way is this: The subject has a firm belief about what the unity-relation is; he surveys how in the two situations the various events that are ascribed to A and B and the A-body person and the B-body person are related; then he works out which of these patterns of interrelatedness exemplify the unity-relation he believes in; and then, on the basis of these calculations, he answers the questions that the thought-experiments require him to decide if they are to yield decisive results. Now it may very well be that the answers such a subject gives will conform to what the assumptions predict: they will be ready, consistent over time and with one another, and confident. They may even be true. Nevertheless in responding in this way the subject has not kept to the rule of the thought-experiment, and it is crucial to see why. That rule requires that the subject should respond to the questions put to him by bringing his intuitions to bear on certain relational facts, such as that an event ascribed to A stands in such-and-such a relation to another event ascribed to the B-body person. And he offends against this rule when he introduces as information not a relational fact but a fact about relations, such as that such-and-such a relation is the unity-relation.

This may seem a very fine point. But it isn't. For if the information that the subject makes use of consists of facts about relations as well as relational facts, the only way in which he can draw upon them conjointly is to construct an argument in which the former constitute the major, and the latter the minor, premise. The subject will then answer the questions put to him syllogistically, not on the basis of intuition.

But why does this matter? Is the subject more than in minor default of a rule? And the answer is that it is only if the thought-experiments yield decisive results, and do so on the basis of the kind of intuition that the rule specifies, that they confirm relational theory. For it is only then that they presuppose relational theory. Then they presuppose relational theory because then they draw upon intuitions that would not be feasible unless relational theory were true. If the thought-experiments yield decisive results by any means other than subjects' intuitions, relational theory is left, confirmationally, just where it was before such thought-experiments were introduced into the argument.

But if the thought-experiments yield decisive results through a syllogism in which the major premise is the fact that such-and-such a relation is the unity-relation, and the minor premise is that this relation holds or doesn't hold between certain events, doesn't that also, to some degree or other, confirm relational theory? And the answer is that it doesn't. The mere existence of a unity-relation does not confirm relational theory. For the unity-relation might not give the essence of a person's life, which is what relational theory requires. What confirms relational theory is not the existence of a unity-relation, but the register of this relation in our psychology in the form of a capacity for intuitions of a certain kind. And this we seem not to have.

But have I shown this?

For, it might be maintained, the most I have shown is that we do not have intuitions about death. In cases where death can be dismissed as a likelihood, do we not have intuitions, which, brought to bear solely upon relational facts, identify the course of a life?

The crucial question is whether it is possible that there should be intuitions that adjudicate the application of some concept — say, a person's life — but are declarative only under certain conditions — say, when death is not a likelihood. If we do not have intuitions based on relational information that indicate the intervention of death, how can we have corresponding intuitions about the course of life? I conclude that we cannot. We cannot, that is to say, have intuitions whose existence shows us anything about what a person's life essentially is. We may have certain impure or hybrid intuitions, whose character is hard to grasp, and which I had in mind in saying that, of relations holding within a life, psychological relations must be crucial.

Thus far my argument has been that, the evidence of certain thought-experiments seemingly to the contrary, we do not have intuitions that, basing themselves exclusively on relational information, pronounce decisively about the course of a person's life. Accordingly, relational theory is deprived of a form of support that the existence of such intuitions would have given it. But does from the absence of such intuitions the falsity of relational theory follow? Relational theory is a necessary condition of such intuitions, but is it a sufficient condition?

This is what relational theorists themselves assume, or at least those who favour the kind of thought-experiment that I have been discussing. In thinking that we can, at least in principle, find the true relational theory by appeal to such thought-experiments, they must believe that, if one relational theory is true, hence if relational theory is true, then what these thought-experiments presuppose — that is, the existence of the intuitions upon which they rely — must be the case. And I am inclined to think that they are right. I am inclined to think that, if persons' lives were essentially relational, then the recognitional skill that we would have for lives would take the form of intuitions that dispensed with everything except relational information. If that is so, then the foregoing considerations amount to a weighty argument against relational theory.

I started this section with a consideration of death, and how inadequately relational theory is obliged to construe it. I shall return to the topic of death only at the end of these lectures, and then with some further thoughts about our intuitions on the topic, or the absence of them.

8.  The time has come when I must say something, however brief or schematic, about what it is to lead the life of a person.

But first a word on my right to say it. It is clear that in talking about the way persons live, I have some authority, and that is connected with the way I live. But what is the connection? There are two versions of what my authority is, and they differ in the order of the explanation they offer. On one version, I live as a person, and my authority derives from this fact. My authority consists in the knowledge that I have of the way I live. On the other version, I live as I live, and the fact that this counts as living as a person itself derives from the authority I have: though from this fact I derive further authority, which consists in knowledge of how I live. The second version can be purged of its worst features. It is not necessary to say that I decide or stipulate that the way I live shall be the way persons live. Nor is it necessary to say that the phrase 'living as a person' is covertly indexical, or always contains a reference to the way in which the speaker or writer lives. It could simply be that a preoccupation with our own interests and needs, an inescapable commitment to our own perspective, compels us to see the world in such a way that only we and those who live like us can be regarded as persons. But, however purified, the second account seems to me wrong: for it cannot give a coherent account of what this preoccupation, or this commitment, is without falling back into some much cruder, or more overtly relativistic, version of itself. This is not to say that the first version is without its real difficulties.

I move to my preliminary account of what it is to live as a person.

A person leads his life at a crossroads: at the point where a past that has affected him and a future that lies open meet in the present. But this, if true of the person, is true of every other thing, animate creature and inanimate object.

To see why the posture of hanging between the past and the future is so special for a person, we have to introduce another interaction: that between a person's occurrent transient mental states and his underlying persistent mental dispositions. For the influence of the past is carried by mental dispositions that are set up in the person and persist. Examples of such dispositions would be beliefs, desires, emotions, memories, phantasies. However, when the influence of the past, stored in the dispositions, is actually exerted over the person, it is not exercised directly by the dispositions — or, if it is, this is just a marginal case. Standardly the influence passes through present mental states in which the dispositions manifest themselves. This can come about in two ways. One way is this: The past can colour the mental state — of which it can therefore be said that it, the mental state, wouldn't be as it is if it weren't for the past. When this happens the past doesn't obtrude into the mental state, though the mental state may somehow put the person in mind of the past. This happens to varying degrees in perception, emotion, and phantasy. But the other way in which the influence of the past percolates through mental states requires the past to be more obtrusive. The past doesn't merely colour the mental state, but it or its delegate comes to occupy it, and the person is aware that this is so. This happens in recollection — or memory in the narrow sense of the term. And there are ways in which the past can influence the person which are intermediate between or combinatory of these two ways.

That the past influences the person largely through mental states is responsible for much of how we live. It means that this influence has a peculiar vivacity and a peculiar variability. Vivacity is secured by the mysterious fact that mental states have a phenomenology. Variability is secured by the fact that one and the same mental disposition can manifest itself in mental states with varying degrees of vivacity. And vivacity accentuates variability in that not only do mental dispositions manifest themselves in mental states, but mental states can modify mental dispositions. Outbursts of jealousy can strengthen jealousy: love satisfied can weaken love: hope can reinforce optimism: the exploration of phantasy can shake the hold of phantasy.

But to understand fully, properly, how the interaction between a person's past, present, and future is realized through the interaction between his mental dispositions and his mental states, we have to introduce a third case of interaction: that between the various systems of the mind: between the conscious, the preconscious, and the unconscious.

# II On the Mind

1. In my first lecture I said that the topic of these lectures would be living, or what it is to lead the life of a person. And I distinguished living from, on the one hand, the person who lives and, on the other hand, the life that is led. The person is a thing, the life is a product, and my topic is a process — a process which occurs in the person and from which the life issues. To understand the process we have to take account of three characteristic interactions which influence how we live. They are the interactions between the person's past, present, and future: between his mental dispositions and his mental states: and between the conscious, the preconscious, and the unconscious systems of his mind. And these interactions occur at once in the mind and in a body. Living is an embodied mental process.

In this lecture I want to produce a schematic description of the mind, a taxonomy of mental phenomena which in later lectures I shall draw upon and elaborate somewhat. My present task is to expound it, not to employ it.

2. Mental phenomena may initially be divided into three broad categories: *mental states, mental dispositions,* and *mental activities.*

Mental states are episodic or transient phenomena. They occur at a time. More than one mental state may occur in the same mind at the same time, but there are very real limits of load on the mind, and in the case of certain types of mental state (for instance, thoughts) there cannot ordinarily be more than one such state at the same time in the same mind. The occurrence of a mental state is one example of what in the last lecture I spoke of as an event in a person's life. Examples of mental states other than thoughts are perceptual experiences, attacks of dizziness, dreams, and moments of terror, amusement, lust, or despair. Alongside mental states we should think of partly mental states, which are events in a person's life that include but are not identical with a mental state of his: examples of partly mental states are actions and painful injuries.

Mental dispositions, by contrast, are persistent phenomena, which manifest themselves intermittently. They do not occur, nor are they events. They are mutable. Dispositions have histories, which are made up of events, and these histories are varied. Dispositions differ from one another in their beginnings, in their ends, and in what lies in between. Dispositions differ in their beginnings, for some are innate, some arise in the mind, and some are acquired. They persist in different ways, for some remain constant and some change, and they may mature or decline or fluctuate. And dispositions differ in their ends, for some last out the person and some come to an end within his life, and they may do so through decay, or through consummation, or they may be eradicated. Different kinds of history go with different kinds of disposition. And a word on the word 'disposition' itself. By calling a mental phenomenon a disposition I am not in any way impugning its reality: I am not suggesting that a dispositional property is less than a categorical property, or that the logical form of sentences attributing dispositions to persons is conditional. Examples of mental dispositions are knowledge and belief, emotions, desires, habits, virtues and vices, and skills.

Mental activities are activities by means of which we bring about mental states or bring mental dispositions into being or initiate bodily movements. They are not necessarily free, nor does it necessarily make sense to ask whether they are voluntary or intentional. Examples of mental activity are thinking a thought, volition or trying to perform an action, attention, repression, introjection.

If these lists of examples of the different mental phenomena seem heterogeneous, this is so because they are, and they are so, in part, for a reason worth considering. In compiling them I have mixed up, as happens in taxonomies of the mind, formal and concrete mental concepts. Formal mental concepts don't pick out actual mental entities at all but serve as cross-headings in a more extended classification: they classify mental concepts rather than mental entities. Examples of formal mental concepts are 'mental state', 'mental disposition', and 'mental activity'; also 'virtue', 'emotion', and, on the normal understanding, 'perception'. Concrete mental concepts pick out determinable mental entities. Examples would be 'pain', 'desire', 'thought', 'introjection'. And determinate mental entities are then arrived at by adding to these concrete concepts a term for an object. Examples would be 'pain in the ankle', 'the desire to burn down the library', 'the belief that winter is upon us', 'introjecting a parental figure'. We do not reach determinate mental entities by adding a term for an object to a formal mental concept, such as 'emotion' or 'virtue'.

3. There are various important attributes that characterise mental phenomena, and in doing so help to determine their nature. I shall consider five such attributes. They are *intentionality: subjectivity: psychic force* and *psychic function: quality of consciousness:* and *significance.* I shall go through this list item by item, to explain what I mean by the terms as well as to say what the attributes are.

4. First, intentionality.

The intentionality of a mental phenomenon is its thought-content.

That mental phenomena have a thought-content receives confirmation from two different sources: from reflection and its deliverances, on the one hand, and, on the other hand, from the fact of opacity, or that characteristically (though certainly not invariably) reports of mental phenomena — that is to say, both first- and third-person reports — contain contexts in which substitution of one expression for another describing or designating the same thing does not necessarily preserve truth-value.

How does opacity provide evidence for intentionality? It does so because the likeliest explanation for the occurrence of such contexts in reports of mental phenomena is that we want our reports to capture and preserve a thought: and we want them to capture and preserve not just what the thought is of, or its object, but how the thought presents its object — we want to capture the very thought itself. By refusing to let us, in reporting a friend's beliefs and desires, be indifferent between saying 'Tom believes that the figure is triangular' and 'Tom believes that the figure is trilateral', or between saying 'Tom would like the author of the pamphlet brought to trial' and 'Tom would like his brother brought to trial' (where his brother wrote the pamphlet), opacity enables us in each case to bring how a certain thought presents what it is of—it allows us to bring the very thought itself—into the report. And since the thought that opacity enables us to capture can only be a thought on the part of the person to whom the mental phenomenon belongs, a thought (in these examples) that Tom has, and not a thought that we have, the natural conclusion to draw is that the thought belongs to, or is a part of, the mental phenomenon itself. The thought that opacity holds captive is part of Tom's belief, or part of Tom's desire. Since opacity always leads us to some thought that the mental phenomenon that is being reported contains, the fact of opacity leads us to conclude that every mental phenomenon has a thought-content, has intentionality.

That intentionality is revealed by language—that is, by the language that we use to report mental phenomena—does not show that intentionality is dependent on language—that is, dependent on possession of language by the person to whom the mental phenomena belong. A language-user reporting on the intentionality of another can pair off fine differences in thought-content with fine differences in language. But that doesn't require that the thought whose differences he thereby records must itself be in language or even that the thinker must possess a language. On the contrary, we have much reason to believe that there are creatures who don't have language but can entertain mental phenomena with a thought-content, though perhaps one without fine differences. Infants must be like this, unless their lives are radically discontinuous with what happens to them later: and so also, it would seem, are some kinds of animal. Language, then, is not necessary for intentionality. Nor is it sufficient. More specifically, the possession of language is not sufficient for a rich form of intentionality. The difference that I have in mind here is between a form of intentionality where the thought-content of a mental phenomenon can allow reference to individuals or permits singular reference, and one where it doesn't or is purely general. The difference between the two forms of intentionality corresponds, I am inclined to think, to the difference between a creature who can think thoughts and one to whom thoughts merely occur, but my present point is solely that the possession of language does not suffice for the creature to have mental phenomena whose thought-content includes reference to individuals. For a rich form of intentionality the possession of a language is ineffectual unless the person has a history such that he has, at however many removes, been in touch with the individual that he refers to. Singular reference may exploit language, but it is not one of its natural resources. Language may enable a person to communicate just what person or thing he has in mind, but it does not by itself enable him to have it in mind.

The intentionality of mental phenomena is important because it is their intentionality that allows them to be internally related to one another or that makes for what has been called the holism of the mental. Examples of such internal relations are when two beliefs conflict, or when a desire and a belief generate a more specific desire, or when a desire is consistent with a fear, or when a perception confirms a hope.

Do all mental phenomena have intentionality? Some have claimed that there are exceptions, at least among mental states, and they usually cite sensations. Against this I am inclined to think, though what I say does not hang on it, that intentionality is one factor in the minimal homogeneity of mental states. If one mental state has intentionality, homogeneity seems to require that its successor does too. And universal intentionality would secure the integrity of mental holism. But, if it is claimed that all mental phenomena have intentionality, the claim doesn't have to be that they invariably contain whole thoughts. The application of a concept may be all that there is to it. Pain, or perceptual illusions once they have been recognized as such — the Muller-Lyer illusion seen for the hundredth time, so that there is no belief that the lines are unequal — are, I believe, well thought of as an amalgam of a stimulus and a concept: the concept pain, or the concept of unequal lines. And in many cases, where a concept provides the intentionality of a mental phenomenon, as in veridical perception, the concept is not the concept that we ordinarily use in thought. Instead of a natural-kind concept, we apply its sensory correlate. When I see something as a tiger, the concept 'tiger' that I apply is a sensory concept whose sense is roughly 'an animal with the appearance of a tiger'.

In later lectures, beginning with Lecture IV, I shall suggest an extension of the concept of intentionality as this applies to mental states to include more than the thought-content of the state. When extended, the concept will include some information about the state which the state carries as part of its thought-content.

5. Secondly, subjectivity.

The subjectivity of a mental phenomenon is how the phenomenon is for the subject: it is, in a phrase that I owe to Thomas Nagel, what it is like for the subject to have that particular mental phenomenon.

An initial difficulty with subjectivity that has far-reaching consequences is that by and large subjectivity cannot be described in any direct fashion. We get nowhere when we try to say either what subjectivity is in itself or what it is in the case of a given mental state — unless we do this obliquely. But for me to have said this much is to reveal two features of subjectivity as I see it. The first feature is that subjectivity is a determinable attribute of mental phenomena, or that every mental phenomenon that has subjectivity has its own particular subjectivity. In this respect subjectivity is like colour, for every object that has colour has a particular colour. But, just as two objects can have the same colour, so two mental phenomena can, I presume, have the same subjectivity: though in both cases, that of colour and that of subjectivity, sameness of attribute is always relative to a specific degree of resolution. Not all contemporary philosophers think of subjectivity as a determinable. The second feature of subjectivity as I see it is that, of the three categories of mental phenomenon, only mental states have subjectivity directly. Mental dispositions lack it, and mental activities acquire it by courtesy — that is, through whatever mental states are their vehicles.

The best way of isolating subjectivity is for us to take a mental state that has intentionality — or, if we think that all mental states have intentionality, then to take one that indubitably has it — and then to ask ourselves whether there could be a mental state that had the same total thought-content, or the same thought-content no matter to what degree this is specified, but that seemed somehow different. So, seeing the eucalyptus trees bending in the wind, we ask ourselves whether we could see just what we currently think we are seeing but do so through having a different kind of experience. Or, in pain, we ask ourselves whether we could be in just the same amount of pain, locatable in just the same part of the body, and it could feel unlike the way it currently does. The answer Yes must not be understood to commit us to envisaging just what it would be like if it did change: all the question asks us is whether in the broadest terms change is conceivable. And it is also imperative that total intentionality, not just a fragment of it, is held constant — otherwise we shall drift into imagining a second experience that simply includes the original experience or partially overlaps with it. If, with these conditions respected, the answer is still Yes, then we have isolated subjectivity, for subjectivity is what in such circumstances would change.

Of course, if in such a case the answer is No, it does not follow that the mental state in question is without subjectivity, or that there is no such thing as subjectivity. All that follows is that the particular mental state is not suitable as an example for introducing subjectivity or explaining what it is. The way to show that a particular mental state is without subjectivity would be first to introduce subjectivity or explain what it is — presumbly by reference to a mental state that is suitable for these purposes — and then to show that in the case under scrutiny it is absent. As for showing that there is no such thing as subjectivity, I can conceive of nothing that we could do or say that might be expected to serve this purpose.

However in seeing what subjectivity is we have also seen something else about subjectivity. For if it is difficult, as I suggest it is, to imagine in anything except the broadest terms, Same intentionality, different subjectivity, this very strongly implies that subjectivity and intentionality interpenetrate one another. They are not to be thought of on the analogy of an inscription and the typographical fount in which it is set: for there is nothing easier than to imagine an inscription set in another face and size. However, when we try to run the thought-experiment the other way round, and imagine, Same subjectivity, different intentionality, or we ask, Could something feel just like pain and we be in a quite different mental state, not pain at all? we find that this is something all but impossible to do even in the broadest terms. And this strongly implies that, though subjectivity and intentionality interpenetrate, intentionality penetrates subjectivity deeper.

This last finding receives confirmation from the way we describe subjectivity — describe, that is, the subjectivity of a particular mental state. Ordinarily we don't even try to do this: we give the intentionality of a mental state and anticipate that the subjectivity will convey itself. I simply say that I see the eucalyptus trees bending in the wind or that I have a stabbing pain in my ankle. However sometimes we go for the subjectivity, but, when we do, we go indirectly and we exploit intentionality. Typical of the way in which we try to capture subjectivity is the 'looks'-locution. I may say, as I see them bending in the wind, 'The eucalyptus trees look black'. That is an attempt upon subjectivity. But the attempt exploits intentionality and does so twice over: once for purposes of identification, once for purposes of description. In the first place, the subjectivity that is to be captured is identified by reference to intentionality. It is the subjectivity of my experience of the eucalyptus trees: of that and of no other object of my experience. But, secondly, and more importantly, subjectivity, once identified, is then described by reference to intentionality. For what the 'looks'-locution does is to say that the subjectivity of my present experience — or, rather, of some part of my present experience — is a certain way, and that way is the very way in which the subjectivity of some other experience is. The subjectivity of my experience of the trees is the same as the subjectivity of those very experiences which I have when I look at black things in normal circumstances. And these latter experiences are identified through their intentionality.

This last point, or how the 'looks'-locution makes its second appeal to intentionality, needs clarification, or else the very claim that the 'looks'-locution does describe subjectivity will lose plausibility. For the truth is that the 'looks'-locution has more than one use, and it is necessary to distinguish the use that I now am concerned with, or the subjective use, from the comparative use, which is also concerned with subjectivity, but differently: in the comparative use the 'looks'-locution does not describe subjectivity. If I said that the trees looked black in the comparative use of 'looks', what I would be saying is that the trees look as black things look in normal circumstances however that may be. But when I employ the subjective use of 'looks' I am saying that the trees look some particular way, which is the very way that black things happen to look in normal circumstances. In other words, of two subjectivites I am not simply reporting that they have a property in common, as I would be doing with the comparative use: I am attributing that actual property to one of them. I am describing subjectivity, a determinate subjectivity, not just alluding to it, but I have to do it indirectly.

There are, I know, objections to thinking that the 'looks'-locution, even in the subjective use, does report subjectivity. The two most cogent would be that the 'looks'-locution doesn't capture the total subjectivity of a mental state, or even of some part of a mental state — a lot gets away — and that the 'looks'-locution communicates subjectivity only on the condition that speaker and hearer share a common subjectivity. One of these objections concerns the capture, the other the communication, of subjectivity, and these are two very different things. But it must be pointed out that parallel objections can be made to the attempt upon intentionality. Total intentionality cannot be captured, and what is captured can be communicated only on the basis of a shared intentionality. Yet it is a matter of agreement that we can report intentionality.

So far I have been talking not about subjectivity itself but about how we talk about subjectivity, and saying that of necessity we talk about it indirectly. If however we turn, briefly, to subjectivity itself, we see that it has a characteristic which accords with the indirection of our speech about it. That we cannot make a frontal assault upon subjectivity goes well with the fact that there is no uniform front that it presents to us. The subjectivity of a mental state is relative to a number of different factors. It is relative to the preceding mental state and its subjectivity: it is relative to our expectations: and it is relative to the object and degree of our attention. The point comes out clearest in connection with visual perception. A scene unfolds before us: a river with wooded banks, some families picnicking, a few sailing boats at odd angles to one another, a jetty and a small hotel with a high-pitched roof — the scene of an Impressionist painting. Can we ask of each of these things in turn not only what it is but how it looks? The Impressionists, we know, would have said Yes, but I think not. I think that we can ask the question only of some of these things, and which they are will depend on such matters as whether they have just come into sight, whether we previously had firm expectations about how they looked, whether we are concentrating on them.

This is what I mean by the relativity of subjectivity, and any account of subjectivity that presents it as something like a vast sumptuous tapestry hung before the eyes, in which, even if the contours are murky and the figures that are depicted can only be inferred, nevertheless the patches of colour glow unmistakably, is simply talking about something quite else.

How, it might be asked, do the indirection of our speech about subjectivity and the relativity of subjectivity fit together, as I have suggested that they do? Indeed, I have also suggested that they fit together in a way that supports our intuitive sense that intentionality penetrates subjectivity deeper than subjectivity penetrates intentionality. How is this?

The answer is impossible to frame adequately, and hard to frame at all, and for reasons that confirm it. For to state the answer would require that we should be able to employ intentionality to describe what subjectivity is like in general, and part of the answer is that subjectivity is not aptly described by intentionality. The other part of the answer is that why subjectivity is not aptly described by intentionality is because of the very way in which subjectivity carries intentionality. There are two features that are relevant here. Subjectivity is replete with intentionality: there is no clear upper limit set upon the thought-content that can be retrieved from a mental state. And subjectivity is instinct with intentionality: subjectivity delivers intentionality in an immediate fashion, so that we do not decipher subjectivity. A rough analogy might be with the way in which the pigment in a painting of a landscape is the perspicuous vehicle of innumerable thoughts about the landscape: which in turn can be connected with the difficulty we have in using thought to describe the lie of the pigment.

6.  I turn next to psychic force and psychic function. (I distinguish them.)

Let us first think of intentionality and subjectivity as conjointly forming something called phenomenology. Since subjectivity applies (at any rate directly) only to mental states, so too does phenomenology.

Psychic force can then be introduced in terms of phenomenology. It will follow that, since only mental states have phenomenology, only they have psychic force, though both mental dispositions and mental activities in their different ways exploit it. Dispositions exploit it (as we shall see) through the mental states that manifest them, activities exploit it through the mental states that are their vehicles. Psychic force holds primarily of type mental states, and indeed it serves as one way of collecting token mental states into types.

What is it for a mental state to have psychic force? Psychic force is one kind of causal efficacy that a mental state has. The causal efficacy of a mental state reveals itself in the relations of the state, on the one hand, to behaviour, and, on the other hand, to other mental phenomena: a state has causal efficacy if it causes the person to behave in certain ways or to feel, think, and believe, certain things. And the causal efficacy of a mental state is a case of psychic force when it accrues to the state because of its phenomenology.

Examples of mental states that have psychic force — and here I shall stick to simple examples because in later lectures I shall consider more complex examples at length — would be pain and terror. Pain and terror are mental states that bring about changes both in the behaviour and in the other mental phenomena of the person, and a crucial subset of these changes they bring about because of the experience that they are. Someone who had never been in pain, who had never felt terror, wouldn't be able to comprehend why people in the grip of these feelings tend to be and behave as they do.

If we turn from type mental to token mental states, we must observe that the actual outcome of a state with psychic force is mediated by the other mental states of the person and by his underlying dispositions: it can, indeed, also be affected by mental activity, for the anticipated effects of a mental state can be intensified or inhibited. Obviously a given phenomenology cannot be expected to have exactly the same causal consequences no matter what the other attendant mental phenomena. Functionalists have taught us to be suspicious of single-track causal pathways running through the mind from input to output, and have familiarised us with mental mediation, but not with its full complexity. For there are three distinct points at which background mental conditions can affect the character of such pathways. They can affect the type mental state that is instantiated, given a particular input: they can affect the phenomenology that the token mental states have, given the type that they instantiate: and now we see that they can affect what output occurs, given the phenomenology that these states have.

I turn now from psychic force to psychic function.

The psychic force of a mental state becomes its psychic function when the mental state occurs because of its psychic force: when its tendency to bring about certain mental or behavioural changes through its phenomenology is the explanation of its occurrence. If, when we are asked, Why is a certain person in such-and-such a mental state? we say something like, Because states of that type induce a person to act in this way or to feel in that way, then, in thinking of this as an answer to the question, we thereby attribute to the mental state psychic function.

But how can psychic force become psychic function? Or in what circumstances can the fact that the phenomenology of a mental state has a certain causal efficacy account for that state's coming to be?

There are in fact two distinct ways in which this can happen. There is the way of intention, and there is the way of disposition.

First, then, there is the way of intention. A mental state of a certain type has psychic force. There are certain effects that it is capable of bringing about through its phenomenology. A person is aware of this, and there is something that he wishes to achieve which falls within the causal efficacy of that mental state. So, with this aim in mind, he intentionally brings about such a mental state in himself. The psychic force of the mental state is now its psychic function. An example: Some months ago I ate a purée of vegetables, and I now want to know what was in it. I know that, if I recall eating the purée, this mental state will through its phenomenology give me knowledge of what was in the purée. So I summon up the appropriate memory. What the memory is like has and is known to have certain cognitive consequences, and it is because of these consequences that I bring it about, hence that it occurs.

Of course it isn't the case that just anyone would, from remembering eating a purée, come to know what it was made of. It also requires experience and discrimination. But that only illustrates the point that the psychic force of a token mental state is mediated by other mental phenomena in the form either of other mental states or of underlying mental dispositions.

Next, there is the way of disposition. But I am in no position to characterize this until I have first said something about the relations between mental states and mental dispositions, which I shall do when the discussion of mental attributes is over.

7. Fourthly, consciousness.

We think of consciousness in two different ways: broadly and narrowly. When it is used broadly, as in psychoanalytic theory, consciousness is a determinable with three different determinate qualities: conscious, preconscious, and unconscious. When it is used narrowly, it picks out the property of being conscious in the determinate sense. Consciousness (in the broad sense) is an attribute certainly of mental states and mental dispositions: whether it applies to mental activities directly, or only in virtue of the mental states that are their vehicles, is more problematic.

It is common to equate consciousness in the narrow sense with subjectivity. This I believe to be a mistake, and I think that consciousness is neither identical nor even co-extensive with subjectivity. This view indeed seems forced upon us if we consider that the most general reason that we have for positing unconscious mental states is their explanatory value. More specifically, we believe an unconscious mental state of a certain type to have occurred because, if a conscious mental state of that type had occurred, it would, *mutatis mutandis,* have accounted for what we have to explain. For example, we ascribe unconscious rage to someone because he behaved in the way that, *mutatis mutandis,* conscious rage would have explained. I say *mutatis mutandis* because there are three broad differences in the causal efficacy of conscious and of unconscious mental states. In the first place, unconscious mental states explain what they do in conjunction with other unconscious, but not with conscious, mental phenomena, for they do not conjoin with conscious states to produce their effects: secondly, the effects of unconscious mental states are, by and large, much grosser than those of conscious mental states of the same type: and, thirdly, the effects of unconscious mental states are generally masked, and their disguise has to be lifted before their similarity to those of the counterpart conscious mental states can be exhibited. However none of these differences dispute the basic match in causal efficacy between conscious and unconscious mental states of the same type. And since in many cases — for instance, states of anxiety, rage, guilt, fear — the conscious mental states are efficacious through their psychic force, or their effects partly depend upon their subjectivity, it seems natural to assume that the unconscious counterparts also have subjectivity. They must have subjectivity since this is how they are efficacious. If they don't have subjectivity, then either they don't have explanatory value, or their efficacy is differently explained from that of their conscious counterparts. If they don't have explanatory force, then the case for positing them is considerably weakened: if their efficacy is differently explained from that of their conscious counterparts, a reason is due why the two sets of states — conscious and unconscious — are held to be counterparts or are tokens of the same type.

Once we recognize consciousness the determinate as something distinct from subjectivity, the problem is to give an account of it that respects and clarifies this distinction and also promises an understanding of consciousness the determinable.

Freud, who provides a natural starting point, presented a basically systemic account of consciousness, according to which mental states and dispositions are classified as conscious, preconscious, or unconscious in virtue of the system of mental phenomena to which they belong. What makes a set of mental phenomena a system is that facilitations obtain within it and barriers are set up around it. What makes such a system the very system that it is are the set of principles that regulate mental functioning within it and the nature of the barriers that separate it from the other systems. So Freud appealed to a twofold difference of principle between the system Unconscious and the system Conscious. The system Unconscious obeys the pleasure principle and exhibits primary process thinking: the system Conscious obeys the reality principle and exhibits secondary process thinking. And as to the barriers, censorship allows movement of mental phenomena from the system

Conscious to the system Unconscious but not vice versa, except in special circumstances.

Any adequate account of consciousness must, I am sure, contain some systemic account, whatever its detail, but there is also something that a systemic account appears to leave out and that we need to have in. Given that, at any given moment, certain mental phenomena of a person are conscious and others unconscious, how does the fact that one set is conscious and the other unconscious stand to, or impinge upon, the person? For instance, a natural if not ultimately tenable view is that, if certain mental states or dispositions of a person are conscious, then not only will access between these states be facilitated (as Freud's systemic account insists) but so will access between them and him. Freud frequently inveighed against Janet's equation of the unconscious with a second consciousness, but what he failed to see is that Janet's view is a plausible reaction to a purely systemic account of consciousness and its qualities.

Generally, attempts to supplement a purely systemic account of consciousness appeal to epistemological considerations. On this approach, to which Freud showed himself sympathetic, the difference between conscious and unconscious mental states lies in the person's knowledge of the states that are conscious. But any epistemic account is bound to fail for three reasons. The first is that we can ask of the knowledge that allegedly makes all the difference whether it itself is conscious or unconscious. If it is unconscious, how could it make the difference expected of it? But if it is conscious, then *ex hypothesi* the person has knowledge of it, and this knowledge too must be conscious, that is, the person must have knowledge of it, and so on indefinitely: and since in each case the higher-order knowledge is not a consequence, but a precondition, of the lower-order knowledge, this establishes a vicious regress. Secondly, a point that Freud often raised in connection with therapeutic efficacy, and to which I shall return, is that a person can have knowledge of his unconscious mental states in a way that is clearly compatible with their remaining unconscious. Knowledge does not suffice for consciousness. Some might think that this difficulty can be overcome by insisting that the knowledge that makes all the difference should be direct rather than indirect —

since that knowledge of unconscious mental states which leaves them as unconscious as they were before must be indirect. But this tactic assumes that the distinction between direct and indirect knowledge is above suspicion — and that the use of it to explicate consciousness is above suspicion of circularity. And this is not clearly the case: the circularity seems endemic. The third reason why an epistemic account must fail comes out most strikingly in the case of feelings, though its application is broader. Insofar as a person doesn't have knowledge of his unconscious feelings, this seems like a consequence rather than the essence of their unconsciousness. The essence seems to lie more in something experiential, or in the way in which the subjectivity of the mental state is registered, and this an epistemic account omits.

Another account constructs itself on the ruins of the epistemic account and attempts to do justice both to the cognitive and to the experiential aspects of consciousness. It is this: A mental state of a certain type is conscious just in case it provides the person with the conditions under which he can acquire the appropriate psychological concept — that is, the concrete psychological concept under which that state falls. This account, which can be extended to mental dispositions, exploits a — some would say the — distinctive feature of a psychological, as opposed to a non-psychological, concept: that is, that we cannot grasp such a concept unless we have been exposed to the phenomenon that it conceptualises.

8.  Finally, I turn to significance.

By significance I have in mind the private meaning that mental phenomena may come to possess for the person. Significance comes about through the conjunction of intentionality and the tendency of thought-contents to be linked by association. The significance of a mental phenomenon lies in the deep associations to its content, and the deep associations to a phenomenon are those which were laid down with the phenomenon either at the time of its occurrence or inception or at the time of a strong recurrence of the phenomenon, as in a certain kind of memory or a dream.

Significance requires us to distinguish between deep associations, which can be retrieved only with difficulty, and those associations which we can make at any time to anything brought to our attention — for instance, the associations that word-association tests test. The distinction shows up clearly in the fact that our dreams have significance for us but other people's don't, though we can, of course, associate to reports of other people's dreams. It is largely a result of the baneful influence of Jung over Freud that the distinction between the two types of association got lost as an explicit element in psychoanalytic theory. It is a related error to think that in a deep association the ground of each of the links in an associative chain can be made explicit in the form of, say, a visual match, or a trope of language; though this is likely to be true of a shallow association.

9. I move from mental states to the relations between mental states and mental dispositions. The subject, on which I have already touched, is very complex, but for an understanding of what it is to lead the life of a person the interaction between the two is central.

If we take any disposition, we need to distinguish between three questions that may be asked of it: what that disposition is; the way in which the disposition modifies the creature who has it, or what I shall call its role; and how it brings about that modification. So, for example, of desire we can ask, What is a desire? In what way does a desire modify the desirer? and, How does the desire bring about that modification?

The three questions that we can ask of a disposition differ in their scope or degree of generality, and this we can follow by continuing to take desire as our example. The first question, or what a desire is, is the most general: it is a conceptual question, and a good answer must hold true for all creatures of whom desires can be predicated, no matter what their psychology. The third question, or the means by which desire brings about the modifications associated with it, has the least generality, and the answer will vary from psychology to psychology. There are, for instance, as we shall see, within the psychology of the person, distinctive means to which desires resort in order to achieve their role. The second question, or the way in which a desire modifies the creature who has it, is a question of intervening generality. Desire does not have the same role across all psychologies, from that of an angel to that of a bird, but equally a differerence in role should not be expected just because of a difference in psychology. It is perhaps only where the difference in psychology amounts to a difference in the kinds or types of way in which the creature can be modified — as is, for instance, the case with the difference between a psychology that includes language and one that lacks it — that we should expect a difference in psychology to be accompanied by a difference in role.

I shall not concern myself with the first question, or the nature of, say, desire, or fear. We can see that what desire or fear are, or the nature of desire and fear, must be different from the way or ways in which they modify the creature by thinking of the use that we make of such dispositions in explanation. We appeal to the desires or fears that a person has in order to account for why he feels or acts as he does. And the kind of explanation is not that provided by mere subsumption, in which we subsume detail of feeling or action under a larger pattern of feeling and action. It is the kind of explanation that, like causal explanation, requires non-identity of explicans and explicandum: it requires, then, that a person's desires or fears are different from what, in the grip of desire or in the grip of fear, he feels or does.

The ways in which a disposition modifies a person, or its role, can be brought under three broad headings: the disposition may constrain his mental states, it may regulate his behaviour, or it may generate new or reinforce existing dispositions. Every disposition does not necessarily modify a person in all these ways — and, in whichever way it does, it does so only in conjunction with other mental phenomena. Take belief. A belief may limit what thoughts a person has about how the world is: it may influence him to act in ways that the truth of the belief would make reasonable: and it may from time to time engender desires — and none of these things will it do on its own. To affect a person's thoughts a belief must conjoin with other beliefs: to guide his behaviour or to influence his desires it must conjoin not only with other beliefs but also with desires.

For any disposition the question, What is its role? will prove very difficult to answer. No answer seems quite adequate. Some will think this an objection to asking the question. But the difficulty seems to reproduce the very difficulty we have when we ask of that same disposition, What is it? And this is no accident. For, when we ordinarily ask, What is desire? What is belief? What is fear? we are not asking, as philosophers seem to assume, the conceptual question. What we are asking, I suggest, is a question about the role of the disposition—and this, incidentally, is no less a philosophical question.

Just how, or by what means, within the psychology of the person a disposition fulfils, or seeks to fulfil, its role is highly germane to the topic of these lectures. A rough answer is that a disposition constrains a person's mental states directly, and it then regulates his behaviour and affects his dispositions through the mental states that it constrains. These are the central cases of disposition. There are, it is true, some dispositions which only marginally constrain a person's mental states, and they modify his behaviour or his dispositions directly. Examples of such dispositions would be skills, or the executive virtues like courage or conscientiousness, or knowledge insofar as it does not include belief as a component—for instance, linguistic knowledge. But such dispositions are fringe cases. The error in behaviourism is to take these fringe cases as central cases.

Concentrating then on the central cases of mental disposition, or those which operate through mental states, I shall make some broad distinctions within the ways in which they relate to mental states.

An initial distinction is between states that are reflective upon, and states that manifest, dispositions. Typically I reflect upon my dispositions when I start to examine my life, and it is in the context of the examined life that I shall return to this relation between states and dispositions. States that manifest dispositions may do so in one or other of two ways: the dispositions may serve as background to the state, or the disposition may be foregrounded. When the disposition serves as background, it doesn't enter into, though it conditions, the thought-content or intentionality of the state: when the disposition is foregrounded, it provides the thought-content, and perhaps also the subjectivity, of the state. For an example of the first kind of case, consider a perceptual experience: that I see the trees bending in the wind is made possible for me by a large network of commonsense beliefs about nature which constitute the background to the experience. They don't however figure in the experience. Another case of this kind would be where I think about a philosophical topic, like this one: in such a case there is likely to be a yet larger network of beliefs in the background, though some beliefs will also form the foreground or the thought-content of the mental state. In this example, then, both ways in which a disposition can be manifested in a state are exemplified. But for a purer example of the second kind of case, where a disposition forms the foreground of a mental state, consider a person in whom a long-standing desire is about to be consummated and whose head is now filled to bursting with thoughts of revenge or of orgasm: Macduff, or Tarquin as he works his way into Lucretia's chamber.

The examples that I have selected in order to illustrate the distinction between a disposition in the background and a disposition in the foreground of a mental state also illustrate how in actuality or substantively this distinction sorts dispositions. For it is characteristic of beliefs that they serve as the background to our mental states (as we saw in the first example) though (as we saw in the second example) they may also form the foreground: but the likeliest of dispositions to fill the foreground are (as the third example shows) desires and emotions, though they also and frequently serve as the background.

A parenthesis: This last fact is symptomatic of a very general principle governing our lives, which is that at any given moment we seek to lead them under the aegis of all our beliefs. Of course at any given moment some beliefs, whether because of their irrelevance to what engages us, or because of their low probability, or for reasons that go deeper, will not influence us directly — though it doesn't follow that they won't influence us indirectly, in that but for them some of the beliefs that influence us directly might very well not have been as they are. But with our desires the situation is altogether different. We seek on a given occasion to satisfy some one desire or some set of desires of ours. We shall prefer it if this does not involve the frustration of other desires of ours, and, if it does, this may cause us regret, pain, and longing. Nevertheless there has been no error on our part in preferring one desire to many others, nor will there be any irrationality in our continuing to hold on to these many other desires once we have preferred another to them.

This big difference between beliefs and desires, in what they do for us and what we are prepared to do for them, is closely connected with what has been called the difference in fit between, on the one hand, beliefs, on the other hand, desires, and the world. We require our beliefs to fit the world, but we require the world to fit our desires.

But this difference of fit can be misunderstood. For what we require of our beliefs we require of them distributively and collectively, but what we require for our desires we require for them only distributively. To put it another way, we expect our beliefs to give us a picture of the world as it is, but we do not expect our desires to give us a picture of the world as it should be, or as it should be according to us. Each desire offers us, as it were, a view through a keyhole, but there is no reason that there should emerge from these views a coherent picture of what lies on the far side of the gate or that, should it be thrown open, there would be revealed a garden that we could conceivably enter. Our desires do not generate a possible world.

Indeed, just what it is about our desires that makes us require the world to fit them makes us unwilling to give them up merely because they don't fit one another. In the case of beliefs, we aren't normally attached to our beliefs because they are ours. Our attachment to them is because of what we hope to gain through them — that is, the truth. But just what attaches us to our desires is that they are ours; though sometimes our attachment to them may be affected by reflection either upon what we pay for them — that is, frustration — or upon what we hope to gain through them — that is, satisfaction.

I close this parenthesis — though the asymmetry of belief and desire is something to which I shall return — and I take up, where I left off, the relations between mental dispositions and mental states. Specifically I take up the relation of manifestation, and to understand this relation we must ask, How does a mental disposition select the mental states that manifest it? Or (for those who might be misled by the seeming anthropomorphism of the last question), What restrictions are placed upon the type or types of mental state in which a mental disposition may manifest itself? And the answer is that a disposition manifests itself in, and only in, those mental states which typically further, or contribute to furthering, its role. For a mental state to manifest a mental disposition, the type mental state of which it is a token must have a causal efficacy that coincides with the role of the disposition. When causal efficacy and role thus coincide, I shall say that mental state and mental disposition concur. Concurrence is the core of manifestation.

My claim is not that the relation of manifestation is the relation of concurrence. It isn't. Manifestation is not concurrence. Manifestation is a causal relation, in that a disposition causes, or helps to cause, the mental states that manifest it. But the causality in manifestation follows the lines of concurrence. When a disposition is manifested by a mental state, it causes a mental state that concurs with it, and it causes that mental state because of the concurrence. Initially, unreflectingly, this might seem like a revival of the belief in pre-established harmony. But reflection shows this is wrong. For, if it weren't the case that dispositions and mental states were related in this way, how could dispositions appropriately modify behaviour through mental states?

From the earlier discussion of mental states and their attributes, it follows that there are two different ways in which a mental state can come to manifest a disposition. For there are two different ways in which a mental state can come by the causal efficacy that leads it, the mental state, to concur with the disposition. It can come by its causal efficacy for reasons other than its phenomenology—for instance, its intentionality. Or it can come by it because of its phenomenology. When it comes by it because of its phenomenology, this causal efficacy is its psychic force—and now it should be apparent that I am just about to rejoin, from another direction, a topic that I broached a while back and postponed until we had the relations between mental state and mental disposition before us. This topic is the second way, the way other than the way of intention, by which the psychic force of a mental state can explain its occurrence, and so become its psychic function. For when the causal efficacy of a mental state that leads it to concur with the disposition it manifests is come by through its phenomenology, this is at once its psychic force and that which explains its occurrence. Psychic force has become psychic function along the way of disposition.

For an example of the two ways in which a mental state can come to manifest a disposition, because of something other than its phenomenology and because of its phenomenology, let us take the case of the fear of snakes, and let us think that the role of this disposition is to keep a person who has it as clear of snakes as is otherwise possible. A person, then, has the disposition to fear snakes. One day he finds himself walking down a white cockle path into an overgrown wood which he suddenly realizes is inhabited by moccasins. The place stimulates his fear, and there are two types of mental state whose causal efficacy makes them suitable for manifesting it. One such state would be a thought to the effect, 'Be very careful: watch your step: don't put a foot wrong: keep your eyes skinned: it's very dangerous here'. The other state would be a moment of total terror. Both states further the role of the disposition — that is why they are suitable for manifesting it. But one would do so in virtue of its intentionality: the thought offers itself as a maxim of conduct which, if the man follows it, will lead him to avoid snakes. The other would do so in virtue of its phenomenology: in the grip of terror the man will get out of the wood as fast as his feet can carry him.

There are two important facts about the psychology of the person, two large truths about the interrelation of mental states and mental dispositions, which we are now in a position to put together. The first is that, by and large, mental dispositions fulfil their role indirectly: they bring about the modifications in behaviour and disposition that they seek through causing appropriate mental states, or mental states with the right causal efficacy. The second is that some mental states that manifest dispositions owe their causal efficacy, and hence their appropriateness, to their phenomenology. The first fact ensures within the psychology of the person the indispensability of mental states, the second the indispensability of phenomenology despite all the baneful consequences it also brings in train. The first is overlooked by behaviourists, the second by contemporary functionalists, and both are central to what it is to lead the life of a person.

When a mental state manifests a disposition and does so because of its phenomenology, I shall say that it expresses that disposition. When a mental state expresses a disposition, it also stands in an important further relation to the disposition, which is that it is possible for a person who is in that state to learn from it what it is to have that disposition. He is in a position to learn not just whether he has, but what it is to have, the disposition that his mental state expresses. A man could not learn what it is to have a belief by being in a state in which he is ready to make an assertion, even though assertoric states manifest belief. But he could learn, through experiencing the perturbations of love, which express love, what it is to be in love or to love someone, as Cherubino's aria '*Non so piu cosa son, cosa faccio*' or the recapitulation of it in '*Voi che sapete*' make transparent to us. The young page burns one moment, he freezes the next, he is elated, then he is dejected, and he wishes this state to continue indefinitely. He suffers from an emotion he cannot explain—'*un desio ch'io non posso spiegar*'—and he asks of the ladies, of those who know, whether this is love. But in asking the question, not merely does he reveal the answer, but, more important, he also reveals that he is, for the first time, in a position to ask it. He has a grasp of the concept of love.

10. So far I have concentrated on just one aspect of the relation of manifestation as this holds between mental states and mental dispositions. It is the aspect that arises out of the content of the states and the dispositions: that is, out of the intentionality of the dispositions and the intentionality, subjectivity, phenomenology, of the states. But there is also the causal aspect, to which I now turn.

It seems plausible to think that every mental state has amongst its necessary conditions some underlying disposition or dispositions, particularly if we remember to include dispositions that are backgrounded in the mental state. A possible exception is, once again, sensations, but the case for thinking so weakens when we take account of the capacity that we have to relate sensations to parts of the body or to subsume them under a body-image.

That we cannot, except perhaps marginally, attribute mental states to a person without also attributing to him suitably related dispositions is what I referred to in the first lecture as the strongest consideration against constructionist theories of a person's life: against, that is, theories that hold that mental states do not essentially contain a person. If it is true that for mental states to arise, they must be appropriately linked to mental dispositions, then they must essentially belong to things that can house dispositions, and this is where the person is required.

However there are some mental states of which it seems reasonable to hold that dispositions constitute parts of their sufficient conditions. These would be mental states in which a disposition is foregrounded. But, dispositions being persisting phenomena, which do not occur at a time and are not events, how do they suddenly gain efficacy from one moment to the next? For no one could hold that they are in a condition of permanent manifestation. Conventional wisdom attaches to the disposition something in the way of an initial condition which accounts for the show of efficacy or the coming-to-be of an appropriate mental state. Is this correct?

There are certain cases in which we seem to have no difficulty in accounting for the manifestation of the disposition in terms of some initial condition. Characteristically this condition will be an external stimulus. It will, for instance, be something perceived. A man's anger with his father flares up when he catches sight of his father: the transient perception of the father engages with the persisting disposition of anger and the conjunction occasions a manifestation of the anger, which is an access of rage against the father.

But in many cases, if we are to find an initial condition for the manifestation of a disposition, the only available candidate is an internal stimulus, and it is then tempting to think that internal stimulus and external stimulus fit into the same pattern of explanation. Instead of the passing scene, which casts up an external stimulus, we have the stream of thought, which casts up an internal stimulus, and the two kinds of stimulus play the same explanatory role. A thought of some kind about the father, an access of rage against someone or other occurs, and it engages with the disposition of anger in just the same way as the perception of the father did, and to the same effect: there is a manifestation of anger against the father, which is an access of rage.

But are the two patterns of explanation really the same? In some cases they may be. But in many cases it looks as though the so-called internal stimulus, which is supposed to explain the sudden efficacy of the disposition, actually presupposes it. There are two ways in which this can happen. In the first place, that the mental state engages with the disposition is only because the disposition is already efficacious or close to being so. A man thinks of masturbation, and this thought engages with his anger against his father — but if he hadn't already been close to rage, he might have had the same thought and it not engage with his anger. But, secondly, that the mental state occurred at all might be only because of the waxing strength of the disposition. The man might just not have had the thought about masturbation if his anger against his father hadn't already been on the point of eruption.

Of course, such reservations can also arise in the external case. The man's perception of his father might not have enraged him, indeed he might not have noticed his father, if, independently, his anger had not mounted. We shall have to consider a whole group of such examples, or what I call projective emotions, in Lecture VII. Nevertheless, such reservations seem exceptional in the external case, but regular in the internal case. And this seems to fit in with the rough-hewn thought that, just as external reality irrupts on to our dispositions, our dispositions irrupt on to our mental states.

This last kind of case has the expository advantage that it introduces the mental phenomenon on which I shall end this lecture. It brings me, after mental states, after mental dispositions, to mental activity. For certainly one kind of case in which it seems far-fetched to think of the manifestation of the disposition as in any way stimulus-bound is when a piece of mental activity, or a person by means of a piece of mental activity, brings about a mental state which manifests a disposition.

But before leaving the topic of mental disposition, mental state, and causality, I want to consider briefly the causal impact of mental states upon mental dispositions. Most mental dispositions that are not innate originate in mental states, though often in a confused set of such states. However mental states, as well as generating new dispositions, reinforce existing dispositions. Indeed, characteristically mental states reinforce the dispositions that they manifest. In *De l'Amour* Stendhal traces the way in which certain experiences which are open only to the lover nourish love: this is what he calls crystallization, and he also noted the process of crystallization in envy, hatred, superstition, and the love of gambling. That mental states should reinforce the disposition they manifest is something for which we have been prepared: we have, that is, the materials on which to predict it. For one part of the role of a mental disposition is to preserve itself; and this part of its role too it will characteristically fulfil indirectly, through mental states that manifest it. And of those mental states which reinforce the dispositions that they manifest, a special place is occupied by those which do so through their phenomenology. Once again psychic force coincides with the role of the disposition that the mental state manifests and so is transformed into psychic function. I shall consider such cases in Lecture IV.

11. Mental activity is a puzzling phenomenon.

Its existence is something I cannot doubt. Trying to perform an action, attending to something in the visual field, repressing a desire, introjecting a parental figure, seem clearly things that we *do* — where this is an intuition that is not simply based on grammatical considerations. For these seem things that we do in a way that hating someone, or falling into confusion, or admiring someone's success, which have the same grammatical marker, don't.

But to say of something that it is something that we do is not to say that it is an action. And I don't hold that a mental activity equates with an action. Indeed, we can make a start on understanding mental activity just by seeing how it differs from action.

I accept the view that an action is identified by reference to the explanatory schema that it fits. More specifically, an action is to be explained in terms of a conjunction of a desire, or, more realistically, a set of desires, and a belief, or a set of beliefs, which prompts an intention. The belief interlocks with the desire in such a way as to tie it to the particular action. Actually the conjunction of desire and belief occurs twice over in the explanation of, hence in the identification of something as, an action. One and the same conjunction has to do two things: it must at once make intelligible and cause what the agent does. The conjunction of desire and belief is then fused or mixed in the intention—like pigment on the painter's palette.

A mental activity, by contrast, requires for its explanation and so for its identification desire, but it does not require belief. If I will an action or attend to something in the visual field, I do not have to have a belief about what trying or attention can achieve. I do not have to conjoin to my desire to do something or to find out about something an instrumental belief about certain powers of the mind—though in Lecture V I shall contend that in certain cases of mental activity, and what will undoubtedly seem to some the unlikeliest cases, precisely what we do have in their explanation is such instrumental beliefs.

What takes the place of belief in the explanation of, hence in the identification of something as, a mental activity is something that I shall call instinct. Volition and attention, sometimes repression, come about solely through desire guided by instinct.

Since mental activity does not require belief as well as desire, it equally does not require an intention in which desire and belief are fused or mixed. A mental activity is not prompted by the intention to carry out that activity.

However, just as there is something that takes the place of belief in the genesis of a mental activity, which I have called instinct, so there is also something that takes the place of intention. It is the failure or the refusal to inhibit. Mental activity can be inhibited. Trying to do something, attending to something in the visual field, repressing a desire, are things that I can inhibit, though, here and now, impatience, curiosity, anxiety may be too much for me, and the mental activity takes place.

This view of mental activity is open to the criticism that it is born of the theoretical impulse to find an internal analogue to something that is essentially external. But this criticism can be met by pointing out that the phenomenon I have been talking about is not essentially internal, and that the characteristics I have attributed to mental activity also qualify something external. What I have in mind is expressing, or doing something so as to express, a feeling or emotion: or one of that whole range of things which metamorphosed Io, metamorphosed Actaeon, cannot do, and can attempt only through trial and error. An example would be smiling so as to express pleasure. And my contention is that expressing is an external case of an activity. It is doing something, but it is not an action.

Certain mental activities bring about mental states or changes in mental states: for instance, attention, or trying to retrieve a name. Of these some not only terminate on mental states, they are realized through mental states. They are the mental activities of which I have been saying that mental states are their vehicles. Examples are trying to recall an event where this is realized through a succession of memory experiences, or introjecting an external figure where this is realized through a certain kind of incorporative phantasy. The details of both these examples will concern us later, but I introduce them only to clarify something that I have already said: that, if mental activity has subjectivity, it has it only indirectly. For if mental activity has subjectivity, the subjectivity that it has is the subjectivity of the mental states that are its vehicles.

12. This brings to an end this catalogue of the mind.

# III Iconicity, Imagination, and Desire

1. In this lecture and the next I shall discuss a whole group of mental states which have in common a property that I call iconicity. Iconic mental states have an important part to play in the way in which we lead our lives. They are crucial to the way in which the past exercises an influence over the present, and we draw upon them when in the present we try to predict, or anticipate, or control, the future. Iconic mental states are complex in character, and I begin with examples. Examples of type iconic mental states are a certain kind of imagination, which in the modality of vision is visualising, but to which there are counterparts in the other sense-modalities, insofar, that is, as within imagination the different sense-modalities can be segregated: a certain kind of memory, which is event-memory: dreams: and phantasy.

2. There are various marks of iconicity. These marks can be connected with the attributes of mental phenomena that I considered in the last lecture.

In the first place, iconic mental states may be of mere individuals, but standardly they are of events. These events contain their own characters, and these characters constitute the dramatis personae, in a loose sense of the term: loose in that, though for the most part these characters will be persons — parents, lovers, historical figures — they can also be things like volcanoes, or beasts of prey, or sweet-smelling plants, or pieces of strange clothing. Iconic mental states regularly occur in sequences and, as the states succeed one another, so the dramatis personae interact, the events make up a story, a narrative unfolds. This first mark of iconicity concerns the intentionality of iconic mental states.

Secondly, the individuals, the events, the sequences of events, the stories that iconic mental states are of, they represent. This second mark of iconicity concerns the relationship between the intentionality and the subjectivity of iconic mental states, or how the intentionality is conveyed. Exactly how representation is to be understood gives rise to very real difficulties. Negatively, representation means that why the mental state is of what it is of is not by reason of, or at any rate not primarily by reason of, convention: that is not the way it secures its intentionality. An iconic mental state is not like an internal inscription of a sentence. A positive characterization is harder to give. Imagery by and large functions representationally, but to be able to generalize from this example, we have first to be certain that we have got right how imagery, and specifically how mental imagery, functions when it is a medium of intentionality. This requires us to guard against certain demands that we are somehow tempted to make of images, though they would not even occur to us if we were thinking about language as a medium of intentionality. So we should not think that we have to observe our images before we can know what they are, any more than we have to listen to the words we think in before we can know what they are: nor that we have to decide what our images mean before we can know what they are of, any more than we have to decide what the words we think in mean before we can know what they are about: nor that our images have to be as determinate as experience, any more than the words we think in have to be concatenated into well-formed sentences.

Thirdly, iconic mental states have a causal efficacy over the behaviour and the mental dispositions of the person who has them that they owe exclusively to their complex phenomenology — and quite how complex it is we shall have a chance to see. Iconic mental states have, in other words, psychic force.

In addition to these three marks, there is a linguistic clue to iconicity, or a clue contained in the way in which iconic mental states are reported, whether it be by those whose states they are or by others. This clue is however only of limited value, for the form of report that it favours gives us neither a sufficient nor a necessary condition of iconicity. Where a type mental state has both iconic and non-iconic instances, the clue works in that the favoured form of report is available only for the iconic instances. But there are also type mental states all of whose instances are iconic, yet for them the favoured form of report is not available: hence it isn't a necessary condition of iconicity. And, further, there are type mental states none of whose instances are iconic, yet for them the favoured form of report is available: hence it isn't a sufficient condition of iconicity. Specifically the linguistic clue will enable us to pick out iconic from non-iconic imaginings or iconic from non-iconic memories: but applied in the domain of dreams, which are uniformly iconic, or in the domain of calculations, which are uniformly non-iconic, the clue can only mislead us.

What is the clue? The clue is a matter of whether the report of the mental state is of the form 'I/you/he/she Vb'ed + that + embedded sentence' or of the form 'I/you/he/she Vb'ed + direct object' (where the direct object is likeliest to be a nominalization). It is the latter form that is the favoured form. So, if I imagine something and imagine it non-iconically, I shall characteristically report this by saying something like, 'I imagined that the horse fell down in the street'. But, if I imagine that same thing iconically, I shall be able to say, 'I imagined the horse's falling down in the street'. And the same holds in the case of second- and third-person reports. 'Hans imagined that the horse fell down in the street' characteristically reports a non-iconic imagining, whereas 'Hans imagined the horse's falling down in the street' is reserved for iconic imaginings. By contrast, we would say of Hans, and he would say of himself, on the one hand, that he dreamt that the horse fell down in the street despite the iconicity of dreams, and, on the other hand, that he calculated the horse's falling down in the street despite the non-iconicity of calculations.

Someone might object to the last example instructively. He might dispute the fact that all calculations are non-iconic on the grounds that, sometimes when he calculates, he does so by visualising the calculation on a page. But this is not a counter-example. For what is represented in such cases is not the calculation itself, but a representation of it: it is numbers that are calculated but what is visualised are numerals, which represent numbers.

The linguistic clue, then, is of utility if used, but only if used, with circumspection.

3. Iconic mental states are those mental states which do most to recommend the traditional comparison of the mind to a theatre. Pains and volitions, for instance, give no support whatsoever to the comparison.

In considering iconic mental states I intend to take this comparison seriously, and to structure an account of iconic mental states on an account of the theatre. But I should emphasise that the utility or value of the comparison lies solely in the realm of description. Modelling an account of some part of the mind on an account of the theatre will, I hope, allow us to see certain things about the mind that we might otherwise miss. But it neither has nor pretends to explanatory force.

4. Understanding the theatre — understanding, that is, the classical western theatre and its varieties — requires us to understand three interdependent roles and how they depend on one another.

These roles are those of the *dramatist,* the *actor,* and the *audience.* These are, it should be noted, roles: roles, not persons. There are three roles here: such roles are filled by persons, but not necessarily in a one-one correspondence. On the same occasion the same role may be filled by more than one person, or on successive occasions more than one role may be filled by the same person. Beaumont and Fletcher were dramatists jointly, and I have watched Lenny Bruce be in turn dramatist, actor, audience, and to amazing effect.

5. Let us look at these three roles in as simple-minded a way as the facts of the matter permit.

First, then, the dramatist. The dramatist makes up actions, makes up lines, which he distributes among the various characters of his drama. But to be able to make up and distribute actions and lines in this way, he has to have characters whose actions and lines they will be. He must first make up the characters themselves. Here, then, are two pieces of invention, and each piece of invention can vary in the degree — as well, of course, as in the quality — of inventiveness it displays. Actions and lines on the one hand, characters on the other hand, can be modelled upon prototypes in the real world, or they can be altogether original, or they can be somewhere in between. And the two pieces of invention are inter-dependent. Actions and lines obviously presuppose the existence of characters to whom they are assigned, but, perhaps less obviously, once a character exists, his nature will heavily constrain the actions and lines that the dramatist can assign him. The dramatist will doubtless experience this as a psychological constraint, but the constraint descends from the fictional reality that he constructs. The dramatist in assigning actions and lines to a character has to work out of that character's *repertoire,* and, in working out of a repertoire, he is in effect working out the consequences of creating that character. However we must remember that creating a character is not itself the work of a moment: a character may take time to acquire its consequences.

Secondly, the actor. The actor is assigned a character—perhaps more than one—and, along with the character, that character's actions and lines, and the actor's task is then to represent the character for the benefit of the audience. Different views have been held about the purely internal requirements that this lays upon the actor: that is to say, about how his mental states should stand to the mental states of the character he represents. Should he replicate them, or should his mental states stand to them in some other relationship? For Stanislavsky it was required that the actor should 'live his part'—that he should think, strive, feel, and act in total unison with his character. Diderot, by contrast, believed that there was nothing more misguided than 'to act from the heart', *'jouer d'âme',* and he found it perfectly all right that the actor who plays the besotted lover in the evening should, while doing so, be brooding over the bitter quarrel he had had with his mistress that morning. But it is common to both Stanislavsky and Diderot that the views they have about the proper relationship of the actor's mental states to the mental states of the character whom he represents are instrumental views: the relationship should be that which best enables the actor to represent the character to the greatest benefit of his audience, for that is his, the actor's, essential task.

So, thirdly, the audience. The audience perceives the different actors representing for its benefit the different characters, it listens to the lines, it notes the actions, it follows the narrative as it unfolds, and it interprets the totality. In this way it gains access to the work of the dramatist.

This is a minimal characterization of the audience. Is there not additionally some particular way in which the audience should respond to the representation? If there is not a requirement on how the mental states of the actors, is there not a requirement on how the mental states of the audience, should be related to the mental states of the various characters?

There are, broadly speaking, three different ways in which it has been held that the two sets of mental states may be related, and, ignoring the question that divides Aristotle and Brecht, and Brecht and the straw man whom he calls 'Aristotle', the question how they ought to be related, I shall indicate the three broad types of audience response, and each type of response I shall personify and present as a type of audience.

In the first place, the audience may note, with varying powers of discrimination, the precise mental state that each character is in, it may try to comprehend that mental state, but it holds back from any further involvement. Above all, it permits itself no affective response. This type of audience is the *detached audience*, and *detachment*, as I intend it, is perfectly compatible with *favour*, or siding with one character rather than with another, just so long as favour doesn't escalate into feeling. For the audience to remain detached, favour must remain a matter of judgment.

Secondly, the audience may not merely note and try to comprehend the mental state that each character is in, but it may respond to such states and respond exactly as it would to those of a fellow human being with whom it shared a common life. This type of audience is the *sympathetic audience*, and *sympathy*, as I intend it, requires that the mental states that the audience has are determined by the mental states that are represented for its benefit and by the favour — that is, the good favour, the disfavour, or indifference — in which it holds the character whose states they are. Judgment upon a character filters the way in which the sympathetic audience reacts to the mental states of that character, and it is in this respect that the sympathetic audience models the normal participant in human intercourse.

Thirdly, there is the audience that from the outset selects one character out of the dramatis personae, responds to the mental states of this character by duplicating them, and then goes on to respond to the mental states of all the other characters — and for that matter to the narrative itself as it unfolds — in the perspective of this one character. It responds as, or as it thinks that, that character would. This type of audience is the *empathic audience,* the character that the audience selects is the *protagonist* — or rather its protagonist, for in this sense of the term a character is a protagonist relative to a particular audience — and *empathy,* as I intend it, en-sures that the audience's mental states and the mental states of the protagonist are in unison. Empathy must be distinguished from favour, and the two are very different. Favour starts in the intellect, and it may or it may not spread to the feelings: in the case of the detached audience it must not, in the case of the sympathetic audience it must. Empathy, by contrast, is a matter of the feelings, and it may or it may not gain support from the intellect: in the case of the empathic audience it needn't, for there is nothing in the specification of the empathic audience to say how, or on what grounds, it selects its protagonist. It doesn't have to look upon him with favour or to side with him rather than with others, let alone with him against the others. A friend of mine, a lawyer of liberal views, of subtle and civilized tastes, judicious, ironical, tells me that he invariably empathises with Clytemnestra.

I illustrate, schematically, these distinctions by taking a charac-ter, assigning to him a variety of mental states, and then predicting the responses of the detached audience, the sympathetic audience that looks upon the character favourably, the sympathetic audi-ence that looks upon him with disfavour, and the empathic audi-ence that selects him for its protagonist. So, assume that the char-acter feels terror, and then we may predict that one kind of sympathetic audience, or that which looks upon him with favour, will feel solicitude, the other kind, or that which looks upon him with disfavour, will feel triumph, and the empathic audience that selects him for its protagonist will feel terror. Next, assume that the character feels sad, and then we may predict that the first kind of sympathetic audience will feel pity, the second kind will feel pleasure, and the relevant empathic audience will feel sad.

Throughout, the detached audience will note with interest just what the character feels, it will try to comprehend it, and it will feel nothing in response.

6. How does this account of the theatre and its constitutive roles illuminate the nature of iconic mental states?

It does so by providing us with a way of describing what goes on in the mind when we entertain such states: for we can think of them as the work, the conjoint work, of internal counterparts to the three roles of the theatre. An iconic mental state, we can say, arises out of a collaboration, though not on equal terms, between an *internal dramatist,* an *internal actor,* and an *internal audience.* The purpose of this comparison is to get clear description, it is not to get sound explanation. It has no explanatory force.

But in what way does this segmentation of iconic mental states or of their formation help? Just what features of this stretch of our mental life am I drawing attention to when I posit the three different internal roles?

In saying that there is an internal dramatist, I refer to the fact that in bringing about an iconic mental state we draw upon and combine a number of dispositions that we have, and we find a sequence of events or a narrative to manifest them. These dispositions may already be in existence, or we may form them expressly for the purpose of bringing about such states — as when, for instance, having decided to regale myself in a prison cell with stories I shall tell myself, I construct repertoires for the different characters. What we do in the role of internal dramatist is a mental activity, of which the vehicle is mental states, though there is no reason to hold that what we do is necessarily freely or even voluntarily done.

In saying that there is an internal actor, I refer to the fact that in iconic mental states we represent to ourselves for our benefit the actions or events that we have made up as internal dramatist.

In saying that there is an internal audience, I refer to the fact that iconic mental states have the power to leave us in some particular condition — cognitive, conative, affective — and this power derives from the actions and events that the internal actor represents. The classification of the real-life audience into different types can be applied to the internal audience, and its application permits, as we shall see, a fine-grained account of just how this power is exercised and to what effect. It will allow us to see how the condition in which an iconic mental state leaves the person, or what I shall call the residual condition, derives from what the mental state is of. Of course the power of an iconic mental state to leave the person in a certain condition is mediated by other or attendant mental phenomena, and therefore it shows itself solely as a tendency. In this respect that power of iconic mental states which is personified by the internal audience is like psychic force. It is like it, but it isn't it. It isn't psychic force, for whereas the effect that the psychic force of a mental state tends to bring about lies outside that state, the residual condition is part of the state. The way in which the two are related is that the residual condition on which the state terminates is the means, or a means, by which the state exerts its psychic force. That iconic mental states have a tendency to leave the person in a residual condition appropriate to what they represent, or that an internal audience fits tellingly into the description of them, is probably the most important single fact about them as far as their contribution to the way in which we lead our lives is concerned.

It is however crucial to recognize that in describing iconic mental states as though they were brought about by an internal dramatist, an internal actor, an internal audience, the modifier 'internal' needs to be taken very seriously. These roles are not to be thought of as those of a dramatist, an actor, an audience, who, in each case, happens to be inside us. Internalize the roles, and what results is something different, systematically different, from the original. The internalization of the role is responsible for at least two striking differences which reveal themselves across all three roles.

In the first place, what the internal roles are directed upon, or the internal counterpart to the drama itself, is something essentially indeterminate or incomplete in the way in which characters or events in the external world are not and could not be. There is no text, there is no systematic sequence of actions and lines, which we compose and enact and respond to in the internal theatre, and which could then be transcribed and studied. The point overlaps with one already made about imagery — overlaps, since imagery is only one possible medium of iconicity — and it can therefore be made by borrowing Sartre's characterization of imagery. There is an 'essential poverty' to iconic mental states whatever the representational medium.

Secondly, the internal roles themselves are finely enmeshed one with another in a way that the counterpart external roles are not and could not be. So, the work of the internal actor is not preceded by that of the internal dramatist: rather, we represent the internal narrative to ourselves even as we concoct it. Again, the work of the internal audience does not follow on that of the internal actor: rather, even as we represent the narrative to ourselves — which is to say, even as we concoct it — we respond to it. And most important of all, it is not required that, in responding to the narrative, we should, like an external audience, actually have those mental states which are appropriately related to the mental states represented for our benefit. It suffices, as we have just seen, that we find ourselves in the condition in which such states would leave an external audience. The residual condition can do duty for the thoughts and feelings that in real life, or in the auditorium of the actual theatre, would induce this condition. A more egregious error yet is to think that the internal audience is or is like an internal observer. It isn't: though, as we shall see, there is, if not in the description of iconic mental states themselves, then in the description of the context or of that stretch of mental life in which they occur, a place that an internal observer can occupy.

A good way of making the general point is to say that internal dramatist, internal actor, internal audience, correspond to different and distinguishable aspects, but not to separable bits, of the dramatic project that iconic mental states may be taken to realize.

7. There is however one distinction to be made within iconic mental states for which the theatrical comparison doesn't prepare us. It doesn't prepare us for it because no corresponding difference exists within the theatre itself: there is no external counterpart to the distinction. Nevertheless the descriptive resources with which our comparison equips us allow us to phrase the distinction adequately.

Basically the distinction is between iconic mental states that possess a point of view and those which don't: more specifically, between those which possess a point of view internal to that which they represent and those which don't. The point of view is the point of view of one of the dramatis personae: generally, but not necessarily, in the stricter sense of that expression. For it is generally, but not necessarily, the point of view of one of the dramatis personae who are persons. Iconic mental states with such a point of view I shall call *centred* and those without one I shall call *acentred,* and to bring the distinction between centred and acentred iconic mental states before us I shall take an example from one particular type of iconic mental state: from imagination, more particularly from visualising. Imagination is a broad term: not all kinds of imagination are iconic, but visualising is.

8.  I have been sitting up reading Gibbon late into the night. I put the book down. I turn off one of the lamps. I start to visualise the celebrated entry of the Sultan Mahomet II into Constantinople, which took place on May 23, 1453.

If I have made myself clear about iconicity, then it should also be clear that the mental states that will realize such an imaginative project will bear all the marks of iconicity as I have set them out. What I imagine will be a sequence of events, ordered into a narrative, and I shall imagine these events by representing them to myself. The complex phenomenology that such mental states are bound to have will ensure them psychic force. If asked what I am doing, it would be natural for me to say, 'I am imagining the Sultan's entering Constantinople'. Further reflection suggests that my project could be described by distributing the credit for what goes on between three internal roles. I am internal dramatist, in that I draw upon a number of different dispositions that I have, even though in doing so I am heavily constrained by what I have recently acquired from Gibbon: reading Gibbon has provided me with repertoires for the various characters he writes of and I imagine. I am internal actor, in that I represent to myself the various characters, the animate and the inanimate cast of this momentous event, and do so in internal imagery. And I am internal audience, in that at the end of the project, indeed at certain crucial moments in the course of it, which constitute closures in the narrative, I shall tend to find myself in a certain condition — cognitive, conative, affective — which I am in in response to what I have been, or still am, visualising. It is this residual condition which in turn is likely to have causal efficacy over my behaviour or my mental dispositions. So visualising is an iconic mental state.

And now for the distinction that I want to introduce.

In visualising the Sultan's entry into Constantinople, I could visualise it from no point of view — from no point of view, that is, within the historical scene. In that case I would visualise the Sultan and his train of viziers and bashans and guards as they passed through the gates of St. Romanus, paused at the hippodrome, and then rode on to Santa Sofia — and this pageant would be presented to me, or I would represent it to myself, as stretched out, frieze-like, the far side of the invisible chasm of history. However I might not do this: I might visualise the event from a point of view within the scene, and specifically from the point of view of one of the characters involved in the event. So I do this. And let us further suppose that, as is not unusual in such cases, self-aggrandizement sets in, and what strikes me as the most natural point of view to adopt from which to visualise the Sultan's entry into Constantinople is that of the Sultan himself. So I adopt it, and in that case what will happen is that I shall successively represent the sights and sounds and smells and internal sensations as they would have reached the eyes and ears and nose and the proprio-perceptive system of the triumphant Sultan: the noise of the horses, and the clatter of spears and armour behind him, the sight of the column of the twisted serpent as the gaze passes upward over it, the smell of shit and summer dust, the thud as his feet, which have shaken themselves free of the stirrups, hit the ground, the sudden cool of being inside the vast old church, and then twenty, thirty feet away, the Moslem zealot hacking to pieces the ancient marble mosaic is in view, and I the Sultan find myself forbidding him, I the Sultan stop him, words of peremptory command issue from my mouth, the mouth of the Sultan. That is how in the second case the narrative will unfold. Now in the first of these two cases I imagine the event acentrally, in the second I imagine it centrally, and more specifically I centrally imagine what the Sultan says and does and feels or I imagine him from the inside. He is the protagonist of my imaginative project.

A word on terminology, followed by a word on the philosophy of the matter. Centrally imagining contrasts itself with acentrally imagining, and, when I centrally imagine an event, there is someone whom I imagine from the inside. Imagining from the inside naturally contrasts itself with imagining from the outside, but 'imagining from the outside' is not a phrase for which I shall find a use. The reason is that, by grouping together unlike cases, it would blur the very distinction on which I want to insist. For I should have to say that, when I centrally imagine an event, I imagine from the outside everyone except the one whom I imagine from the inside, or the protagonist: and I should also have to say that, when I imagine an event acentrally, I imagine everyone from the outside. But in the first case 'outside' would be relative to a point of view that is internal to the imagined scene and occupied. In the second case the term would be used just to show that there is no point of view that is at once internal and occupied. So, to avoid this ambiguity, I shall prefer to say that, when I centrally imagine an event, I imagine one person centrally — the person whom I imagine from the inside, the protagonist — and I imagine all the others peripherally: and that, when I acentrally imagine an event, I imagine everyone acentrally. In other words, the fundamental distinction, corresponding to a big divide between two modes of imagination, is that between centrally (and peripherally) imagining, on the one hand, and acentrally imagining, on the other hand, and this distinction is something that the phrase 'imagining from the outside' can only obscure.

And now I turn from terminology to philosophy to make a point that thus far has been left implicit. It is shown in the example I used. It is that the only restriction upon whom I can centrally imagine is that it should be, first, someone to whom I can refer and, secondly, someone for whom I have, or have the capacity to form, a repertoire of substance. (The first of these conditions may, as some would hold, entail the second.) Specifically, there is no requirement that the person whom I centrally imagine must be me — any more than, in the theatre, the character whom I take as my protagonist must be me. I can centrally imagine someone other than myself. And, for that matter, when I imagine myself, I do not have to imagine myself centrally: I can imagine myself peripherally or acentrally. Centrally imagining is neither a sufficient nor a necessary condition of imagining myself.

To some however it will seem impossible that I should centrally imagine anyone other than myself, and cases where it might be thought that I can they would reinterpret in one or other of two ways, both of which preserve me as the protagonist and add some further complexity to what I imagine. Both ways, I claim, fail. I shall consider them in turn.

The first interpretation is this: When it might be thought that I am centrally imagining the Sultan Mahomet II's entering Constantinople, what I am really doing is centrally imagining myself being identical with Sultan Mahomet II, or identical with him at least for the duration of his entry into Constantinople. However I query the intelligibility of what this interpretation requires me to imagine: that I am identical with someone else. And it is interesting, and germane, that the support that idiom is supposed to lend to the possibility of my imagining such a thing turns out to be illusory. I can say — there is such an idiom — that I imagine myself being Sultan Mahomet II. But in this idiom, appearances notwithstanding, identity does not occur: I am not saying that I imagine myself being identical with Sultan Mahomet II. And this we can see from the fact that, though identity is symmetrical, 'imagining myself being Sultan Mahomet II' and 'imagining Sultan Mahomet II being me' are not synonyms. They are used to pick out two different imaginative projects. If we now ask how these idioms are to be understood, the answer is as substitution-instances of 'imagining $x$ in $y$'s shoes': so I can imagine the Sultan in my shoes; alternatively (and it is alternate) I can imagine myself in the Sultan's shoes. Identity is eliminated. And this analysis provides us with the materials out of which the second interpretation is constructed.

The second interpretation is this: When it might be thought that I am centrally imagining the Sultan's entering Constantinople, what I am really doing is centrally imagining myself in the Sultan's shoes, at least for the duration of his entry into Constantinople, and therefore doing what I know he did there and then. But, though what this interpretation (unlike what the first interpretation) requires me to imagine is fully intelligible, it seems unconvincing as an account of the case under consideration. For imagining myself in the Sultan's shoes, doing the things that he did, leaves it open to me at any moment to imagine myself brought face to face with the Sultan. And that is something that the imaginative project I have in mind clearly rules out.

That I can centrally imagine someone other than myself is a fact of major importance, and it is a fact of philosophy, not just a point of terminology. It remains undisputed that, in the majority of cases, the person whom I centrally imagine will be myself.

9. I have claimed that, though there is no direct counterpart in the real-life theatre to the distinction between centrally imagining and acentrally imagining, nevertheless the difference can be captured in the terms that I have borrowed from the theatre to describe the formation of iconic mental states. For this claim to be vindicated it is necessary that we should be able, with the use of these terms, to say what it is for someone to select one rather than another of his internal dramatis personae as his protagonist. My claim, therefore, must be that the selection of a protagonist, which lies at the core of centrally imagining, can be seen as a piece of collaboration between the three internal dramatic roles. I believe it can be, with the lion's share going to the internal audience. Let us see how this works out.

As internal dramatist the person has to assign to the character who is to be the protagonist not merely lines and action, but also thoughts, feelings, and experiences. And he must assign lines and actions, but above all thoughts, feelings, and experiences, liberally and systematically. 'Systematically' means as and when they occur in the narrative, and 'liberally' means that there are plenty of them.

It is important to see that the thoughts, feelings, and experiences that are assigned to the protagonist fill two distinct functions. In the first place, they serve as the background to the lines and actions that are the protagonist's own, and secondly they serve as the means — and are the only means — by which the lines and actions, and the thoughts, feelings, and experiences, of other characters, or of those peripherally imagined, can get into the narrative. The mental states, the imagined mental states, of the protagonist, act, in virtue of their intentionality, as windows open on to the world, through which characters other than the protagonist can climb into the story. Now, insofar as the protagonist's thoughts, feelings, and experiences serve the first of these functions, they are constrained solely by the repertoire that the person assigns to the protagonist as his repertoire. But, insofar as they serve the second function, they are also constrained, or constrained in part, by repertoires that are not assigned to the protagonist but are assigned — that is, are imagined assigned — by the protagonist to the other characters who share his world as their repertoires. Not the repertoires themselves, but belief in them belongs to the protagonist's repertoire. Now, if the protagonist is imagined to share his world with others, then of necessity he must have assigned to him as part of his repertoire beliefs about the repertoires of others. Furthermore, if he is imagined not only to share his world with others but also to imagine their sharing their worlds with each other and with him, then the beliefs that he must have assigned to him about the repertoires of others must specifically include beliefs about their beliefs about the repertoires of others, including his own. It is manifest that this embedment of beliefs in the repertoire that has to be assigned to the protagonist will very soon place a limit upon a person's capacity for centrally imagining. Let us for the moment ascribe this difficulty to the mounting complexity of the task, though we shall soon have a way of looking at the matter which is at once more comprehensive and more enlightening.

I return to the question how the selection of a protagonist can be articulated in terms of the three dramatic roles.

As internal actor the person has to represent what the internal dramatist has prepared for him. He must (to recapitulate) represent to himself, for his own benefit, the actions and the lines, the thoughts, feelings, and experiences that have been assigned by the internal dramatist to the protagonist: and through them, through their intentionality, he will introduce whatever in the way of lines and actions, of thought, feeling, and experience, the other characters are imagined, are peripherally imagined, to have. And he must not only represent what the internal dramatist has prepared for him, he must do so in a way that respects the way in which the internal dramatist has prepared it: that is, in the perspective of the protagonist. He must represent the actions, lines, thoughts, feelings, and experiences, of the protagonist as though they were his own. 'As though they were his own', note: not 'as his own'— for it would be inappropriate for him to represent them as his own except in the case where the protagonist is himself, which is only one possibility amongst others, even if it is that which is most often actualized.

It is however as internal audience that the person makes the most significant, indeed the decisive, contribution to the selection of the protagonist. To the internal audience falls, I have said, the lion's share of the work. To grasp this, let us see the form that this contribution takes. Distinctive of centrally imagining is that the internal audience is modelled upon the empathic external audience. It is empathic, and furthermore empathic to the character who is, and is partly in virtue of this fact, the protagonist. And what this in turn ensures is that the residual condition in which the person will tend to find himself after representing to himself the thoughts, feelings, and experiences, of this character as though they were his own, is the very condition that thinking, feeling, experiencing, those things would have left him in. To assert then, as I have done, that the decisive contribution to the selection of the protagonist is that made by the internal audience seems to imply that the identity of the protagonist, or who it is that I centrally imagine, is ultimately a matter of whom, out of the dramatis personae of my imaginings, I finish up, or tend to finish up, in unison with. And that implication is, I suggest, correct. It accords with whatever pretheoretical ideas we have about imagining someone from the inside, and it also fits in, as we shall see, with the uses to which centrally imagining is put.

I have said, and the point needs to be insisted upon, that the residual condition on which centrally imagining terminates is the realization of a tendency. There is an invariable pull in this direction, but there can be countervailing factors. One crucial factor is the state of the repertoire that is assigned to the protagonist. For repertoires, and bits of repertoires, can be arranged on a scale that runs from the replete to the purely nominal, and where any particular bit falls will depend partly on how much the person knows or understands about the protagonist and partly on how far what he imagines the protagonist doing draws on this knowledge and understanding. Three cases where the relevant repertoire, or bit of the repertoire, comes close to the nominal, though for somewhat different reasons, may prove illuminating. The first case is where I try to centrally imagine an old friend, about whom I am not ignorant, reciting to himself Pushkin: but my knowledge of Russian and of Pushkin is zero, so the relevant bit of the repertoire must itself be close to zero, saved, if at all, only by a sense of what Pushkin's poetry, whatever that is actually like, means to my friend. A second case is where I try to centrally imagine my student Kemal taking part in a ceremony at the mosque, and here not merely is my knowledge of Islam hazy, but I also have no idea at all what it means to him in the way of faith or feeling. A third case, of a kind just touched upon, is where I set myself to centrally imagine John's centrally imagining Angus's centrally imagining Stephen's writing his diary, for no matter how much I know about these three friends, no matter how successfully I can speculate about John's understanding of Angus's beliefs about what Stephen thinks worth putting into his diary, I am certain not to have this information in a form in which it would be available for me to use appropriately as the narrative unfolds. Multiply embedded repertoires are not accessible, and that is one powerful reason why such repertoires are in effect nominal. And it is as the repertoire degenerates towards the nominal, for whatever reason, in whatever way, that the tendency for the person to find himself in what I have called the residual condition is increasingly weakened.

10. To summarize the discussion thus far: There are three essential features of centrally imagining. They are *point of view, plenitude,* and *cogency.* Point of view is this: In centrally imagining an event, I imagine it from the point of view, or in the perspective, of some character within that event. This character is the protagonist, and it need not be me. Plenitude is this: As I centrally imagine the protagonist's doing or saying this or that, so I shall tend to imagine his thinking, his experiencing, his feeling this or that. Both point of view and plenitude I attribute to the joint work of internal dramatist and internal actor. Cogency is this: As I centrally imagine the protagonist's thinking, experiencing, feeling this or that, so I shall tend to find myself in the condition — cognitive, cona-

tive, affective — in which the mental states that I imagine, were I actually to have them, would leave me. Cogency is the work of the internal audience. And note that both plenitude and cogency, which derive from powers that centrally imagining possesses, manifest themselves as tendencies.

I have said a certain amount about plenitude and cogency. Point of view, it might be thought, can speak for itself. But I need to distinguish my use of it from broader and from narrower interpretations. On a broad interpretation, every mental state has a point of view just because a person enters into it. The assertion of point of view, thus understood, equates with the denial of constructionism. On a narrow interpretation, only perceptual states have a point of view. The assertion of point of view, thus understood, reflects the perspectival character of the states. However, on my use of the term, in addition to perceptual states, imaginings — and specifically cases where I centrally imagine someone or other thinking, feeling, experiencing this or that — have a point of view: therefore my use is broader than the narrow interpretation. But it is also narrower than the broad interpretation, in that for me what is imagined — the thinking, feeling, experiencing — need not itself have a point of view. If, according to me, centrally imagining someone or other's mental states has a point of view, that is not because the imagined mental states have a point of view: it is because in centrally imagining them, I thereby adopt a point of view. If both centred iconic mental states and ordinary perceptual states have a point of view, they come by it in very different ways. Perceptual states come by theirs through the person's position in nature: iconic mental states come by theirs through mental activity.

By contrast, acentrally imagining essentially lacks point of view. And in lacking point of view, it lacks plenitude and cogency as I have defined them.

Nevertheless in many cases where I acentrally imagine some event there is a residual condition — cognitive, conative, affective — in which the imaginative project will tend to leave me and do so because I have engaged in it. What the issue hangs on is whether the external audience that the internal audience is modelled upon is the sympathetic or the detached audience. It is only if the internal audience is sympathetic rather than detached that the tendency can be posited. And the residual condition will then be that in which I would have been left, had I been present at the imagined event and distributed favour in the way in which I did throughout the imaginative project.

That iconic imagination often leaves the person in a certain residual condition and that, specifically, centred iconic imagination tends to leave him in the condition of the protagonist, is what does most to ensure that iconic imagination generally, and centred iconic imagination invariably, have psychic force. And we can understand this psychic force if we trace, as I have been doing, the route through the imaginative project by which this residual condition comes about. The most general characterization that can be given of the psychic force of iconic imagination is that it simulates to some degree the effect of an event that we might have lived through — either the overall effect of the event, or, more specifically, its effect upon belief, desire, or feeling.

Before I turn to the ways in which the psychic force of iconic imagination can be exploited so as to become psychic function, I want to consider briefly how the boundaries of imaginative iconic states are to be drawn.

11. I have said that the internal audience that enters into the description of iconic imagination is not to be thought of as an internal observer, but that there is a place for an internal observer in the description of our mental life. I shall introduce the internal observer in the context of centrally imagining.

If I centrally imagine someone or other doing something, then I shall, as internal audience, tend to find myself in the condition in which being in the protagonist's overall position would leave me. But when this happens, so much are we, in Montaigne's phrase, *chose ondoyante* that this condition is likely to be overtaken by some new feeling. But, when this in turn happens, this new feeling will be no part of the original imaginative project in the way in which the condition it overtook certainly was. In feeling what I then feel, I shall have abdicated the role of internal audience: I shall have adopted that of internal observer. The internal observer does not belong to, though it belongs to the context or falls within the orbit of, iconic imagination.

I shall use the familiar phenomenon of the erotic daydream,

which invades idle hours, to illustrate the distinction. Let us suppose that I centrally imagine myself engaged in some sexual activity with a strange figure, or a close friend. As I do so, I centrally imagine myself becoming excited over what occurs between us. This is plenitude. And as I centrally imagine myself becoming excited, so I become excited. This is cogency. And then I pause, I reflect on my excited condition, and as I reflect on it — and here much depends on the circumstances, on what kind of a person I am, on who the other person is, on where we both are — I begin to feel, in response to or in reaction against my excitement, one or other of an assortment of feelings. I may feel surprise, or embarrassment, or relief, or disgust, or a fiercer form of excitement, which is excitement at my own excitability. And the point that I am illustrating rules that this feeling, whichever of these it may be, is no part of the erotic daydream, though the original excitement, to which any of this is a response or against which it is a reaction, is. The original excitement is that of the internal audience, the subsequent feeling that of the internal observer.

In *Albertine Disparue* the Narrator starts to speculate about the state of expectation in which in their last weeks together Albertine would have sat at home awaiting the arrival of some young girl with whom she anticipated making love. Drawing upon his own experience, recalling the agitation, the exhilaration, the cold sweat into which *he* would habitually fall when he found himself hoping for some girl who attracted him, he started to imagine — centrally, we may suppose — Albertine feeling just the same fluctuating, tremulous emotions while she waited for, say, Andrée to arrive. And then, in a flash, utter despondency came over him. Re-experiencing in the person of Albertine all the hopes and terrors of desire, all the feverish voluptuousness that accompanied them, so familiar to him from his own life, he was forced to recognize just how little by comparison he could have meant to her, how trivial and insignificant she must have found those long, earnest conversations that he and she used to have together as he discoursed on the merits of Stendhal and Victor Hugo. My claim is that the despondency to which the Narrator succumbs on realizing what Albertine must have felt falls outside the imaginative sequence he initiated; it is the contribution of the internal observer, whereas the sensuous excitement that came over him on the way to this realization and to which the despondency is a reaction is the contribution of the internal audience. It falls firmly within the imaginative project: it is part of it.

12. There are, I claimed in the previous lecture, two distinct ways in which the psychic force of a mental state can get exploited so that the mental state graduates from having psychic force to having psychic function.

The two ways are these: Either the mental state is brought about through an intention which the person forms, or a mental disposition causes it to occur. In the first case some end that the person pursues, in the second case the role of the disposition, coincides with the psychic force of the mental state, and in each case it is this coincidence that is why the state comes about. In the first case the coincidence is why the person forms the intention to bring it about: in the second case it is why the disposition causes it to occur.

Does this apply to iconic imagination? It has psychic force, but can this psychic force graduate to psychic function? The answer is Yes, and I next want to consider how such an intention could be motivated, or what the disposition might be.

13. First, the way of intention.

What motive could a person have for initiating an iconic imaginative project so as to reap the benefit of its psychic force? Given the general characterization of the psychic force of iconic imagination — that it simulates to some degree the effect that the imagined event would have upon the person if he had lived through it — then two obvious suggestions are pleasure and curiosity. So long as the event is attractive to him, or its nature has not been fully investigated, one or other of these motives could lead the person to want to simulate the effect that the event would have upon him.

The argument has been advanced, notably by Sartre, that it cannot be possible for a person to learn anything from imagination, because in imagination — and here the contrast would be between imagination and perception — the intentionality of a person's mental states derives entirely from his knowledge and belief. Everything that is in his imaginings he has put there. This argument is open to the obvious objection that it assumes that knowledge and belief are closed under entailment, or that we know or believe the consequences not only of every single thing that we know or believe but of every conjunction of everything that we know or believe. But, more germanely, the argument overlooks the fact that there is a kind of knowledge that comes with experiencing a thing or an event, and the further fact that iconic imagination because of its phenomenology is uniquely able to understudy experience in the provision of such knowledge. The two points against Sartre's argument are linked in that what experience, or its surrogate, imagination, can distinctively do is to effect a synthesis of what we know by report.

14. Secondly, the way of disposition.

What disposition or dispositions could there be that cause states of iconic imagination and do so because of their phenomenology? My claim is that it is desire that characteristically expresses itself in imagination.

For this claim to hold there must be a coincidence between the psychic force of iconic imagination and the role of desire. There is, I claim, such a coincidence, which is best seen by breaking down both iconic imagination and desire into kinds, and then pairing off kind of iconic imagination and kind of desire as concurrent. Such a pairing is made possible by a structural parallelism between the mental phenomena. For sorting desires by their intentionality, or what kind of object they are directed upon, we find that there are three kinds of desire. There are desires to do something or other: desires that someone, or, more specifically, someone else, should do something or other, where such a desire may or may not impinge upon the person who has the desire: and desires that something or other should be the case. Sorting iconic imagination by its phenomenology, we find that for each of the three kinds of desire there is a corresponding kind of imagination, which is precisely apt to represent its kind of object. So, my desire to do or be something or other pairs with my centrally imagining my doing or being that thing: my desire that someone, someone else, should do or be something or other pairs with my either peripherally or acentrally (depending on whether what I desire impinges on me or doesn't) imagining his doing or being that thing: and my desire that something should be the case pairs with my acentrally imagining that thing to be the case. Wherever acentrally imagining expresses desire, it may be assumed that the internal audience is modelled on the external sympathetic audience rather than the detached audience. Within the orbit of desire, detachment is not a stance that can be maintained.

With this pairing of iconic imagination and desire, let us go back to the claim that the two phenomena concur or that there is a coincidence between the psychic force of one and the role of the other. The concurrence is effected by two different routes, the first and more important of which involves no new material, but the second involves the introduction of a new mental phenomenon, which is the wish. I shall postpone discussion of the second route until the later part of this section.

As far as the first route is concerned, the crucial consideration is that iconically imagining the object of desire in each case serves to bind that object to pleasure. It does so because in each case the residual condition in which the person will tend to be left will be pleasure. Centrally imagining myself doing or being something I want to do or be: peripherally or acentrally imagining someone doing or being something that I want him to do or be, the first when what I want impinges on me, the second when it doesn't: and acentrally imagining something that I want to be the case being the case — all these projects would tend to leave me pleased. And this we can see by returning to the account of imagination in terms of the theatre and seeing that pleasure is what the relevant internal audience will tend to feel. For the internal audience will either be an empathic audience (in the first case and in the second case when the someone else is imagined peripherally) empathising with a character whose desires are being fulfilled; or a sympathetic audience (in the third case and in the second case when the someone else is imagined acentrally) responding to a situation it looks upon with favour. Each situation is cause for pleasure.

But, it may be objected, this account is wrong. Despite its apparent complexity, it rests on an over-simplification: an over-simplification which, in turn, rests upon an over-optimistic view of our psychology. For it assumes that, when a person's desires are satis-

fied, so is he: that, when he gets what he wants, he will be pleased
— it is only such an assumption that would predict that in each case
the internal audience will be pleased. But, though this is sometimes or even mostly the case, it is not invariably the case. The
assumption overlooks not only possible errors of calculation or
mistakes in instrumental belief that a person might make, but the
sombre facts of ambivalence and conflict of desire. As soon as a
person gets what he wants, or sooner, even as he finds himself on
the brink of attaining it, he may experience remorse, apprehension, tedium, humiliation. He may be, in Freud's phrase, 'wrecked
by success'. And once a person recognizes these same sombre facts
or, for that matter, the fallibility of reasoning from ends to means,
once he accepts that there is a gap that can open up between desire
satisfied and satisfaction, this knowledge, this self-knowledge,
must cast a shadow forwards across the imaginative project each
time he tries to imagine the object of his desire realized. It must
disrupt the smooth transition from his iconically imagining the
fulfilment of one of his desires to his experience of pleasure. There
are two specific points in the imaginative project at which awareness of the fallibility of desire will insert itself and ensure that the
project does not automatically terminate on pleasure. In the descriptive account of iconic imagination that I have been employing, the two points are the repertoire and favour.

   To see how this would work, let us divide the iconic imagination of desire not, as I have been doing, into three, but into two. Let
us put together as one the case where a person desires to do or to be
something and the case where he desires that someone else should
do or be something that will impinge on him, for in both these
cases he centrally imagines himself getting what he desires. In
order to accommodate ambivalence and conflict of desire, the
person will correspondingly adjust the repertoire that he assigns to
himself — he will, say, add to anticipation apprehension of desire
fulfilled — and then the imagined he, who is the character with
whom the internal audience will empathise, will not necessarily be
a contented character, nor will the audience itself, and so the
outcome for the person will not necessarily be pleasure. Let us next
put together the case where a person desires that someone else
should do or be something and the case where he desires that

something should come about and neither eventuality affects him directly, for in both these cases he acentrally imagines what he desires. In order to accommodate ambivalence and conflict of desire, what he will now do is to adjust the judgment that he assigns to the internal audience, which is the sympathetic audience — he will, say, mix favour with indifference or disfavour — and then the audience will not necessarily finish up contented, and so once again, the outcome for the person will not automatically be pleasure.

To meet this objection it is not necessary to deny the facts of which it is a salutary reminder. For the objection is at fault in the role that it ascribes to them, so that it in turn can be charged with taking an over-optimistic view of our psychology. Specifically, the objection fails to note the significantly different ways in which iconic imagination is related to our total body of desires, beliefs, and emotions when it expresses desire and when it is invoked in the interest of curiosity — including (it must be noted) curiosity about whether this or that desire will really satisfy us. For, when I invoke iconic imagination in order to learn something about the world or about myself or about myself in relation to the world, I make use of everything that I already know or believe about the world and about myself: I ensure that the repertoire for myself on which I draw is as rich and as complex as self-knowledge allows: I let favour distribute itself across the narrative in as unimpeded a way as possible. For, only if I do this, do I have a chance of finding out what I think I need to learn. However, when iconic imagination expresses desire, the position is very different. The repertoire is heavily abridged, favour is rigidly constrained, so that nothing in my psychology that could disrupt the pleasing effect of imagining desire satisfied is afforded recognition. It is in part because desires that are in conflict with the desire imagined are censored out that iconic imagination not only expresses desire, it reinforces it.

Let me illustrate the differential working of imagination in the two cases. In his *Autobiography* John Stuart Mill tells how one day he asked himself whether the implementation of all the reforms that the Benthamites had urged, social, political, educational, moral — the satisfaction, in effect, of the official desires of his culture circle — would give him total satisfaction, should it come about. In order to answer this question he set himself to imagine such a dawn. So that he should be able to trust the answer that this would give him, he was at pains to draw upon every relevant belief that he had about himself and the world: and just because he did this he laid himself open to the possibility of receiving an unexpected answer. Which is just what he got. To the question that he put to himself, 'an irrepressible self-consciousness distinctly answered "No".' This prefaced the great mental crisis of his life. But when Emma Bovary, in the weeks following the great ball at La Vaubyessard, allows her mind to fill with daydreams in which she returns to the château as the vicomte's favoured guest, travels to Paris, goes to the races and to soirées, frequents society and converses with ambassadors and duchesses, she does not find a place in these imagined scenes for her less congenial dispositions: for her lassitude, for her cloying melancholy, for that dissatisfaction with herself which spread contagiously to every neighbouring thing. Emma Bovary's daydreams were not in the service of inquiry. She wasn't testing these worldly desires, she was expressing them, and in consequence the sickly side of her nature was not allowed to enter in and stain the picture of their fulfilment.

A fact that we considered in the last lecture is that we do not act under the aegis of all our desires. A complementary fact is that in imagining the satisfaction of any one desire we do not do so against the background of all others, and it is the failure of the present objection to recognize the ways in which individual desires entrench themselves in our psychology as though conflict did not exist that led me to charge it with just what it had charged me with: over-optimism.

The point I have been making might now be put by saying that, when iconic imagination expresses desire, it not only represents what the person desires but represents it as desirable overall. Nothing of the same kind holds when iconic imagination serves curiosity, even curiosity about some desire of ours. For it then represents the object of that desire against the background of all our desires — that is, all our other desires *and* it.

The question remains why, even if iconic imagination does bind the object of desire to pleasure in the way I have suggested, this establishes the concurrence of desire and imagination: for that requires that imagination plays a crucial part in bringing about the modifications of behaviour and disposition that, within the psychology of the person, are associated with desire. Why should we believe that what binds desire to pleasure gives causal efficacy to desire?

The primary consideration here is that the representation of desire pleasurably satisfied acts as a lure: it lures the person either into action or into the formation of fresh dispositions. Of course it does this only in consort with beliefs. Ancillary beliefs about the world, inner or outer, are required to fix the action that is to be done, or the disposition that will be formed, given a desire. A secondary consideration is that representation of the desire actually, and pleasurably, satisfied is calculated to erode any residual resistance that may exist in the mind to its pursuit. And, finally, representation of the desire as satisfied reinforces the desire, which is also part of its role or the efficacy it seeks. Even if something pleases us only because we desire it, the more it pleases us, the more will we tend to desire it. And all these services that iconic imagination performs for desire, it does so, it must be emphasised, through its psychic force.

In these last three considerations lies the truth that there undoubtedly is to psychological hedonism. But to recognize this element of truth requires that we reinterpret this ancient doctrine not as a view about the way in which desire is formed, as it is usually taken, but as a view about the way in which desire motivates to action. For even if we think that desire is essentially motivational, the question can arise just how it is so. Does it motivate through recruiting mental states, and, if it does, does it recruit their phenomenology? Seen as an answer to this question, psychological hedonism insists on the place of pleasure in any motivational history running from desire to action, and I have been suggesting that it is right to do so. But on my reinterpretation of the doctrine, pleasure, in accounting for action, presupposes desire: pleasure does not account for desire itself, which is what the doctrine traditionally would have it do.

A problem for my account of the connection between iconic imagination and desire might seem to lie in the fact that desires that are idle or have no role — my desire to have seen the *Oresteia* in the twilight of ancient Athens, my desire to have had another mother—also maintain a close connection with iconic imagination. To what outcome are such imaginings supposed to lure us? Part of the explanation for the continuing connection between desire and imagination in such cases is that the connection is effected on the highest level of generality, it is joined between desire and imagination as such, and therefore it is not sensitive to the distinction between working and idle desires. Furthermore, this distinction itself is, as behaviourists have been ready to see and to exploit, not all that easy to draw, and the difficulty can only increase when the role of desire is recognized to include not only the modification of behaviour but also the modification of disposition—and indeed the reinforcement of itself. This recognition leaves few desires idle.

But the most important consideration as far as the connection between iconic imagination and idle desires is concerned is the fact that, however the line is to be drawn between idle and working desires, there is no firm register in our psychology of this line or of where it runs. The mind tends to be indifferent to the difference. But to understand why this should be so, I turn to the second of the two routes along which, as I said at the beginning of this section in introducing the topic, the concurrence of iconic imagination and desire is effected, for it is in this area that the explanation lies.

The second route along which the concurrence is effected owes everything to the fact that desire never fully emancipates itself from the aegis of the wish. The wish is, in the life-history of the person, an archaic phenomenon, and, whether or not desire actually originates in the wish, the wish exercises a perennial attraction over desire, which, under stress, will degenerate into—and in at least this sense regress to—the more primitive condition of the wish.

What, then, is the wish?

I wish for something rather than merely desire it, when I desire it: and because I desire it I tend to imagine (in the appropriate mode) my desire satisfied: and when I imagine my desire satisfied, it is for me as if that desire were satisfied. (This suggests that, even if the wish is more primitive psychologically than desire, conceptually it is more complex, in that desire enters into the definition of the wish. But it is unclear that this must be so, and the formulation of the definition may simply reflect the fact that we view the wish in our current perspective or from the standpoint of desire.)

But how, we must ask, could it ever be that my having a mental state, which is what imagining is, could be for me like satisfying a desire — except, in the limiting case, when the desire is for that state?

The answer lies in the fact that not merely is the wish an archaic mental phenomenon, but it comes along with an archaic theory of the mind to which the wisher subscribes. Indeed, the archaicism of the latter largely accounts for the archaicism of the former. The theory is to the effect that a mental state suffices by its mere occurrence to bring about that which it is of, or, more specifically — since the theory specifically ranges over iconic mental states — that which it represents.

It is crucial to recognize that this theory involves not only a misrepresentation in the person's mind of mental states and what they can achieve, but also a misrepresentation of desires and what satisfies them. The psychic force of imagination is over-valued, but at the same time the role of desire is etherealized. It is for this reason that it would be wrong to say that this second route by which the concurrence of iconic imagination and desire is effected rests simply on a false instrumental belief or exemplifies magic. What it rests on is an illusion, which, when operative, is pervasive in the psychology of the person and is furthermore something from which desire is never altogether liberated.

The archaic theory of the mind has a name. The name was coined for it by one of Freud's patients, known as the Rat Man, who called the belief a belief in the 'omnipotence of thoughts'. We shall hear more about this belief. I shall refer to it in the next lecture, but I shall talk about it at greater length in Lecture V, when I shall also have something to say about the sorrows and follies of the Rat Man himself. But I hope I have already said enough about the theory to show how under its influence, and specifically under the influence of the wish, the mind is ready to blur the distinction between working and idle desires.

A final point about the relationship of desire and imagination: I have made the familiar point that desire cannot lead to action, however much its motivational force has been inflamed by imagination, except in consort with belief. Belief, belief about how the world is, partially fixes what is the appropriate action for any given desire. It might now be contended that this interlock between desire and belief must be anticipated in imagination. For is it not the case that for any given desire what is imagined as the satisfaction of that desire will always be against a certain background, and this background must be fixed by belief? The answer is, No. Certainly when desire is imagined satisfied, it is always against a background. But this background, this imagined background, need not be believed in: it need only be supposed. Indeed, the background against which one desire is imagined to be satisfied is often nothing other than the representation of the satisfaction of other desires. This will prove a matter of importance when we come to consider a cousin of the wish: phantasy.

15. A woman who lives in the North writes to me that, when she expects friends to arrive for a visit, she finds herself imagining their crashing in hideous ways on the motorway that passes near where she lives. She does so, we must believe, not because this is what she desires, but because this is what she fears. Does not such a case run counter to my views?

The case engages with my views in the following way: Fears are a form of aversion: aversions are the negatives of desire, in that to every aversion there corresponds a desire not to do this or a desire not to do that or a desire that something should not be the case. In consequence of these equivalences, my views might be expected to predict what someone who, like my friend, is in the grip of fear should imagine. She should imagine what she desires, which is the negation of what she is averse to and therefore the negation of what she fears. But in imagining her friends' crashing on the motorway, she imagines what she fears, which is what she is averse to, which is the negation of what she desires. Does this not refute my account? Or, to put the matter the other way round, does not my account, taken in conjunction with what she imagines, require me to believe that what she really desires is for her friends to crash on the motorway?

I start with the last point. If my correspondent did desire that her friends crash on the motorway, what my account would predict her to imagine is something rather more specific than what she tells me she imagines. She would imagine the crashes occurring, and she would imagine them as overall desirable. To employ the descriptive resources of the dramatic analogy, she would represent to herself her friends involved in all kinds of pile-up: she would do so acentrally: the internal audience, which would therefore be of the sympathetic kind, would regard the imagined events with favour: and she would tend, in consequence of what she had represented to herself, to end up pleased. (Of course, she might, after imagining all this, react strongly both against what she had imagined and the delight she had taken in it, and feel revolted. But the revulsion would fall outside the imaginative project, and, though it would testify to her general good feelings, it would do nothing to dispute the nature of the specific desires she had just expressed.)

This now puts us in a better position to see what this woman should be expected to imagine, given that (as she tells me) she fears, and so has an aversion to, her friends' crashing on the motorway. She will imagine the crashes occurring, but now she will imagine them as fearful. She again will represent to herself her friends involved in these hideous pile-ups, again she will do so acentrally, but the internal audience, still the sympathetic audience, will look upon the event with disfavour, and she will tend, as a result of what she has imagined, to end up appalled and terrified. And just this, as I understand it, is what she wrote to tell me she does.

However it might be objected that this is a very indirect and roundabout way for fear, or, more specifically, for aversion, to find expression, and it fails to keep aversion and desire strictly in line in their relations with imagination. If aversion were to be brought into line with desire, then surely my friend should represent to herself not her visitors' crashing on the motorway but her visitors' not crashing on the motorway. In expressing her aversion, she should not have to rely solely, as the previous suggestion would have it, upon the contribution of the internal audience, but she should also have at the disposal of her aversion the contribution of the internal dramatist and that of the internal actor. The aversion should find expression through the imagery that imagination pro-

vides and not only through the attendant feelings — that would be
the nub of the objection.

The objection fails because it does not correctly appreciate the
materials, the mental materials, of imagination. In the first place it
is utterly wrong, as we have seen several times, to think of the
condition in which the person is left as the result of imagining
whatever it is, or the residual condition, as a matter of attendant
feelings. The residual condition and such feelings as it involves are
at least as much a part of the imaginative project as the imagery,
and we have seen that, in one context, that of fixing the protagonist in centrally imagining, they pull more weight. Secondly,
there cannot be — so a feeling cannot find expression through —
negative images or imagery that represents something as not being
the case. Of course, an image can represent that something isn't
the case by representing a contrary state of affairs. There can only
be positive images, images representing this or that as the case.
And, if to this last point it is retorted that, though this holds true of
external images, it cannot also hold true of internal or mental
images if they are to be the medium of intentionality — since a
person in thinking that something is the case must thereby, or
without switching to another medium, be able to think that it isn't
the case — the answer is that positive images can come to represent
something as not being the case. They can come to represent
this — as in the case of the woman who expresses her desire that
something shouldn't happen in images that represent it as happening — through feelings and thoughts which can, from the point of
view of the imagery, be thought of as merely attendant upon it but
which are, from the point of view of the mental state as a whole,
integral to it. These feelings and thoughts operate upon the imagery like the negation sign. Another way of putting the matter is to
say that, whereas representational pictures require interpretation,
the materials that such interpretation calls for, such as thoughts,
beliefs, feelings, are materials that mental images bring with them.
Mental images arise in the mind interpreted.

A final point about aversions: They lie heavily under the shadow
of the wish.

16. Realism requires us to recognize that the neat classification
that I have proposed for imagination fits untidily on to the world.

In life there are constant alternations between centrally imagining and acentrally imagining, and, within centrally imagining, between imagining the event from the point of view of one character and imagining it from the point of view of another character. These oscillations between and within modes of imagination — from viewpoint to no viewpoint, from this viewpoint to that viewpoint — become more striking, more vertiginous, as we shift our attention from the manifest to the latent content of our imaginings, or try to retrieve the significance of what we imagine. On the manifest level the abrupt transitions are apt to get smoothed over.

The point is neatly illustrated, as might be expected, in an essay of Freud's. The title of the essay is 'A Child is Being Beaten', and in it Freud takes one particular phantasy, which he found to be common amongst patients, and which he had reason to believe was first entertained early in life and then persisted and recurred. The phantasy is that a child, or sometimes more than one child, is chastised by being whipped on its bottom. But even amongst those patients who fairly readily revealed that they had such phantasies, there was great difficulty in answering a number of questions about them, which turn out to be the very questions that must be answered if the classification that I have proposed is to be applied. Freud lists such questions:

Who was the child that was being beaten? The one who was himself producing the phantasy or another? Was it always the same child or as often as not a different one? Who was it who was beating the child? A grown-up? And if so, who? Or did the child imagine that he himself was beating another one?

'Nothing', Freud tells us, 'could be ascertained that threw any light upon all these questions.' Pressed harder, the patients gave only the one timid reply, 'I know nothing more about it: a child is being beaten.'

The questions that Freud asked and his patients could not answer touch upon issues that we are in a position to identify as mode of imagination, identity of the dramatis personae, identity of the protagonist, repertoire, and favour. And an explanation that Freud implies for the patients' inability to answer these questions fits in very well with my account of the concurrence between imagination and desire. For Freud suspected that the difficulty that the patients had in describing what they really imagined was a difficulty they had in recognizing what they really desired.

Nevertheless, at least in the case of his women patients, Freud had some success in ordering the phantasies that he was told of into some kind of chronological sequence according to the date from which they originated. He detected three phases. Then by identifying for each phase a characteristic mode of imagination in which the phantasy was cast, a characteristic point of view or absence of it, and characteristic repertoires for the dramatis personae, he was able to reconstruct a fragment of female psycho-sexual history. So in the phantasies that derive from the earliest phase, the girl peripherally imagines her father beating another child in front of her. The other child seems satisfied. Phantasies from this phase express jealously as well as an approximation to sadism. In phantasies deriving from the next phase the girl centrally imagines herself being beaten by her father, and she enjoys it. Now the phantasy expresses masochism. In phantasies of the last phase the situation is confused. The girl fluctuates between acentrally imagining a teacher beating a lot of boys and centrally imagining herself getting a whipping from her father and liking it. The phantasy is now condensed, it possesses more than one point of view, and it combines in ways that I shall not attempt to disentangle both sadism and masochism. But I have, I hope, followed Freud's reconstruction far enough to secure the point that in actuality mode, viewpoint, repertoire, oscillate, and that as a result of these oscillations the same phantasy — same, that is, judged by the identity of the events it represents — can become the expression of different desires or acquire different significance.

In the next lecture I shall pursue iconicity.

# IV Experiential Memory, Introjection, and the Inner World

1. In the last lecture I considered one kind of mental state — it was one kind of imagination — and I attributed to type mental states of this kind and to token mental states of those types the property of iconicity. Token iconic mental states present in a singularly vivid fashion — they represent — the individuals, the events, the sequences of events, the stories, that they are of. In this lecture I want to consider two further kinds of mental state. One is a kind of memory, the other is a kind of phantasy. Type mental states of these kinds, and their tokens, are also iconic. And, like states of iconic imagination, they play a very important if not properly recognized role in the way we lead our lives.

2. The kind of memory and the kind of phantasy that I have in mind differ from iconic imagination in one important respect. They are dependent phenomena: that is to say, for every token mental state of either kind there is an earlier event — an earlier event in the life of the person whose mental state it is — to which it is related in a special way. Returning the phrase to its etymology, I shall say that every dependent event depends from some original event. And note that, if the original event and the dependent mental state must be, as I have said, events in the life of the same person, this necessity is not analytic nor is it a mere matter of definition.

Dependence, or the relation between the dependent mental state and the original event, is a causal relation. It is a causal relation of some complexity in that causality enters into it in two distinct ways. In the first place, there is the causal connection between the original event and the mental state. This relation is invariably mediated. It is mediated by a disposition. The disposition arises in the original event, and the mental state manifests the disposition, and both the two constituent relations that are thereby formed, that between event and disposition and that between disposition and state, are causal: the original event causes the disposition to be, and the disposition causes the mental state to occur. And, secondly, causality appears within the role of the mediating disposition. Not only is the disposition a causal effect of the original event, but it has as its role the preservation and transmission of the causal influence of the original event. Its role is to keep the event causally alive. And since a mental state that manifests a disposition furthers its role, every dependent mental state preserves and transmits the causal influence of the original event from which it depends. Dependence, then, is at once an instance of causality and an agent of causality: it exemplifies and it diffuses one and the same causal influence.

Dependence, thus understood, and iconicity, as I introduced it in the last lecture, are, of course, mutually independent. Not all iconic states are dependent: visualising is an obvious example. Nor are all dependent states iconic, for, if one kind of memory is iconic, other kinds aren't, yet all memory is dependent. However, when dependence and iconicity conjoin, a remarkable situation supervenes, for which we are fully prepared.

Any mental state that is at once iconic and dependent has psychic force: iconicity ensures this. But the superimposition of dependence upon iconicity ensures more than this. It ensures two further things. In the first place, this psychic force is not idle. It is it that accounts for the concurrence of mental state and the disposition it manifests, and it therefore accounts for the occurrence of the mental state. In the case of a mental state that is at once iconic and dependent, psychic force is invariably psychic function. And, secondly, this psychic force is at the service of an earlier event. It perpetuates and transmits the causal influence of this event. Or to put it the other way round, the way in which an earlier event is kept causally alive is through the phenomenology of a later mental state.

The core of what I have to say about one kind of memory and

one kind of phantasy is this: Mental states of these kinds preserve and transmit the influence of some earlier event. They do so through, or partly through, their psychic force. And when, as is characteristically the case, the original event had psychic force, they preserve and transmit its psychic force through their psychic force.

3. I should like to make two preliminary observations about the kind of memory, the kind of phantasy, I have in mind, and how it functions.

The first observation is that, if it is true that the occurrent memory or the occurrent phantasy, when it occurs, perpetuates the influence of an original event, this does not mean that it faithfully reproduces the original influence of that event. The event itself remains the same, it continues to exert an influence, but the influence of the event can, indeed in normal circumstances will, change. The crucial factor here is that later mental states exert the influence of the earlier event not immediately, but mediately, through a disposition; and, as we saw in Lecture II, dispositions have, contrary to what some philosophers would have us believe, histories. Indeed, they have very complex histories. (Some philosophers, who have allowed dispositions histories, have given them histories of only the simplest or most basic kind: they have allowed them histories of steady secular decay.) Just what permits the influence of a person's past to survive also prevents this influence from surviving unchanged.

It is furthermore an oversimplification to think that the survival of the influence of a past event consists solely in the establishment of a disposition, which, so long as it survives, manifests itself from time to time, for one reason or another, in concurrent mental states, which enforce this influence. For such is the nature of these mental states — and here their iconicity is important — that they can have the effect of modifying or refashioning the dispositions that they manifest as well as the more standard effect of reinforcing them. They can impinge not only on the strength of the dispositions, or the way in which they bind the energies of the person, but also on their content or intentionality. And they can bring about these changes through their mere occurrence if the circumstances are propitious — Proust's 'involuntary' memories, Freud's 'abreaction' are examples — or through their deliberate exploitation in conditions cunningly organized — the confessional or the transference. The feedback from mental state to mental disposition is an essential element in the way in which we try to control the lives that we lead.

Another relevant factor in the way in which the influence of a past event in our lives can change is the mental attribute that I have called significance. The significance of an event, I claimed, is contained within the deep associations to it, and for associations to be deep they have to have been laid down with the event. But, though this is so, these associations can and will ramify during the after-life of the event. A familiar phenomenon is the capacity of an isolated, perhaps a trivial, event to come to stand in for, or be the delegate of, a whole stretch of events to which historically it belonged: a single picnic with tomatoes and small curly leaves of basil and the crunch of salt can signify a complete Tuscan summer, or a period of turbulence and disorder in middle life can be carried by the memory of one brief encounter. And, when this happens, inevitably the influence of the delegate event will change somewhat in deference to the new significance that it now carries. But when the delegation is unconscious, or the person cannot retrieve the set of associated events or situations for which the remembered event is standing in, as in the case of Goethe's childhood memory of his throwing his parents' plates out of the window of their house, the influence of this event is likely to change beyond the person's powers of recognition and comprehension.

The second observation that I have to make is that the kind of memory and the kind of phantasy that I have in mind, though they share all the features that I have thus far considered, differ from one another in the mode in which they preserve and transmit the influence of the original event. In the case of memory the original event is represented in the later mental state, in the case of phantasy it isn't. Both the occurrent memory and the occurrent phantasy are representational, or they represent what they are of — this follows from their iconicity — but memory represents, and phantasy doesn't, the event whose influence it conveys. This is because memory, in addition to exerting the influence of the earlier event, conveys information about it. Indeed, it exerts the influence of the remembered event through conveying information about it — a fact which has led most philosophers altogether to overlook the role of memory as the transmitter of influence and to concentrate upon it exclusively as the conveyor of information. Phantasy, by contrast, only exerts the influence of the earlier event: it conveys no information about it, although a sufficiently skilled observer can infer such information from the phantasy. In doing so he is likely to draw upon further, perhaps theoretical, premises.

4. The kind of memory I have in mind I shall call *event-memory*, though, as the title of this lecture discloses, I shall pay special attention to one species of event-memory, for that is what *experiential memory* is. Event-memory is that memory of events in which a person doesn't simply remember that some event occurred, he remembers that event itself. And event-memory is characteristically reported — though I have stressed the fallibility of such linguistic clues — not by a sentence of the form 'I remember (or he remembers) + that + embedded sentence' but by a sentence of the form 'I remember (or he remembers) + direct object', where the direct object is likely to be a nominalization of some embedded sentence. So the sun goes down over the Indian Ocean, two friends have a fight, I read a poem of Hardy's, and if later I have event-memories of these events, if I remember them and not just that they occurred, I am likeliest to report such memories by saying 'I remember the sun's going down over the Indian Ocean', 'I remember John's pulling a knife on James', 'I remember reading (or perhaps my reading) "At Castle Boterel"' — and what I report on in saying such things will be an iconic mental state.

In the last lecture, I claimed that iconicity not merely suggests a very general analogy between the mind and a theatre, it also allows mental states that have it to be described in terms of three roles which are constitutive of the theatre. What occurs in iconic imagination can be brought out on the level of description by thinking of it as a collaboration, though not necessarily on equal terms, between an internal dramatist, an internal actor, and an internal audience.

Does the same hold true for event-memory? Reflection suggests the answer, Yes. Event-memory too can be fruitfully described in terms of the work of an internal dramatist, an internal actor, and an internal audience.

In connection with iconic imagination I claimed that the theatrical analogy can do more. Combining the three internal roles in some appropriate fashion, we can also do justice to an important distinction within iconic imagination—though the distinction does not hold within the analogue, or the theatre itself. That distinction is between centrally imagining something or other and acentrally imagining it: between imagining some event from a point of view—that is, a point of view within the imagined event—and imagining it from no such point of view.

Does this distinction between a centred and an acentred mental state hold for event-memory? When I remember an event, is it the case that either I remember it centrally or I remember it acentrally? The distinction holds within event-memory, but there are differences in the way it applies, and these must be remarked if a faithful picture of event-memory is to emerge.

Let us look at this.

5. First, then, acentred event-memory.

There is such a thing. In remembering a certain event I may remember it from no point of view within that event. But unlike acentred imagination, this is a marginal phenomenon: there is very little of it within the domain of event-memory.

Why this is so has to do with the dependent character of event-memory. Every event that I remember, as opposed to every event of which I remember that it happened, was an event in my life, it was an event that I experienced or lived through. Of necessity I was amongst the dramatis personae of the event, even if the part that I played in it was very minor, down to that of a mere passive observer. In consequence, if I am not amongst the dramatis personae of the memory—and I cannot be if I acentrally remember it—this must be because I have edited myself out of it. But not far out of it: I wait in the wings. The situation is unstable, and at any moment I may, I am likely to, reassume in the representation of the past event the very part that I played in the event itself. And when this happens, acentred event-memory converts itself into centred event-memory.

But why do I say that I cannot figure in acentred memory? And why do I say that if, in remembering an event that I experienced, I represent it with myself out of it, this is unstable?

The explanation of these two features of acentred memory, which are in turn what make it marginal, is the same. It lies in this fact: that in event-memory not only must the event that I remember be an event that I experienced, but I must remember it as I experienced it. Now it is a clear consequence of this that, when I acentrally remember an event, I can't figure in the memory. For if I were to, then for the memory to be acentred would require that I be represented as from the outside, but the fact that it is an event-memory forbids this, for this isn't how I experienced myself in the course of the event. With other persons and objects that constitute an event that I acentrally remember, there is, of course, no conflict between the requirement that they be represented as from the outside and the requirement that they should be remembered as I experienced them. For how I experienced them was — of necessity — from the outside. But with me it is different.

Actually it is an exaggeration to say that in event-memory not only must the event that I remember be an event that I experienced, but I must also remember it as I experienced it. (Note: 'as I experienced it.' I am not considering the view that in event-memory I must remember an event as it actually was. That is a yet more exaggerated view.) The view that I am considering exaggerates the real situation in two ways. In the first place, it isn't necessary that I should remember an event in every single way in which I experienced it: event-memory may obviously fall short of experience. But, secondly, it isn't necessary that every single way in which I remember the event should correspond to a way in which I experienced it: event-memory may, less obviously perhaps, distort or deviate from experience. I could remember John as wearing a blue shirt when this isn't how I experienced him. Nevertheless, there are limits to this, and there couldn't be gross deviations within memory. There couldn't be what might be thought of as structural deviations, or deviations in identity. If I seem to remember someone as John but how I remember him corresponds to some degree to how I experienced James, then there are two possibilities: if the deviations are not too gross, then I remember, though I falsely remember, John; if the deviations are too gross, then it is not the case that I remember John. These distinctions are not stipulative. They attempt to capture the actual histories of mnemic disposition and the mental states that manifest them.

However there is a distinction easy to miss, but not hard to hang on to when caught, between my remembering an event as I experienced it and my remembering it as experienced by me — between my remembering the event in the way I experienced it and my remembering it as something that I experienced. Now, if it is essential to acentred memory, since it is a form of event-memory, that I should, or should within broad limits, remember the event as I experienced it, it is also essential that I should not remember it as experienced by me. For to remember an event as experienced by me would be just to introduce, or to re-introduce, a representation of the point of view from which the event was experienced, and that is what acentred memory forbids. However, if in acentred memory no point of view is represented, a point of view is heavily suggested. It is heavily suggested by the uniform perspective in which everything in the remembered event is represented, in broad conformity with the uniform perspective in which everything in the remembered event was originally experienced. So long as I stick to acentred memory, this uniformity of perspective must seem fortuitous; nothing appears to account for it. So it is only natural that the suggestion of a point of view should give way to the representation of a point of view, or that, once my absence from the memory becomes conspicuous, it should give way to presence: the point of view becomes explicit, and I come to occupy it. In this way I find myself centrally remembering an event that I began by acentrally remembering. This is the instability of acentred event-memory, and also the explanation of why acentred event-memory is marginal.

6. I turn now to centred event-memory.

I centrally remember an event when I remember an event and not just that it occurred: the event is one that I have lived through: I remember it from a point of view: and this point of view is represented within the memory. Centrally remembering an event is the standard case of event-memory.

Centred event-memory parallels centred imagination, and like it has plenitude and cogency. In other words, when I centrally remember someone doing something or other, I shall tend, liberally and systematically, to remember his feeling, his experiencing, and his thinking, certain things: that is plenitude. And when I centrally remember someone feeling, experiencing, and thinking, certain things, I shall tend to find myself in the condition I would be in if I had felt, experienced, thought, those things myself: that is cogency. However there is a point where the parallel between centred event-memory and centred imagination ends and the two mental phenomena diverge. It is that, whereas there are only very broad epistemic constraints upon the point of view from which I can centrally imagine an event, the only point of view from which I can centrally remember an event is mine. Centred event-memory in which the point of view is that of the rememberer I shall call experiential memory, as in the title of this lecture, and my present claim is that all centred event-memory is experiential memory. (In consequence, nearly all event-memory is experiential memory.) Centred event-memory has, in addition to plenitude and cogency, egocentricity. I am necessarily the protagonist of my event-memories — if, that is to say, they have one.

Let me briefly distinguish a triad of claims that I have now made about event-memory. The first claim was that event-memory is always memory of some event that the person lived through. The second claim was that a person in remembering an event, whether centrally or acentrally, always remembers it as the person who lived through it — that is, himself — experienced it. And now the third and last claim is that in centrally remembering an event, which is the normal version of event-memory, a person always remembers it from his point of view. Let me insist that none of these claims is true stipulatively, or simply in virtue of the definition of 'event-memory'. All that is true stipulatively is that in event-memory a person remembers an event, and not just that this event occurred.

Some philosophers would challenge these three claims. That is, they would agree that these claims hold for event-memory as it is, but they would dispute that they hold for event-memory as it must be.

I shall return to these claims and the challenge to them, but first

let me try to bring centred event-memory as we have it so far—
that is, if I am right, experiential memory—into focus, by means
of an example. I use one from my own experience.

On a hot dusty night in August 1944 I drove my jeep, by mistake,
into the German lines. This event I remember from time to time,
and, when I do, I remember it experientially. I centrally remember
driving along a cratered road in the almost pitch-dark, trying to
make out the line of the hedgerow to keep myself straight: then
hearing a rifleshot, then hearing a fusillade of shots from the side
of the road, then trying, and failing, to turn the car round, then
hearing the petrol gush out of the car, then a torch was shone in my
eyes. And as I remember doing these things, or having them done
to me, I remember some of the thoughts and feelings that I had at
the time: for instance, thinking that someone had let off his rifle
while trying to clean it, then realizing that it must be the enemy,
then feeling that I was totally lost, then experiencing utter terror.
And as I remember feeling these feelings, the sense of loss, the
sense of terror, the sense of being on my own, the upsurge of
rebellion against my fate, come over me, so that I am affected by
them in some such way as I was when I felt them on that remote
summer night. This, as I say, is a recurrent experiential memory,
and it displays plenitude, cogency, and egocentricity.

So much for the experiential memory itself.

In the last lecture, in discussing iconic imagination, I said that
we should distinguish between, on the one hand, the imaginative
project, which realizes itself in mental states of the appropriate
kind, and which can be described in terms of an internal dramatist,
an internal actor, and an internal audience, and, on the other hand,
a response to, or a reaction against, this project, which is no part of
it and falls outside it, and which can be described in terms of an
internal observer. The same distinction applies to event-memory.
For if, as often happens, when I remember this event and in consequence of doing so, I feel relief that in the moment of confusion
when the soldiers seized me, they did not kill me; or I am aware
that I have never been so terrified before or since; or I concede that
terror has for me some comforting, some reassuring, side to it; or I
suddenly feel ridiculous at having lost my way on a battlefield of

all places; or through having done so I transmute myself into a character of fiction in another campaign, on another field of battle — I am Fabrice, I am Pierre, I am the Cornet Rilke — then in any such case, these thoughts, these feelings, which might be of deep importance for me, are no part of the memory itself though it is the memory that provokes them. They are responses to it. They fall outside it just as the feelings of surprise, or disgust, or vainglory, or the excitement at getting excited, fall outside the erotic daydream to which they are the response.

7. In the first lecture I talked of relational theories of a life. I talked of theories that, having decomposed a life into parts — necessarily into temporal parts, which would be events — then try to find a relation that, holding between such events just in case they are parts of one and the same life, would thereby give the nature of a person's life.

A number of such theories, I pointed out, propose for the unity-relation, or the relation that gives the essence of a person's life, a psychological relation. (I distinguished between theories that put forward a psychological relation as primary and those which do so as secondary.) As an example of a psychological relation, and to show what I had in mind, I cited memory. And I left it at that.

Now it must be obvious that any relational theorist who proposed memory as the unity-relation must have been thinking of event-memory. There are different kinds of memory, and to propose some as unity-relations, outside let alone inside relational theory, could only invite ridicule. Such kinds of memory don't hold, let alone hold of necessity, throughout and just throughout a single life. The fact that I was once told and haven't forgotten that Alexander the Great burnt Persepolis does nothing to make my present memory and Alexander's burning of Persepolis events in the same life, or to make me identical with Alexander the Great, in my eyes or in anyone's else's. The only kind of memory that could seem convincing in this context is event-memory.

The point that I am now concerned to make is that memory-theorists, having seen that only event-memory could be a plausible candidate for the unity-relation, have failed to go on to see just

why it is plausible. They have failed to see this for two intercon-
nected reasons. One reason is to do with the nature of event-memory: the other reason is to do with the nature of a unity-relation.

In the first place, then, memory-theorists have failed to see what
event-memory really is. They have treated it as an exclusively
cognitive phenomenon, or as a way in which we come to gain or
preserve knowledge and belief. They have not recognized that
feature of event-memory which I have called cogency, and, more
particularly, they have not recognized the affective aspect of cogency as this is found in event-memory. They have failed to see
that event-memory can touch the heart as well as the head. And a
corollary of this is that they have thought of event-memory as a
purely backward-directed phenomenon: so that at a certain moment I look back over the past and I acquire a belief about some
event that occurred in it — for instance, amongst other things, that
it was mine. They have not seen that event-memory is also a
forward-directed phenomenon, so that an event occurs, and then
at a later moment, or when I centrally remember it, it thereby
exerts an influence over me. One of the most forceful criticisms of
memory-theory remains that of Thomas Reid, and Reid in effect
pointed out that, if event-memory is purely cognitive and purely
backward-directed — and he did not see how it could be otherwise — then it could not conceivably make a contribution to the
issue that it was attempting to solve. It could not account for, even
if it went along with, the unity of a person's life. If it was a
unity-relation, it presupposed another unity-relation, in just the
way in which knowledge of a proposition presupposes truth of the
proposition known.

Secondly, memory-theorists have underestimated what a unity-
relation can provide. Like all relational theorists, psychological
and corporeal, they have looked to it to provide a criterion of
identity for a person's life, but by a criterion they have understood
what might be thought of as a merely indicative criterion: in other
words, a criterion such that, when it holds, that for which it is a
criterion must be presumed to exist. A merely indicative criterion
of identity for a life would be one such that, when it holds, we can
be certain that what we have under scrutiny is one and the same
life. A merely indicative criterion may be contrasted with a cre-

ative criterion, and memory-theorists have failed to pursue — failed indeed to see that it was an option for them to pursue — a creative criterion for a life. By a creative criterion I mean one that is certainly indicative but not merely so: it is creative in that, when it holds, it brings about or helps to bring about that for which it is a criterion. So a creative criterion of identity for a life would be one such that when it holds, we can indeed be certain that what we have under scrutiny is one and the same life, but that is because its holding has brought about or helped to bring about that this is so.

An example may help to make clear the distinction I have in mind between a merely indicative and a creative criterion of identity. Imagine three things: some beads made of paste soft enough to be pierced by a needle; a needle threaded with a strong piece of thread which cannot be removed from the needle; and, finally, a necklace formed by running the threaded needle through a number of these beads. Then imagine this necklace thrown down into a casket where there are other beads, other necklaces made in the same way, and someone dips both hands into the casket and comes up with a section of a necklace in each. He tugs at each section, but he cannot get either to come free. He then asks, 'Is *this* (what he is holding in his left hand) part of the same necklace as *this* (what he is holding in his right hand)?' Two suggestions are put to him for answering the question. The first: 'Yes, but only if you can move stepwise, from bead to adjacent bead, starting from what you hold in one hand and finishing up with what you have in the other.' The second answer: 'Yes, but only if the needle that pierced the beads in one hand also pierced the beads in the other'. The first answer gives a merely indicative criterion, but the second answer gives a creative criterion. It gives a creative criterion because the suggestion that it makes for determining whether the two sections of necklace are indeed parts of one and the same necklace appeals to the process that would have made them so. If they are parts of the same necklace, this can be so only because the needle that ran through one section went on to run through the other section. In transfixing first one set of beads, and then, when the time came round, the other set, it combined them, and the intervening beads, into a single necklace.

The two failures of the memory-theorist — the failure to appreciate that event-memory is an affective as well as a cognitive phenomenon, or that it is not just backward-directed, it is also forward-directed, and the failure to appreciate the possibility of a criterion of identity for a life that would be not merely indicative but also creative, or that would account or partially account for how events fit together to form a single life — these two failures are, as I said, linked. They reinforce one another: and righting one would go a long way towards righting the other. For once event-memory is properly understood — that is, as a phenomenon that is amongst other things affective and forward-directed — then it is easier to recognize that, if it is criterial of the identity of a life, what it could furnish is a creative criterion. For event-memory, by bringing us under the influence of the past, brings it about, or helps to bring it about, that our life, even as we lead it, is of a piece. Conversely, once event-memory is recognized as being a possibly creative criterion for the identity of a life, then it should become easier to understand it as a phenomenon that is, amongst other things, affective and forward-directed. For these very properties could account for whatever capacity event-memory has for uniting into a whole the different events that compose a life.

I have been arguing for a better view of what relational theorists, or more specifically, memory-theorists might have achieved, not so as to reinstate relational theory — in Lecture I I gave my reasons why I think that we should not do that — but so as to lay out the material that someone interested in the process rather than the product might be able to inherit from relational theory.

8.  However, even if centred event-memory is best studied for the contribution it makes to the way in which persons lead their lives, what has been believed of it by relational theorists must still be true. Difficulties of formulation apart, centred event-memory must be a unity-relation, even if that is not the most interesting thing about it. Specifically, it must be sufficient for the identity of a person's life. For if it weren't, or if centred event-memories could run across as well as along persons' lives, how could such memories have a crucial role to play in the way in which those lives are led?

So the question arises, Could centred event-memories cross persons' lives?

Some philosophers think that the answer to this question is, Yes. There could be, they say, Q-memories, and Q-memories are defined as being just like centred event-memories as we know them except that they need not follow the course of a single person's life. A person has a Q-memory when he centrally remembers an event that another person lived through.

(Perhaps it would be wiser to say that some philosophers appear to think that centred event-memories could cross persons' lives. For it is not clear how much weight they attach to the concept 'person' as it occurs in this question. Their view may merely be that centered event-memories could run across lives, or that there could be creatures, but not necessarily persons, in whose lives Q-memories might figure. The difficulty of settling what advocates of Q-memories really think on this issue arises because they typically say nothing at all about how such memories would fit into, or form part of, the lives of those who have them. Therefore we cannot tell whether they even *think* they are talking about persons. However I shall assume that the argument for Q-memories is an argument that persons could have them.)

There are two ways of arguing against the possibility of Q-memories as events in the lives of persons.

One argument, the broader argument, claims that persons couldn't have Q-memories because Q-memories are incompatible with the way in which persons lead their lives. More specifically, Q-memories are incompatible with the way — that is, the specific way — in which persons, even as they live in the present, can be brought under the influence of their past. For what is essential to the way in which the influence of their past is transmitted is not only that centred event-memory should have all the features that we have been considering — features which taken together make it altogether inappropriate to think of the reception of this influence as being like the retrieval of information — but that these features could not attach to the way in which the influence of anything other than their past in transmitted. They couldn't attach to the way in which the influence of another's past is brought into their lives. Yet this is exactly what would be the case if persons could have Q-memories.

To my mind an argument of this broader sort gives the best

rationale for rejecting Q-memory, but patently it is not open for me at this juncture to use it under pain of circularity. And that is because in trying to characterise what it is to lead the life of a person I have drawn heavily upon experiential memory.

The narrower argument against the possibility of Q-memory considers not so much the consequence of Q-memory as Q-memory itself. It considers whether Q-memory is intelligible—though the argument can be predicted to establish nothing of interest if it is so narrow as to fasten exclusively on the question whether the definition of Q-memory does or doesn't involve self-contradiction. Without discussion I concede the point that Q-memory is not self-contradictory.

A consideration of Q-memory as such might start with the triad of claims that I have made about centred event-memory. If these claims are taken to give not just how things are but how they must be, advocates of Q-memory are clearly compelled to deny them as a conjunction, but in assessing the intelligibility of Q-memory we might inquire which of these claims they are likely to deny individually and where this gets them. The claims, reformulated so as to achieve mutual independence, are as follows: Every centred event-memory is a memory of an event in the life of the person who has the memory; the event is remembered as the person in whose life it occurred experienced it; and the person who remembers the event not only centrally remembers it, he remembers it from his point of view. Advocates of Q-memory have no reason to reject the second claim, and their quarrel must therefore be with the other two. Of these they surely deny the first claim, and on the third claim their position is radically unclear. The first claim concerns, in effect, centred event-memory as a disposition: the third concerns centred event-memory as a mental state, and the question is, How would Q-memory require us to re-think these two phenomena?

If the claim that every centred event-memory must be of an event in the life of the rememberer is rejected, then we have to think that mnemic dispositions could originate in one person and be transferred to another. So if, for instance, I were to Q-remember my father as a boy walking to school through the streets of Breslau, it would have to be the case that a mnemic disposition, established

in him by his living through the event that I then come to remember, migrates at some moment in its history from him to me.
In principle there is no restriction upon when this might occur,
and in the present example it would have to be at least forty years
on in the life of the disposition: it would have to be some time after
my birth. From the moment of this migration I would house the
disposition, and the disposition would then be free to manifest
itself in some appropriate mental state of mine.

There are two difficulties with this supposition. In the first
place, there is nothing in what we already know about mental
dispositions that could encourage us to think that mental dispositions could shift from one person to another and remain intact:
after all, we do know certain central features of the history of
mental dispositions. Least of all should we, having identified
within the functioning body of the person a physical correlate to
the disposition, rush to conclude that the subsequent transplant of
this corporeal bit from one body to another would automatically
amount to a transfer of the disposition itself from one person to
another. Everything would depend on whether, once the transplant had been effected, the result would be for the second person
as if he was endowed with the memory: and the trouble is that as
yet we have no idea what that would come to. Secondly — and the
two difficulties are closely connected — dispositions form, within
the psychology of the person, a web or network: they are ancillary
to one another, and there seems no method for determining what
in the way of other dispositions, what in the way of beliefs, emotions, desires, fears, and other memories, would have to be transferred along with it if the original memory is to run across persons.
It seems plausible to hold that, if I am to Q-remember my father's
childhood walks, I should also have to have, and to have because he
had them, a native speaker's knowledge of German: a capacity to
imagine intense cold: a sense of the aspirations of a late nineteenth-century Central European schoolboy: a familiarity, which
did not depend upon something I had been told, with the details of
my father's family, with the books he would have read, with the
thoughts he would be inclined to have when he looked up into the
sky, or smelled the smell of soup, with the religion, if any, in
which he was brought up, and many other such dispositions which

would be backgrounded, if not foregrounded, in the Q-memory. And there is the related problem of those of my existing dispositions which would, presumably, have to disappear if room was to be found in my mind for the new dispositions: such as, in the present case, my ignorance of and my consequential curiosity about my father's parents. Would these dispositions vanish for ever, or for the duration of the Q-memory, and how would this be engineered?

Once the transfer of the mnemic disposition had been effected, by whatever means, the disposition would then, on suitable occasions, manifest itself in appropriate mental states. But what would a mental state that was appropriate for the manifestation of Q-memory be like? It is in trying to answer this question that advocates of Q-memory are led to reconsider the third of the claims that I made about centred event-memory: that the person remembers the event from his point of view. How should they regard this claim, and what can they substitute for it?

One suggestion about the phenomenology of Q-memory states must be rejected: it is that it precisely mimics that of centred event-memories as we know them. So on a particular occasion Q-remembering my father's walks through the streets of Breslau, I would have an experience of a sort that I would be happy — happy, that is, about the implications of what I said — to report by some such form of words as 'I remember walking, or my walking, through the streets of Breslau'. But how could such a mental state further the role of, hence how could it manifest, the memory that I allegedly have inherited from my father? Its psychic force could only be the same as that of the mental state whose phenomenology it mimics, and therefore it must engender the belief, the false belief, that I as a child walked through the streets of Breslau. It is not possible to see how on the proposed phenomenology the Q-memory could perpetuate the psychic force of the event from which it allegedly depends.

Some advocates of Q-memory concede that initially — that is, in the wake of the transfer — the Q-memory state that is of my father's walking through the streets of Breslau would have the same psychic force as some illusory memory of my walking through the streets of Breslau, but with time I would learn to correct for the anomaly and then the Q-memory would come to

effect in me the appropriate modifications. But, even if we concede that this correction could occur, the Q-memory will not then
work as event-memory currently does. It wouldn't be through its
phenomenology that it brought about these revised modifications:
indeed, if it did come to modify the person in this new way, it
would do so despite its phenomenology. It was only once its
phenomenology had been overcome that a mental state of mine
that represented my father's walking through the streets of Breslau
exactly as though this were something that I had done could serve
to bring me under the influence of the event that had actually
occurred.

A second suggestion, which would be in immediate reaction
against the first, clearly fares no better and can be dismissed
straightaway. It is that the mental states in which Q-memories
would manifest themselves would be exactly like acentred event-
memories. This suggestion runs counter to the hypothesis of Q-
memory. Definitionally, Q-memories are centered.

A third suggestion, and that which recommends itself most
strongly, is that Q-memory states would be modelled on those
states in which we centrally imagine someone other than ourselves. In ascribing such a phenomenology to Q-memory, this
suggestion seeks to do justice to two features that Q-memory
would have to exhibit: I remember some event from the inside, but
I don't believe it to have been part of my life. However it is this
suggestion that brings advocates of Q-memory into direct dispute
with the claim that in centred event-memory the person remembers the event from his point of view: or so it seems. Is this so?
And if it is so, what effect does this have upon the intelligibility of
Q-memory?

It is clear that to satisfy its definition, a Q-memory state must be
a first-person state. This is what the second suggestion overlooks.
But a first-person mental state does not have to have the point of
view of the person who has it: centrally imagining someone else
shows this, and this is what the first suggestion overlooks. But can
a mental state be first-person and mnemic and not have the point of
view of the person who has it?

Let us try to envisage such a mental state. We can see that there
are grave difficulties in doing so; but it is harder to see what they
are.

One difficulty that suggests itself concerns the repertoire, and the way in which the repertoire would become available to the memory. Let us go back to centrally imagining, and the difference between my centrally imagining myself and my centrally imagining someone else. For corresponding to the difference in protagonist that this difference involves, there is not merely, as there is with every difference in protagonist, a difference in repertoire, there is also a difference in the way in which the repertoire comes to play its part in the imaginative project. There is a difference in the way in which the repertoire becomes available to the imagination. For when I centrally imagine myself, I draw upon the repertoire that I have for myself. (I draw, as we saw in the last lecture, upon more or less of the repertoire depending on whether I induce the imaginative project in the interest of curiosity or whether the imaginative project manifests desire.) But it is not the case that before I draw upon this repertoire, I have first to select or adopt it. But when I centrally imagine someone else, not only do I draw upon the repertoire that I have for that person, but before I can draw upon that repertoire just what I have to do is to select or assume it. Unless I assume it, it is not there for me to draw upon. (An analogy is with the way in which in order for me to make singular reference to someone else I have to have that person in mind, but to refer to myself I do not have to have myself in mind.)

So when I centrally imagine someone, sometimes I have to assume a repertoire (when someone other than me is the protagonist) and sometimes I don't (when I am the protagonist). When I don't assume a repertoire, I slip into it.

Now when we turn from imagination to memory, it looks as though, if I were to centrally remember someone else, then, by parity of reason, I should have to assume that person's repertoire. But what also seems the case is that it would be incompatible with the character of memory that, before some kind of memory state could occur, I should first have to assume a repertoire. It seems impossible that before a repertoire becomes available to memory, it should have to be assumed. Why should this be impossible?

There are two candidate reasons.

The first reason, which is more general and more problematic, is the difficulty in seeing how any mental state that draws upon a repertoire could both manifest a disposition and be such that the repertoire upon which it draws should be assumed. For the assumption of a repertoire seems to get in the way of the causal link between disposition and mental state that manifestation involves. We have already anticipated this difficulty, for it will be recalled that, in considering the ways in which iconic imagination manifests desire, I found no role for the kind of iconic imagination in which a person centrally imagines someone other than himself. There is, of course, imagination of this kind, but can it manifest desire? If the answer is, as I implied, No, the explanation, I suggest, lies in the fact that this kind of imagination requires the assumption of a repertoire, and that would interfere with manifestation.

The second reason, which is more specific, comes to the fore if we consider something which I have thus far said nothing about. This is the nature of the occasion on which a mnemic disposition manifests itself, or what I called in Lecture II the initial condition. Such occasions are of two different kinds. One kind of occasion is the product of mental activity and is, in effect, when the rememberer asks of himself just what happened, what he did or what was done to him, at some particular moment or period of time. But it is the other kind of occasion that is relevant here, and this is when the memory state arises involuntarily. For Proust such memory states were the quintessence of memory, but, whether or not we agree with this, we must concede that memories stimulated in this way form a significant feature of our lives. Now it is clear that with involuntary memory there is a special or additional difficulty in conceiving how, inside its genesis, there is room for the assumption of a repertoire. But any memory, identified by its content, can, in appropriate circumstances, arise involuntarily. Q-memories would have to be able to arise involuntarily — how, then, would a repertoire attach to them?

This completes the case against the possibility of Q-memories. I conclude that there are powerful reasons for thinking that iconic event-memory must run along, and cannot run across, lives that are the lives of persons.

9. I have talked at some length about one respect in which the phenomenology of iconic memory does and must differ from that

of iconic imagination. It is that there is no equivalent within iconic memory to centrally imagining someone else doing something or other, and this plays a substantial role in the case against the possibility of Q-memory.

There is another major difference. This difference falls within the intentionality of iconic memory, and a further interest that it has is that it provides that expansion of the concept of intentionality which I mentioned in Lecture II. It is that, not merely does every iconic memory state — indeed, every memory state — manifest a mnemic disposition that depends from an earlier event which the person has lived through and which the state itself is of, but it also contains a thought to this effect. Every memory state comes labelled as such. In the case of iconic memory, this thought has a representational counterpart in the sense of familiarity with which the remembered event is invested.

It is because of this thought that the psychic force of iconic memory allows itself to be characterized in the way I suggested, as that of preserving the influence of a past event, in contrast to the psychic force of iconic imagination, which I characterized as that of simulating the influence of an event. For it is the thought that the memory state has the causal history it has that accounts for this differential in psychic force.

The reason for postulating such a thought is that it gives the only convincing account of how we distinguish memory states from other, closely related, mental states. The account that we get by postulating such thoughts could then be put by saying that memory states distinguish themselves. Of course, they do not always do so successfully, but such mistakes could then be explained by assuming that the distinguishing thoughts have been repressed, or interfered with, or misplaced. The alternative kind of account, favoured by traditional empiricism, is that we distinguish memory states from other mental states on the basis of some distinctive aspect of the subjectivity of memory states. Such an account not only makes the discrimination an unduly inferential process, it also has shown itself unable to come up with any indication of what this relevant aspect might be.

The account that I propose fits into a general picture of the mind once it is recognized that there are other cases of mental states that are partially identified by their causal history and where their cause has a double effect: the cause brings them about, either immediately or mediately, and it also brings about the thought that they have such a causal history. One such case is that of perception. For it is one mark of a perceptual state that it is caused by something in the external world which it is also of, and another mark that it comes with the thought that it has arisen in this way.

10. Just as in the discussion of iconic imagination in Lecture III, realism required us to note the fact that different modes of iconic imagination can alternate, so in a discussion of iconic memory we must recognize that different modes of iconic memory can alternate. More ominously, iconic memory in its different modes and iconic imagination in its different modes can alternate, indeed they can interpenetrate. I want to look at some of the ways in which this occurs.

But first an observation. It has traditionally been thought that imagination has to be introduced in order to account for the fact that a mental state that seems in all other respects to be a memory state may to some degree misrepresent the event that it is of. For it is imagination that accounts for that part of the state which is non-veridical. But unless 'imagination' is simply used as equivalent to 'the non-veridical', as it is by Hume, its introduction here is gratuitous. I have already contended that error can be a perfectly legitimate part of a memory state. For what makes a mental state of the appropriate phenomenology a memory of a certain event is that it has the right causal history or that it manifests a mnemic disposition, and this is brought in doubt only if the misrepresentation of the event from which the disposition allegedly depends is so gross as to prevent the transmission or reinfocement of its influence. Within these limits, misrepresentation can be fully explained by reference to the specific history of either the mnemic disposition or the ancillary dispositions whose presence is integral to manifestation.

However there are mental states, and above all, sequences of mental states, which manifest the entanglement of iconic memory with bona fide iconic imagination. They are a potential source of confusion for those who have them as well as for those who try to give a philosophical account of them.

Several kinds of case may be itemized. One kind of case would be where I remember, peripherally or acentrally, someone doing something or other: then straightaway, I set myself to centrally imagine his doing just what I remembered his doing, and this is then projected beyond the point at which my memory of the event gives out. A disposition to imagine the person in this way is then established. A fragmentary memory of a friend beginning to tell a story leads me to imagine from the inside his telling a long anecdote, which I now frequently visualize in florid detail. A second kind of case is where I centrally imagine someone doing something or other: then some time much later I find myself centrally remembering this imaginative activity, and once again a new disposition, this time a mnemic disposition, is established. I imagine a friend arriving for the first time in Venice and I centrally imagine from the inside her delight at the new sights and sounds: and now, whenever I think of Venice, I tend to remember myself imagining her at that magic moment. A third kind of case is where I start to remember my having done something, something quite trivial, and then, as a result of an associative link between this incident and some powerful early event in my life, which was far from trivial, I start to centrally imagine myself doing what I did or what was done to me on the earlier occasion but re-casting it in the setting of the later occasion. And this again sets up a disposition.

The third kind of case is what Freud called a screen-memory. The first two kinds of case are of just the sort that helps to give rise to the illusion of Q-memory. All three cases, hybrid of memory and imagination, are cases of dispositions whose role is only to be grasped through an understanding of their origins.

11. The other mental phenomenon that I want to consider in this lecture is a kind of phantasy, of which I shall take as my example *introjection*.

Introjection is a psychic mechanism. Its working exhibits on the face of it the same pattern as experiential memory. There is a disposition which arises in or out of an event that the person lives through. The role of the disposition is to preserve and transmit the influence of this event. The disposition manifests itself in iconic mental states which forward this role. They do so through their psychic force, and therefore they express the disposition. Since the original event is — is invariably — itself an iconic mental state, the way in which the later states perpetuate its influence is that they preserve and transmit its psychic force through their psychic force. However, in perpetuating the influence of the original event, they perpetuate not the original influence of that event but a changing influence, and these changes are to be accounted for by the history of the disposition that carries it. What ensures that the influence survives ensures that it does not survive unchanged.

But there are also two big differences between introjection and experiential memory. The first, which I have already mentioned, is that in experiential memory the original event obtrudes into the later mental states. The memories represent the event from which they depend. In introjection there is no similar obtrusion of the past. The later phantasies do not represent the event from which they depend, nor indeed do they carry information about it: though what they are of, or represent, has much in common with what the original event — which was also a phantasy — was of, or represented. The second difference is that, in the case of introjection, though not in the case of experiential memory, the original event from which the disposition depends is, and is as such, part of the mental phenomenon. The original phantasy itself belongs to introjection: whereas the remembered event does not, or does not as such, belong to experiential memory. Let me start with a description of introjection.

12. In the best available account of introjection, which can partly be derived from Freud's writings but needs to be supplemented from later writers (notably Karl Abraham and Melanie Klein), phantasy appears twice over. On its first appearance, we have occurrent phantasy, or phantasy as a mental state: on its second appearance, we have phantasy as a disposition, or the disposition to phantasise in a certain way.

Schematically the account goes like this: A person, or more specifically a child — I shall say from now onwards a child — perceives some figure in the environment either as exceptionally loving and benign or as singularly frightening and malign. (This perception, being so extreme, is probably itself, at least in part, due to phantasy, but, if it is, the phantasy would belong to projection, and so would lie outside the phenomenon we are now considering: we can therefore for our present purposes forget about how the perception originates and simply treat it as the occasion for introjection.) In whichever of the two extreme ways the figure is perceived, and in each case because it is perceived the particular way it is, the child engages in a phantasy, and in this phantasy he imagines himself taking the figure into his own body. If the figure is loving, he does so in order to protect the figure from harm: if the figures is malign, he does so in order to protect himself from the harm that the figure might do him. Typically entry into the body is effected—that is to say, typically the phantasy represents the figure as entering the body—through the mouth, but sometimes through the anus. This, which constitutes the first appearance of phantasy in the account of introjection, I shall call the incorporative phantasy.

The incorporative phantasy is the vehicle of incorporation, incorporation is a mental activity, and we have returned to what I was talking of in Lecture II when I spoke of mental activity being realized through, or having as its vehicle, mental states. Freud caught the perspective of the child who engages in incorporation when he described it as a piece of 'psychic cannibalism'.

The incorporative phantasy has two significant consequences. It has one short-term consequence, and this is relief from the anxiety that motivated it. And it has a long-term consequence, which is the establishment of a disposition: and the two consequences are associated in that what the establishment of the disposition does is, amongst other things, to help avoid the recurrence of the initial or motivating anxiety. This is a crucial part, though only one part, of the influence of the original phantasy that later phantasies aim to preserve and transmit.

What is the disposition that the incorporative phantasy establishes? It is a disposition to phantasise in a certain way. The figure whom in the incorporative phantasy the child took into his body is now phantasised as engaging in a variety of activities, all of which will be drawn from a repertoire, and all of which are sited within the confines of the child. Just how the repertoire is fixed is something which will continue to occupy our attention over several lectures—it is no simple issue—and just how the locus of the various activities is represented within the phantasies that the infant entertains, or what makes us say that they occur within the child, is something to which I shall return later in this lecture. The disposition to phantasise in this way, about a figure inside one, constitutes the second appearance of phantasy in the account of introjection, and I shall call it internalization. Phantasies of internalization perpetuate, largely through their psychic force, the influence of incorporation. In other words, they serve to allay the anxiety against which incorporation was a defence: but because of the way in which they do so, they also tend to preserve the anxiety itself.

What we have learnt about iconic imagination and its modes, when mapped on to phantasy, puts us in a very good position to note a big difference, a grade, within internalization. For ordinarily when the child entertains phantasies about the figure whom he has incorporated and imagines it engaging in various activities, he will imagine its doing so either peripherally or acentrally. In such phantasies he may make an appearance himself or he may not — though, as we had a chance to see in the last lecture in connection with the phantasies of chastisement that Freud analyzed, there is a fine line to draw between phantasies in which the child doesn't represent himself at all and phantasies in which he represents himself as a still, silent spectator, a pair of eyes whose gaze misses nothing of what is going on. However in certain circumstances the child will imagine the figure neither peripherally nor acentrally, he will imagine the figure from the inside or centrally, and, when this comes about not haphazardly but as the manifestation, indeed as the expression, of the disposition, mere internalization has graduated to identification. In introjecting a figure the child has identified with it.

Just what determines whether internalization does or doesn't graduate to identification is, once again, a highly complex matter. Sometimes the issue is decided straightaway — it is implicit in the content of the incorporative phantasy itself — and sometimes it is the result of a lengthy process in which the phantasies of internalization gradually modulate, but the distinctive effects of identification should not be difficult to calculate. For they reproduce, indeed they exaggerate, the distinctive effects of centrally imagining: the exaggeration being connected with the fact that unconsciousness shrouds the phantasies. In identifying with an incorporated figure the child, in consequence of being empathic audience to what he phantasises, gradually comes to be fashioned or refashioned in the image of that figure. Freud charmingly illustrates this process in his account of how the youthful Leonardo becomes a homosexual, and I cannot do better than recapitulate Freud's version of what happened.

Brought up in the house of his mother, Leonardo, the illegitimate son of the notary Ser Piero da Vince and the servant-girl Caterina, found himself at the age of five required to move to the more elevated household maintained by his father and his young stepmother. For him the move was a clear threat to the intense bliss he had experienced in his mother's undivided love. To defend himself against the threatened loss of her love for him — as well as (or so it turns out, for nothing in these matters is simple) against the excess of his love for her, which must in turn have increased in his mind the chances of her turning away from his demands upon her — the young Leonardo resorts to introjection. He takes his mother — that is, he phantasises taking her — into his person. And this incorporative phantasy establishes a disposition to phantasise about her as inside himself, and, in the phantasies he is now disposed to have, he centrally imagines her doing this or that. He identifies with her. Crucially for the future course of his emotional life, he centrally imagines her loving boys just as — the most precious thought he possesses — she loved him: where 'just as' means not only 'just as much as', but also (we must understand) 'in just the way in which', he has at any rate come to believe she loved him — that is, in a pure or idealized fashion. And as he entertains these phantasies, so the empathic audience within him responds to the feelings of the protagonist first by giving way to those feelings, then by adopting those feelings. He is destined to become (we might say) a father to nothing except his mother's feelings. Identification with the mother initiates Leonardo into the *amor socraticus*.

Freud's essay on Leonardo illustrates many things very well, and amongst them a point I referred to in introducing introjection: that, if introjection is primarily a defence mechanism, or, if the incorporative phantasy is basically motivated by the child's, the person's, desire to protect himself against anxiety, the phantasies of internalization, as they persist and recur, serve other purposes — purposes which, given the way we lead our lives, require for their attainment the recurrence of phantasy and the reiterated efficacy of psychic force. Analysing the narrative content of a typical phantasy that the homosexual is disposed to entertain, Freud writes, 'In this manner he [the homosexual] repeats over and over again the mechanism by which he acquired his homosexuality.'

13. Internalization follows upon an incorporative phantasy, and I have spoken of internalization as the disposition to phantasise about the figure who in the incorporative phantasy is represented as being brought inside the person. But this way of putting it appears to imply that there is an identity of figure across the two phantasies, and this is not quite right. The incorporative phantasy is a phantasy about an external figure and the taking of it into oneself: phantasies of internalization are phantasies about an internal figure and its doings inside one. The relation between the two figures is not one of identity, it is the relation of counterpart, and perhaps the best way of modelling the relationship is as that between a real-life figure and a fictional character based on that figure.

What can we say about either relation?

The most general thing that we can say about the two relations is that each is at once causal and intentional.

The hypothesis of internal objects is well developed in a number of Freud's writings — 'On Narcissism', 'Mourning and Melancholia', *The Ego and the Id, Outline of Psychoanalysis* — but it is in the work of Melanie Klein that it receives a powerful elaboration as well as a much broader application, and criticism of her work commonly takes the form of assuming that she simply misplaced the property of internality. Instead of attributing it to phantasies, where indeed it belongs, she erroneously attributed it to what phantasies are of: rather as though she had made the opposite mistake to that of which Moore accused the Idealists when he charged them with attributing to consciousness what really applies to that which consciousness is of, with thinking, say, of the consciousness of blue as itself blue. But in Klein's case certainly the criticism misconceives what she was doing. She was in no way concerned with the general nature of phantasy, nor was she even interested in establishing something that was true of all phantasies. On the contrary: she was concerned with a distinction within phantasies, dividing some from others, and this distinction applied to phantasies in virtue of their objects, not their nature. Quite explicitly she gave recognition to the fact that there were phantasies about external objects, and her concern was to contrast with them phantasies that in her opinion had to be thought of as phantasies about internal objects — and her first point about these latter phantasies and what is distinctive of them is that they derive by an appropriate causal route from incorporative phantasies. She makes the point in the form of a rule of technique. 'I do not', she writes in a note in the *Narrative of a Child Analysis,* 'interpret in terms of internal objects and relationships until I have explicit material showing phantasies of internalizing the object in concrete and physical terms'. By 'phantasies of internalizing the object in concrete and physical terms' Klein means what I mean by 'incorporative phantasies', and she clearly assigns such phantasies causal responsibility for phantasies about internal objects.

Now it might seem paradoxical that Klein should have insisted on the causal character of the distinction in connection with, of all things, technique: for though it may not be hard to believe that phantasies of internal objects do have distinctive causal histories, or even that they have the very causal histories that Klein proposes, it is surely all but impossible in practice to sort phantasies on the basis of their actual histories, just because those histories are not practically retrievable.

At this stage intentionality, the other aspect of the counterpart relation, to the details of which I turn in a moment, needs to be invoked. For this seems to be another case, like memory, like perception, like (to add a new example) sublimated desire, where the cause is traceable through the intentionality of the effect. Of course, the trace is not sufficient evidence, nor is the inference from it to the cause incorrigible.

The form that the intentional linkage between the external figure and the internal figure that derives from its incorporation takes is twofold. In the first place, the linkage reveals itself in the repertoire which constrains how the internal figure may be phantasised. For this repertoire matches, up to a point, a sub-set of the beliefs that the person has or had about the external figure. I take the two crucial phrases, 'a sub-set' and 'up to a point', in turn. 'A sub-set': for the internal figure most often corresponds not to an external figure as such but to some particular aspect of an external figure or to an external figure as experienced or perceived at some particular moment; to, for instance, the hypercritical father, or the deprived brother, or the phallic mother. And the set of beliefs that forms the repertoire of the internal figure is correspondingly restricted: it consists of those beliefs held true of the external figure at the relevant moment, and under the relevant aspect or in the relevant role. 'Up to a point': for even within these limits the beliefs are subject to the distortions and condensations characteristic of unconscious processes, though they may also be readjusted over a period of time to cohere with reality. Internal figures as well as external figures lead lives. And the second way in which the intentional linkage between the external figure and the counterpart internal figure reveals itself is this: that the person believes the internal figure to be the counterpart to that external figure from which in point of fact it derives — though this belief may not be conscious.

Just how the relationship between internal and external figure is indeed modelled by that between a fictional character and its original, I now entrust to your reflection.

14. The difficulties with internal objects are not over, and they can be brought out by emphasising first one, then the other, constituent of the phrase. So: How are internal objects internal? How are internal objects objects?

First, then, How are internal objects internal?

The marks of internality are complex, and they can conveniently be brought under two broad headings, which I have already employed in a different context: concrete and formal.

Introjection is a psychic mechanism that is tied to a very early phase of psychological development — the very earliest indeed: the oral phase. And internal figures have in consequence attributed to them certain traits or characteristics which inhere in an imagination ineradicably rooted in that phase. These characteristics include ambivalence: the pursuit of archaic sexual aims: and the alternation between an utter implacability and an unnatural radiance of character. And in calling such characteristics concrete marks of internality, what I have in mind is that they are characteristics that the internal object is represented as having. They belong to his repertoire. By contrast, the formal marks of internality are characteristics that qualify not so much the internal object itself as the mode in which it is represented. And here again the analogy with fiction should help: for the formal marks of internality reproduce, while grossly exaggerating, the marks of fictionality. These characteristics include a radical incompleteness or indeterminacy of character, so that certain questions (they will vary from figure to figure) do not arise: deathlessness, or rather a permanent renewability of existence: an unlimited power to attract to itself novel significance through expanded associations: and a relative imperviousness to reality-testing, or at any rate to any matching of a given figure against its external original.

And, secondly, How are internal objects objects?

A person's internal objects make up his inner world, and someone coming fresh to these ideas might well think that it is necessary to have a theory about the kind of object an internal object is. For instance, he might ask what sort of identity-conditions govern them or whether *de re* assertions can be made about them.

But once again reflection upon fictional characters should be of help. For though we might be tempted to ask analogous questions about fictional characters, it is not so hard to see that this is a misguided approach. To understand fictional characters, we need to understand two things. We need to understand our ordinary thought about those things which fiction is about—persons mostly, but also houses, and animals, and the sea—and we need to understand the nature of fiction. In fiction, our ordinary thought about persons and other things goes through a few systematic and many more unsystematic transformations. And these transformations sometimes bring our thought under pressures which affect its coherence. We all know and are habituated to the fact that we cannot ask how many children Lady Macbeth had: but more ominously, it seems not to be determinate whether the Figaro whose arias Mozart composed is or is not identical with the Figaro whose lines Beaumarchais wrote. Similarly, then, with internal objects. To understand internal objects we need to understand two things. We need to understand our ordinary thought about those things which phantasy is about — again, persons mostly, but creatures and objects as well — and we need to understand the nature of phantasy. And in phantasy too, indeed to a far greater extent than in fiction, the nature of our ordinary thought is under pressure, and sometimes this pressure is so great that the form of the thought has become unrecognizable. On such occasions both the individuation and the identity of internal objects cannot be made out. But none of this seems to me to justify the idea that a different logic constrains phantasy. On the contrary. I do not quite see how the defensive or regressive character of such fragmentation of the inner world can be appreciated unless it is recognized that the ground-rules of phantasy are provided by our ordinary thought. Just what is under assault in phantasy is the very thing that rules undisputed in the realms of science or common sense.

# V The Tyranny of the Past

1. In the first of these lectures I announced my topic for the series. It would be what it is to live as a person: what it is to lead the life of a person. My enquiry would be into the nature of a process, which unfolds in a thing, which is the person, and out of which a product, which is a person's life, emerges. And the core of this process is to be found in three characteristic interactions: one, between the person's past and his present, and between his present and his future; two, between his mental dispositions and his mental states; and, three, between the conscious, preconscious, and unconscious, systems of his mind. And these interactions, which take place in a continuing body, interrelate: for instance, they collude.

We have already observed a fragment of this: An event, a mental or partly mental event, occurs in a person's life. It affects him. It affects him in a variety of ways, but one way in which it affects him is that it establishes a mental disposition, more specifically a mnemic disposition. This disposition from time to time manifests itself: when and why is a further question. There is more than one way in which the disposition may manifest itself, but one way in which it does so is in a mental state that has a distinctive phenomenology. The mental state, which is a memory and, more specifically, an experiential memory, represents the original event, and its phenomenology is characterized by plenitude, cogency, and egocentricity. Through having this distinctive phenomenology, the experiential memory can have an impact, can make an impression, upon the person which resembles that of the original event. This power of the memory I call its psychic force. The psychic force of a memory is always in the service of a mnemic disposition which causes it, and causes it just because it has this psychic force. Thus its psychic force is always its psychic function, and when this psychic function is felt, thereby the original event exercises its influence. The influence of the past over the present, and the manifestation, indeed the expression, of mental disposition in mental states, collude to a highly specific effect. The effect is not simply that we live under the influence of the past—how could we not, if we have one?—but it is that the past influences our lives through obtruding itself into the present. And this obtrusion is made possible by two very general facts about the psychology of the person: that mental dispositions manifest themselves in mental states, and that mental states, or some of them, possess phenomenology.

Once we grasp this mechanism by which the past exerts its influence over the present, we appear to be in a position to understand two further things: how the influence of the past over the present can become excessive, and how, once the influence of the past over the present has become excessive, it can be curbed and reduced to normality. For the rise and fall of the influence of the past, it might seem, can be accounted for through one and the same mechanism. The expression of mnemic dispositions in iconic mental states permits the influence of the past to get out of hand and also enables it to be brought back under control.

So it might seem. However, if something like this is in fact true, what is true is something rather more complex, and something rather less obvious. In this lecture I shall talk about how the influence of the past can break its bounds, about the tyranny of the past: and I shall talk about how this influence can be brought under control, about the overcoming of the past, in Lecture VIII.

2. The most obvious way in which the influence of the past—the influence, that is of some past event or some set of past events— might get out of hand, and do so through the very mechanism that transmits the normal influence of the past, is this: that an experiential memory of the events should become excessively forceful or should occur with excessive frequency. The past comes to dominate the present, and the concerns of the present go unattended. The phenomenon is familiar from life and from fiction.

For years after the event, during his exile in Siberia and after his return to Russia, Dostoevsky's mind was haunted by the moment when he stood below the scaffold, waiting his call for execution, and his reprieve was suddenly announced. At the end of the second book of the *Confessions,* Rousseau tells the story of how he falsely accused an innocent young servant girl of stealing a piece of blue and silver ribbon, an object of no value, which he had taken himself and had not even troubled to conceal. Not a day passed, he writes, without the memory of what he chose to call the 'sole offence' he had ever committed returning to plague him, and at various points he claimed that his writing the *Confessions* was chiefly motivated by the desire to rid himself of this burden on his conscience, which he had been unable to disclose even to his most intimate friends.

3. When Freud began his psychotherapeutic practice in the late 1880s, he started with a view about the genesis of mental illness which is superficially in line with this simple and obvious conception of how the tyranny of the past asserts itself. Mental illness is due to the excessive influence of past events, and past events acquire an excessive influence through the incorruptibility of memories that recall them. An event occurs, and what normally happens to memories — that is, they are abreacted or flushed away in the attendant emotion, or they are swept up into some network of associations, or they are simply forgotten — does not happen in this particular case. On the contrary, the memory survives as if fixed in ambergris. In 1892 Freud produced his famous maxim 'Hysterics suffer mainly from reminiscences', and five years later he was ready to generalize this maxim from the hysteric to other types of neurotic, assigning to each type its own form of pathogenic reminiscence. Just what it was that the person remembered in this singularly persistent fashion determined just how, or of what, he fell ill. But at this moment, as Freud was extending his maxim to provide a differential diagnosis of the various psychoneuroses, he lost confidence in the maxim. He was convinced that experience had refuted it, and that it did not give the mechanism through which the past exerted its tyranny.

What I propose to do is to reconstruct the way in which Freud's mind changed, not once, but twice over, in the course of those five years, in the hope that theory can learn something from the history of theory. The first thing to note however is that during the period in which Freud did believe first that hysterics, then that hysterics and others, suffered mainly from reminiscences, the evidence to which he appealed had a certain peculiarity to it, enough to show that what he then had in mind was rather different from what we see in the case of Dostoevsky or Rousseau. We need to turn to the *Studies on Hysteria,* a joint work of Freud and Josef Breuer, which appeared in 1895, to get the measure of the difference. For in this book there are set out a number of case-histories of hysterical patients, and one feature of these case-histories is that where we should naturally expect to find, if the maxim is to be justified, a memory of gross persistence, we are presented with just the opposite: a piece of forgetfulness which resists all attempts to dissolve it. More precisely, what we find is a piece of forgetfulness and a bodily symptom. The symptom is hysterical in that it has no organic base and it represents, somatically, some aspect or constituent of the forgotten event. So long as the symptom is there, the forgotten event cannot be ignored. Freud called the hysterical symptom a 'mnemic symbol' of the event.

Let us look at one such case-history.

Fräulein Elizabeth von R. — as Freud calls her — had been referred to him by a Viennese doctor in the autumn of 1892. At their first interview she seemed intelligent, mentally alert, and cheerful, though she also complained of great pain in walking and of an aching lassitude which came over her whenever she had to walk or stand any length of time: the painful sensations seemed to radiate outward from some rather ill-defined area of the right thigh. Apart from the fact that they had no evident organic source, the patient's symptoms evinced what turned out to be two other characteristics of the hysterical: she had immense difficulty in describing these symptoms, and she seemed to experience pleasure rather than pain when the affected area was touched. The patient's family history had in recent years been full of misfortunes: her father, whose companion she had been, had died of a heart attack; her mother had undergone a serious eye operation; and the sister to whom she was close had died, also of a cardiac condition, after giving birth to her second child. During these various trials Fräulein Elizabeth had done a great deal of nursing, though she could not forgive herself for having arrived at her sister's sickbed only to find her dead.

What, Freud asked himself, were the forgotten events that un-
derlay this woman's hysteria and that her symptoms mnemically
symbolized? It was not hard for Freud to establish connections
between the different affected areas of her body and the different
phases of her recent life as they were darkened by her different
family misfortunes. The patient herself volunteered the connection between the focus of pain in her right thigh and the period in
which she nursed her father: the link being effected by the fact that
this was the very place on which every morning her father used to
rest his leg while she replaced his bandage. But what Freud was
looking for were detailed events within the confines of those
general connections from which the symptoms could be seen to
derive.

Gradually he found them. He found them because his patient
retrieved them — not fully realizing what she was doing, but responding to the pressure of Freud's authority, which was at this
period symbolized, within the reigning conventions that gov-
erned the analytic session, by the pressure of his hand upon her
forehead: a vestige of the now abandoned hypnotism.

The first event that Fräulein Elizabeth retrieved did indeed belong to the period of her father's illness, though it was no part of,
indeed it stood out from, the general regime that her father's
illness had imposed upon her. One evening she had, at the insis-
tence of her family, gone to a party. There she had met a friend of
her own age to whom she found herself increasingly attracted: she
was happy in his company: he walked home with her: and on
arrival at her house she found that her father's condition had
seriously deteriorated while she had been out. The event signified
a conflict between her duty to her family, which she fully accepted, and her own erotic longings. However Freud did not think
that this was the crucial event that the symptoms symbolized and
that had caused the hysteria, largely because it had occurred too
early on in the history of the illness: though he was ready to believe
that a vivid memory of it had played a contributory role in the
formation of her hysteria. So he continued to look for another
event, or set of events, which might be expected also to exemplify
conflict of duty and desire. Then he found precisely what he was
looking for. His patient produced for their joint scrutiny a series of

events, this time from the period of her sister's illness, events in which the physical acts of walking, sitting, standing, were prominent, and which culminated abruptly in the moment when, standing by her sister's deathbed, looking across at her widowed brother-in-law, she found herself saying to herself, 'Now he is free again, and I can become his wife'. The inadvertent recall of this event filled Fräulein Elizabeth with horror, but out of this horror Freud won what at this period he thought of as cure: namely, the cessation of symptoms.

The question that this case-history provokes is, How could Freud have thought that the fact that a hysterical patient had forgotten some event conformed to, let alone confirmed, the maxim: Hysterics suffer mainly from reminiscences? And the answer, of course, is that Freud thought that hysterics suffer mainly from unconscious reminiscences, and that their seeming forgetfulness of events, when so powerfully reinforced, indicates that they do remember them, only unconsciously. And that introduces a new element. For so far in considering the tyranny of the past, I have confined myself to the way in which the influence of the past over the present and the expression of mental disposition in iconic mental states collude. Freud added to this the third of the three interactions that qualify the way we lead our lives: that between the conscious, the preconscious, and the unconscious. The event whose influence in the hysteric's life turns out to be excessive was at the time it occurred conscious or preconscious. It is the memory of it that is unconscious, and it is the discrepancy between the two that explains the excessive influence of the event—an influence that far exceeded that of those events of which Dostoevsky and Rousseau retained forceful but conscious memories. Up to this point Freud and Breuer were in total agreement.

The next step was to ask what it was about certain events and not others which accounted for the fact that they were unconsciously remembered, and it was at this point that Freud and Breuer found themselves in disagreement. The theoretical sections of *Studies on Hysteria* preserve the views of each. Breuer thought that the explanation lay in a transient condition which the person was in at the time that the event occurred. For the memory to be retained unconsciously the person had to be in what Breuer called a hypnoid state, which resembles a state of hypnosis except that it is self-generated; in such states splits of consciousness are only to be expected. The tendency to hypnoid states was held to be constitutional. Freud, by contrast, sought an explanation in, first, the character of the event itself, or what actually happened, something which was more or less irrelevant to Breuer, and, secondly, a piece of mental activity on the part of the person, which occurred either at the time or later and was in clear response to the character of the event. When this mental activity was called forth, the memory of the event was defended against or repressed, and when I said a moment ago that what, according to Freud, explains the excessive influence of the event is that, though the event was conscious, the memory of it is unconscious, that is not the whole story. Crucial to the explanation he provides, in contrast to that of Breuer, is the fact that the memory of the event has been made unconscious, or that, presumably for some good reason, the mental activity of defence has been invoked.

But what is the character of the event such that it provokes this response? Advancing from a very vague characterization of what was found objectionable about the event, a characterization cast in terms of incompatibility, Freud gradually moved towards a much more precise answer, which cited two specific characteristics of such events: they must be sexual (this is already accepted in *Studies on Hysteria*), and they must be infantile (this is a later development). And it was this success that in turn emboldened Freud to try to extend the maxim of hysteria to all of the psychoneuroses. Perhaps all neurotics, we can imagine him thinking, suffer mainly from reminiscences — that is, from unconscious reminiscences — and the differences lie, therefore, in the character of the reminisced — that is, the repressed — event. And within six months of the publication of the *Studies on Hysteria,* or in late 1895, Freud produced a differential aetiology of the various psychoneuroses in terms of the event that proved traumatic: everything hinged, he was prone to believe, on its specific sexual character and the specific moment of childhood at which it occurred. So hysteria is traced back to a passive sexual experience, or seduction by an adult, at some time between the ages of five and seven: and obsessional neurosis, which is always overlaid on top of hysteria, to an active sexual experience, or seduction of another child, which is carried out in mimicry of the original experience and so occurs at a somewhat later age.

This is the notorious seduction hypothesis, for which Freud thought that he found direct evidence in the memories that his patients retrieved, and whose virtue, or one of whose virtues, in his eyes, was that it firmly rooted neurosis in the infantile and the sexual, in line with what the analytic material suggested — but it did not require, indeed it implicitly denied, any such thing as infantile sexuality, or that the child had any sexual desires. Neither of the two primal scenes, as Freud called them — neither the passive sexual experience that hysteria presupposes nor the active sexual experience that obsessional neurosis additionally requires — depended upon sexual motivation on the part of the child. There is only suffering, or imitation. And since, according to him, even the emotional impact of these experiences is not felt until puberty, by which time it is too late to absorb it, or to work it over — and indeed that is why repression occurs — the chastity of the young mind is further secured. 'The traumas of childhood operate in a deferred fashion' is another maxim of this period, and the deferment attests to childhood innocence.

Then within eighteen months this whole structure was in ruins. In two letters written to the person who at this time was closer to him than anyone he knew, Wilhelm Fliess, one dated May 2, 1897, the other September 21 of the same year, Freud disclaimed two constituent theses of the seduction hypothesis. In the earlier letter he gave it as his view that memories are made unconscious not because of the character of the event they are of, but because of the impulses or desires that are expressed in, or associated with, those events: it is through guilt by association, as it were, that memories get repressed, the primary target of repression being impulse or desire. In the later letter he said he no longer believed in the seduction stories, passive or active, that the patients retailed to him. He could no longer regard his *neurotica,* as he called them because he had looked to them to provide the materials for a differential aetiology of the neuroses, as memories: they were phantasies, though phantasies deriving from the period that they purport to record. Either of the two disclaimers by itself, with other beliefs held constant, but certainly the conjunction of the two, point powerfully to the reality of infantile sexuality — a fact that Freud was now condemned to absorb. From now onwards, in thinking that the tyranny of the past involved the infantile and the sexual and the unconscious and, most recently of all, desire, he could scarcely avoid the most economical hypothesis of all: that how the past tyrannizes over us is through unconscious infantile sexual desires.

4. On October 1, 1907, a youngish man, aged 29, educated as a lawyer, shrewd and clear-headed, came to see Freud. He complained of certain obsessions, which had intensified in the previous four years, and which, he said, dated from childhood. Specifically, he suffered from, one, certain fears relating to people he loved — in particular, his father and (as he put it) a lady to whom he was devoted, who constituted the two important relations of his life: two, certain compulsions, such as the sudden impulse to cut his throat with a razor: and, three, various prohibitions, which were generally very minor but so related as to make joint compliance with them impossible. He had wasted years fighting with these ideas. He had tried several forms of treatment, but the only one that had had any success was a course of hydro-therapy and that (he himself made the suggestion) probably only because in the sanitorium he had had regular sexual intercourse with the woman who had the room next to his. Otherwise his sexual life had been attenuated. What had driven him into treatment by Freud was the shock he had experienced a few weeks earlier, when, on summer manoeuvres, he had been told by a fellow officer of a Chinese torture in which a pot was strapped on to the buttocks and was then filled with rats, and the rats bored their way into the criminal's anus. Horrified at the story, the young man had immediately found himself imagining the torture applied to his lady — indeed, though he tried to gloss over this fact, to both the two people who were dear to him. The next few days had been spent in futile attempts to carry out incredibly complex instructions which he imposed upon himself, too complex indeed for Freud himself to comprehend, but which the young man had thought of as a way of averting the fulfilment of his fears — or wishes, as we might care

to see them — concerning the torture. Thoughts about the torture played a sizeable part in the analysis, so the case is known as that of the Rat Man. The patient's name was Ernst Lehrs, and the suitability of this case for close study comes from the fact that, in addition to the case-history that Freud wrote up under the title 'Notes upon a Case of Obsessional Neurosis', we also possess something unique, which is Freud's original notes on the case, kept session by session, a selection of which appears in the Standard Edition and which have been published in full in a French translation.

Freud's case-history was written in the summer of 1909, and many of the interpretations that it conserves attest to the enormous gain in insight that he had achieved for himself when, twelve years earlier, he had substituted the phenomenon of desire for that of memory as the basic pathogenic entity. Indeed, when we read the Rat Man case, it calls for a herculean effort of the imagination to reconstruct how the history would have gone if it had been written in the style of *Studies on Hysteria,* with memories marking the nodal points at once in the Rat Man's development and in Freud's explanation of his illness.

It did not take Freud long to extract the overall pattern of the Rat Man's predicament. And the flow of material that was made available to him, even in the first session, ensured that he was never to be at a loss for evidence. In this first session the Rat Man, guided only by his commitment to the first rule of analysis — that is, that he would say everything that came into his head, even if it was unpleasant for him, or seemed to him senseless or irrelevant or trivial — introduced, one after another, the following topics: the part played in his life by male friends whom he was used to admiring for their intelligence, for their judgment, and for the interest they took in him; his childhood experiences with a series of young governesses, whose genitals he fingered, and his persisting intense desire to inspect any woman who attracted him and to look at her naked; the conviction that his parents knew of these thoughts of his without his having to utter them, or alternatively that in their presence he invariably did utter them without his realizing it; and the fear that, if his father did know the kind of thing that occupied his mind, he (the father) might suffer some terrible misfortune — for instance, though the idea was vague, he might die — unless the

Rat Man could think up some effective way of averting this consequence. Thoughts of his father's death had indeed depressed the Rat Man for long periods, he said.

By the end of the session Freud had concluded that the Rat Man was the victim of two general conflicts: there was the conflict between his father, or his father's wishes, and his lady; and there was the conflict, which qualified both the important relations in which he was involved, between love and hate. The two conflicts joined up in various ways, and in particular love of the lady coupled itself with hatred of the father, who appeared as the interferer in his son's erotic desires. The first time he had an orgasm with a woman, he found himself thinking, 'This is glorious! One might murder one's father for this!' The Rat Man's situation had in no way benefited from the fact — which Freud did not learn of until the last minutes of the session — that his father was dead. He had been dead some eight years.

The material in the case-history is much richer about the Rat Man's relations with his father than about those with his lady, and there is at least one clear case where a communication of the patient's that would have been taken some years earlier by Freud as reporting a pathogenic memory is now reconstrued and found of intense interest solely for the desire or desires it reveals in eruption.

At a point well on in the treatment, the Rat Man managed to recall with great difficulty an incident in which his father had given him a beating. The boy had flown into a terrible rage and had hurled abuse at his father. The abuse was peculiar in that the imprecations that he used were chosen at random. He shouted, 'You lamp! You towel! You plate!' and so on. The father had been so frightened that he stopped and (according to the Rat Man, though other events in the case do not seem to substantiate this) never beat him again. The Rat Man was very ready to believe that the punishment was for a sexual act or, specifically, masturbation. Now the significance of this event for the psychology of the Rat Man was that it brought together, as it were into a single frame, his sexual desires and his hatred of his father. If the Rat Man's communication is taken as a memory, or as the record of something that happened, then the incident that it recalls is one that certainly contains these two desires, but in it the two desires are separated by a punishment which figures as the proximate cause of the hatred. The young man, we would find ourselves believing, was bound to hate his father for the cruel suffering his father caused him, and the occasion of the suffering, or the reason for the punishment, would drop out of account in our thinking: for no matter what the offence, the punishment sufficed to bring about the hatred. If however the informational content of the Rat Man's communication is taken to be the desires to which it makes reference, and the incident is of interest only because it contains them, then what is significant about the communication is that it brings together desires that ordinarily the Rat Man had strenuously denied had anything to do with one another: it was a recurrent theme of the Rat Man's talk that he had never had any hostile feelings towards his father. Taken in this way the communication tells us that the two desires are directly, not indirectly, linked. It is, in other words, the Rat Man's sexuality that leads him to hate his father.

The appropriateness of taking the Rat Man's communication this second way was enhanced for Freud by two further facts that he learned about the incident. The first was that, though the Rat Man claimed that the incident lay on the farthest frontier of his memory and he certainly had no iconic recall of it, it was something that both his father and his mother had talked to him about on many occasions. The second was that, when the Rat Man confirmed the incident with his mother, everything that she said, even with modesty fully discounted, disputed the fact that the boy's misdeed had been of a sexual nature. The Rat Man had as likely as not, Freud wrote, italicising the phrase, *'sexualized his memory':* and what Freud must have meant by this is that the Rat Man replaced the heavy sexual aura that pervaded his childhood by a particular sexual aspect which he ascribed to a single isolated event, chosen because the event already contained, as another aspect, hostility towards his father.

5. However, when, in September 1897, Freud had been forced to the conclusion — and we do not know exactly why or on what evidence — that the memories of childhood seductions, passive and active, that his patients had claimed to retrieve for him were in fact devoid of historical accuracy, he at one and the same time

discovered a new way of thinking about such phenomena and opened up for investigation a new way in which the past exerts a hold over the present. The seduction stories were, he decided, phantasies, and phantasy was the hitherto unidentified means by which a person came to live under the influence of the past.

I have already referred to phantasy in these lectures: once in connection with the wish, once in connection with introjection. If now is a good moment to survey the phenomenon as a whole, two out of the three salient features of phantasy have in point of fact already emerged. In the first place, phantasy is to be found within all the different categories of mental phenomenon. There are occurrent phantasies, which are mental states, and there are dispositional phantasies, and, if there is no mental activity which is itself a phantasy, there are mental activities whose vehicle is an occurrent phantasy — introjection is an example. Secondly, phantasy in all its realizations — that is, as mental state, as mental disposition, and as vehicle for mental activity — is intimately connected with that archaic theory of the mind for which the term 'omnipotence of thoughts' seemed appropriate, first to the Rat Man, then to Freud himself. Phantasy presupposes a mind that is prone to accept this theory. The third salient feature of phantasy, about which I have so far said nothing, though it derives from the second feature, is its weak relation with action. Unlike desire, on the one hand, and imagination, on the other hand, phantasy is not characteristically motivational: it does not conjoin with belief so that an intention is formed.

In order to elucidate the nature of phantasy I shall first discuss the archaic theory of the mind, thus redeeming a promise twice postponed: then I shall return to the varieties of phantasy which shelter under it: and then I shall consider the relation of phantasy to the exteral world.

6. Of the archaic theory of the mind I have said that it generates in the minds of those who subscribe to it a characteristic misunderstanding of their mental life. The theory can be understood in terms of this misunderstanding. For the misunderstanding is brought about by the self-presentations, or presentations of them-

selves, that subscription to the theory imposes upon mental phenomena: for these self-presentations are self-mispresentations. In
other words, the theory causes mental phenomena to present
themselves falsely or as they are not. I have already in Lecture III
considered two parts of this process, such that, when both are
accomplished, desire has regressed to the condition of the wish.
One part of the processs is that certain mental states, specifically
imaginings, mispresent themselves as capable of bringing about
through their mere occurrence the event or the series of events that
they are of — or, specifically, since the imaginings to which this
happens are invariably iconic, the event or the series of events that
they represent. The other part of the process is that certain dispositions, specifically desires, mispresent themselves as having their
role fulfilled when there occurs in the mind a mere representation
of what would fulfil the role. These two stages accomplished, the
mind is felt to be omnipotent or desire self-fulfilling.

Two questions arise straightaway. One is, How is such a theory
registered in the psychology of the person who subscribes to it?
What is it to hold it? The other is, Why should anyone hold it?
How does such a theory recommend itself for adoption?

I have used the word 'theory' because it suggests an obvious way
in which this conception of the mind — either it as a whole or
some constituent application of it — could engage, through their
intentionality, with mental phenomena that fall under it. Theory
is a word that the holism of the mental recommends. But I am also
aware that the use of the word may suggest a totally inappropriate,
or intellectualist, picture of the archaic mind, and an alternative
way of characterizing how the archaic mind conceives of itself is
through, in the first instance, an overarching image of the mind as
a whole, and then, derivatively, through various applications of
this image to the different phenomena of the mind: to dispositions,
and to occurrent states, and to activities and their vehicles. Each
such application of the image, or each self-presentation of a mental
phenomenon, would be iconic. In consequence it would be not
just a self-presentation but a self-representation, or, since it involves error, a self-misrepresentation, of the phenomenon. And
just so long as, or to the degree to which, the person's mind is

working in the archaic fashion, he cannot but present, represent, misrepresent, his mind, his mental phenomena, to himself in this way.

But how can self-presentations of mental phonomena be iconic? How can anything so ghostly as mental phenomena be representable, as I have been using that notion? There seems nothing on which imagery, or any similar medium of thought, can get a grip. What would a picture of a thought look like?

An answer to this question will not only take us deeper into the detail of how the archaic conception of the mind is registered in the mind, it will also explain how it is that the theory recommends itself. For this answer I turn back to Freud, for Freud offers a specific account of how the archaic conception of the mind represents the mind, or how the overarching image, which lies at its centre, is configured, and this account also goes some way towards showing why the mind is conceived of as omnipotent, even though it demonstrably isn't. Freud's account makes use of what I have spoken of as the central truth about leading the life of a person: namely, that it is an embodied mental process, that it is a process, mental or partly mental, that goes on in, though not necessarily inside, a body. For the archaic mind is said to conceive of itself in corporeal terms. It represents its contents and its activities as, variously, parts, products, and processes, of the body.

Freud illustrates his account in the essay 'Negation', where he considers the origins of judgment, or assent and denial: thinking a thought true or thinking it false. Before this can happen, a thought is first assimilated to a physical thing that can at one moment be in, and at another moment be out of, the body: for instance, a piece of food, or a faeces. The next step is to assimilate thinking to a physical activity which can bring this thing into, or expel it from, the body: for instance, swallowing, vomiting, retaining, defaecating. Bringing the thing into the body is the origin of assent: expelling the thing from the body is the origin of denial. A step beyond this, which extends further the corporealization of our mental life, is, having assimilated a thought to a physical thing and thinking to a bodily activity which is directed on to thoughts, then to assimilate thinking thoughts to a more complex bodily acitivity, which is directed on to the world. A child, curious about its mother's body, assimilates its curiosity to a physical exploration.

It is, then, because the archaic conception of the mind presents mental phenomena as corporeal that it can be said to represent them. The corporeality, we might say, fleshes them out so as to make them susceptible to representation. It is in this way that mental self-presentation can be iconic.

But if the assimilation of the mind to the body, of mental phenomena to bodily parts, processes, and products, is accepted, it may still be disputed how this contributes to, or makes more plausible, a belief in the omnipotence of thoughts. For there isn't, after all, a corresponding belief in the omnipotence of the body. Why shouldn't thoughts be represented corporeally but nevertheless presented as at least at fallible as infantile digestion or infantile locomotion?

The answer is twofold. The first part is that, within the archaic theory, the processes of the mind are modelled upon physical processes that have been idealized. So they start off as omnipotent. But why doesn't experience serve to correct this misconception and result in, at any rate, some mental processes being conceived of as fallible? The second part of the answer is that, once the mind's conception of itself is treated as testable against reality in the way that this question assumes, the archaic theory has already lost its hold. The person is no longer under its influence — though, of course, its influence may reassert itself. Indeed, it is not hard to think that traces persist into our adult life of this corporealization of mind, which are singularly in evidence when we start to reflect upon the deeper parts of our nature or the fundamental emotions of love and hate. We corporealize these phenomena when, for instance, we think of hate as something that tears us apart, or we regard love as necessarily diminished or divided when it is shared or we love two people at once. These thoughts are shadows cast by a certain image of the mind upon its workings. But they are shadows that succeed in staining that on which they fall, for the mental phenomena become as they are imaged. Hate keeps us awake at night: divided love can come to seem an inadequate gift. The mind starts to conform to its own prejudices about itself.

It is a reasonable assumption that the area of mental life where the archaic theory of the mind dies hardest is those mental states which are the vehicles of the different mechanisms of defence: for instance, the phantasies that carry introjection or projection. Indeed, the persisting corporealization of such phantasies enters into the explanation of what they achieve. Part of the reason why phantasies of incorporation are so effective in setting up dispositions to phantasise about the internal figure upon which they are directed is because they represent themselves as activities of actually taking the person into oneself.

The thesis of 'the bodily ego', as we may call this archaic conception of the mind, appropriating a striking phrase of Freud's, can be reconstructed as the conjunction of two claims. Each claim is a claim about mental self-presentations. The first or more general claim is that, so long as the archaic conception of the mind holds sway, the mind as a whole, and mental phenomena individually, will have built into them presentations of what they are. They come labelled. The second and more specific claim is that these self-presentations are expressed in terms of an image, which is a corporeal image, of the mental: they are, in effect, self-representations, for they present iconically what they are of. Furthermore, since the mind isn't corporeal or as those labels represent it, they are not merely self-representations, they are self-misrepresentations.

With the thesis of the bodily ego thus segmented, a question that arises is whether the first claim should be restricted in the way it is, or whether it is not a proper part of any theory of the mind at whatever stage of psychological development, in that the mind and mental phenomena always have self-presentations — though not, of course, self-representations — built into them. The contents of the mind, in other words, invariably come labelled. We have already had reason to believe that something of this sort is the case with certain mental phenomena, like memory or perception, that depend for being the phenomena that they are upon their causal history. There is strong reason to think that all such states must come labelled with their causal histories, for if they didn't, how else could the causal histories that they have become accessible to the person? And to suppose that they do come labelled in this way does not involve an appeal to mystery in our mental life, for we may, as we have seen, believe that these labels are another effect of that causal history which they record.

7. That phantasy is to be found both as occurrent mental state and as underlying mental disposition is something that we have observed from a consideration of the wish and of introjection. But a consideration of these two phenomena also shows us something else: that sometimes occurrent phantasy manifests dispositional phantasy, but sometimes it occurs in a way that is causally independent of dispositional phantasy. When it occurs in this latter way, it is generally to be attributed to mental activity, which in turn may be motivated in various ways. Phantasy in its relations with desire provides examples of this kind of occurrence: for phantasy occurs in connection with desire but without manifesting desire. Occurrent phantasy is not apt for manifesting desire because the psychic force of phantasy concurs with the role of desire only up to a point: phantasy can reinforce desire, but, unlike imagination, it does not lure to action. A likelier relation of occurrent phantasy to desire is that phantasy is induced in order to savour the prospect of desire assuaged — without doing anything to bring that prospect any nearer. Of the Rat Man we read:

Believing, for instance, that the lady set great store by the social standing of the suitor, he made up a phantasy in which she was married to a man of that kind, who was in some government office. He himself then entered the same department and rose much more rapidly than her husband, who eventually became his subordinate. One day, his phantasy proceeded, the man committed some act of dishonesty. The lady threw herself at his feet and implored him to save her husband. He promised to do so, and informed her that it had only been for love of her that he had entered the service, because he had foreseen that such an event would occur: and now that her husband was saved his own mission was fulfilled and he would resign his post.

It is not hard to see how the rehearsal of such a phantasy, by bringing to mind so vividly the humiliation of a rival, could keep revenge alive, but there is nothing in it to encourage action. The hyperbolic character of phantasy which makes phantasy so well adapted to one purpose unfits it for the other.

There is one significant difference between the case where an occurrent phantasy is causally independent of dispositional phantasy, as when occurrent phantasy merely reinforces desire, and the case where occurrent phantasy manifests dispositional phantasy, as when occurrent phantasy manifests, indeed expresses, the wish. In the former case it is only the mental state, not the disposition, that lies under the influence of the archaic theory of the mind, and, even then, only in an attenuated fashion. By contrast, in the latter case, to which I shall now turn, both mental state and mental disposition are suspended in the archaic theory.

An initial point to make about dispositional phantasies is that they exhibit considerable differences in complexity, in, that is, the complexity of their intentionality, and that two distinct levels can be made out.

On the lower, or the less complex, level, there are dispositional phantasies of the kind that an incorporative phantasy serves to establish. These are phantasies which reveal themselves in a tendency to phantasise about an internal figure or character who may be, but need not be, the counterpart to an external figure. Each such figure will be circumscribed by a repertoire which will be written into the disposition. These repertoires will place constraints of a mild kind upon the kind of event in which the figures may appear, but they will place more powerful constraints upon the manner in which they may appear in these events or upon the roles that they are licensed to play.

Then on the higher, or more complex, level, there will be dispositional phantasies that reveal themselves in a tendency to phantasise about events or, standardly, sequences of events, arranged in such an order as to unfold a narrative. These more complex dispositional phantasies will rest, to some degree or other, upon dispositional phantasies of the less complex kind, this being a matter of the extent to which the latter provide the former with their dramatis personae. The events that a person is disposed to phantasise about need not exclusively contain internal figures: they can also contain external figures. The crucial, the indicative, consideration is how repetitive the phantasies turn out to be. Highly florid phantasies, which tend to repeat themselves with meticulous exactitude, very strongly suggest the presence of internal figures. For the explanation of repetition is the extremely detailed repertoires that constrain the dramatis personae, and the explanation of these repertoires in turn must be that it is only through them that the original nature of the characters, or the beliefs under which their external counterparts were incorporated, can be conserved. Highly restrictive repertoires indicate internal figures, whose distinctive aspects they embalm.

I have already, in connection with introjection, said something about the first kind of dispositional phantasy, or those which are about characters or figures: I have indicated their origins, and the subsequent role or roles they play in our lives, benign and malign. So I turn now to the second kind of dispositional phantasy, or those which are about events and sequences of events, which I shall call dispositional event-phantasies. Their origins lie not in anxiety, or not directly in anxiety, but in wish and archaic desire. Each event-phantasy contains many or innumerable wishes and desires, each of which has the characteristic that it is no longer intelligible, or fully intelligible, to the person who has it. Furthermore, the different wishes and desires that a single phantasy contains are in conflict, and therefore in addition to containing them the phantasy amalgamates them. That the wishes and desires that a given phantasy contains both lack full intelligibility and are in conflict or stand in need of amalgamation is no coincidence. We shall see this better by the end of this lecture.

The role of a dispositional event-phantasy is to preserve the desires that it contains against the three hazards to which desires are most exposed: testing, frustration, and felt conflict. And for the discharge of this role, event-phantasies, for all the pain they can cause, for all the energies they absorb — we have seen that the Rat Man was very much aware that he had wasted some of his best years struggling with his obsessions — have two things to offer. They can provide substitute-satisfaction, and they can provide concealment.

How event-phantasies provide substitute-satisfaction for the desires they contain is twofold. One way we have already noted, the other I shall come to in a short while when I consider the relation of phantasy to the external world. The first way is when the phantasy manifests itself in the guise of the wish, or when the archaic theory represents, misrepresents, the occurrent phantasy as the realization of itself. Here the substitute-satisfaction remains entirely inward. By contrast, the second way in which event-phantasy can provide substitute-satisfaction, or acting out, is, as the term suggests, not wholly inward.

The way in which event-phantasies provide concealment for the desires that they contain — that is to say, they disguise both the object of the desires, so as to preserve them from testing, and the opposition between them, so as to remove felt conflict — is through exploiting various essential features of narrative, which in turn provides the structure of event-phantasy. Let us look at three features of narrative which ease the amalgamation of desire.

One feature we have already considered in connection with beating phantasies — though at that juncture phantasy was of interest to us only as a variant of iconic imagination. For we saw how switches in mode of imagination, shifts in point of view, changes of protagonist, all of which are possibilities intrinsic to narrative, allow one and the same phantasised event to exemplify competing desires at one and the same moment. It superimposes one desire upon another, and so the phantasy is able, for instance, to represent simultaneously the satisfaction of sadistic and masochistic desires.

Another intrinsic feature of narrative is that it is sequential. The events that compose it are distributed across time, and these events are held in place in the narrative by links of cause and motive and reason as well as identity of dramatis personae. Phantasy can then exploit this feature by using these links to disguise the relationship in which the different desires actually stand to one another. We saw one simple case of this in the Rat Man's 'sexualized' memory of being punished by his father. The phantasy contains sexual desire and hatred of the father, but the narrative organizes the events that exemplify these two desires in such a way that the direct relation between the two is denied. The Rat Man's sexual desires can, according to the narrative, lead him into hating his father, but this will happen only when the father chooses to punish him for his sexuality and moreover to do so in an unnecessarily, in a meaninglessly, cruel way, which is bound to arouse, even if only in the heat of the moment, rage and fury.

A more complex example comes out of the relations between

the Rat Man and his lady. One day, when the Rat Man's lady was leaving for the country and he was taking a walk, he noticed a stone in the road and, knowing that his lady would be passing that way in a few hours' time, he was afraid that her carriage would come to grief against the stone and he felt compelled to kick it to one side. Twenty minutes or so later this struck him as absurd, and he then felt obliged to walk back to the spot and to replace the stone where he had originally found it. (Though this is an occurrent phantasy, Freud gives us reason to believe that it manifests an underlying disposition to phantasise events of this general type — events, that is to say, falling into two distinct parts, which are related as action and rectification.) Now in this phantasy are amalgamated the Rat Man's love for his lady, distilled in this instance into the desire to protect her, and his hatred for her. However narrative does its work, and the phantasy, having represented the Rat Man's love as such, if in an exaggerated form, then goes on to tell a story which misrepresents his hatred as mere critical repudiation of his previous excessive concern. The sense of compulsion with which the Rat Man undoes his original action betrays the fact that it is archaic desire rather than judgment that motivates him, but the narrative, by disrupting the two parts into which it falls, helps to conceal this fact and hence to conceal the further fact that the desires which the phantasy contains are competing desires.

And a third intrinsic feature of narrative is that it employs a distinction, though of no exact sort, between the plot and its setting, between foreground and background. Once again phantasy exploits this feature in the interest of concealment. We have already considered this feature in the case of imagination serving desire, for I pointed out that, when the foreground represents the satisfaction of desire, the background does not have to represent the fulfilment of belief: it can represent the fulfilment of mere supposition. With phantasy this is also the case, but a further possibility is opened up. It is that the supposition fulfilled in the background can in turn correspond to the satisfaction of prior desire. When this happens, phantasy will represent desire satisfied in a world that is itself the object of desire. But how does this help amalgamation? For thus far all that seems to follow is that phantasy, by exploiting the distinction between foreground and background, can amalgamate desires that are mutually compatible. How can it derive from this feature of narrative a capacity to amalgamate desires that are in opposition? Again, an example from the Rat Man case makes the point.

At the time that the Rat Man was working for an examination, he engaged in the following routine. He worked late into the night. Between midnight and one o'clock in the morning he would interrupt his work and open the front door of the house as though the ghost of his father were standing outside. Then, coming back into the hall, he would take out his penis and examine it in a small mirror which he placed between his legs.

The phantasy that underlies this routine clearly manifests a dispositional phantasy since the routine was repeated on several occasions, and of this routine Freud says that it enables us to see in 'one single unintelligible obsessional act' the two sides of his relation to his father. There is the desire to placate his father by working late into the night: and there is also the desire to assert over and against his father his rights to sexual pleasure. Indeed, if we scrutinize the second part of the routine, I believe that we can see the same conflict of love for and hatred of the father patterned over its finer detail. For the sexual pleasure to which the Rat Man lays claim is at this point pleasure with himself—that is, pleasure with someone of his father's sex—but at the same time it is the very sexual offence for which, as we have already seen, the Rat Man had phantasised himself being so severely chastised as a child by his father. Now both the two desires that the phantasy amalgamates are desires that the Rat Man has upon a father whom he certainly recognizes as dead. But, since for the purpose of representing the satisfaction of these two desires, the Rat Man has resuscitated a belief that goes against the whole grain of his thinking—the belief, which he would normally think of as superstition, that his father, though dead, still survives, that he lives on in an after-life from which he can haunt the real world—what he in effect does is to represent the satisfaction of these two desires against a background that corresponds to the satisfaction of a more basic desire: the desire, that is, that his father should be actually alive, alive in such a way that he could really return and could see his son one moment at work, the next moment masturbating, and could experience alternations of pride and rage. The superstition contains such a desire. But the Rat Man had already recognized that this desire was frustrated beyond redemption when he went on to form the desire to gain the love or to defy the authority of a dead father. These new desires, in other words, presuppose the supersession of the old desire. This allows us to see how the distinction which narrative imports into phantasy between plot and setting, between foreground and background, and which initially seemed capable only of amalgamating mutually compatible desires, turns out to be capable of amalgamating desires that stand in opposition to one another. Indeed, it permits phantasy to amalgamate desires that are ranged against one another in what is the most poignant of all conflicts; the conflict between desires that we actively pursue and desires that these desires assume us to have abandoned in their favour — the conflict, broadly, between new loves and old loves.

The most general way in which the various intrinsic features of narrative allow phantasy at once to contain and to conceal archaic desire is best grasped through seeing what is involved in any attempt to retrieve the desires from the phantasy. Of the dream, which is in certain ways the paradigm of phantasy, Freud said that it resembled a rebus. To arrive at what it contained it was necessary to segment the dream into items or elements, which could then be paired off with the various desires. The structure, the interrelations, the links that narrative supplies, could by and large be ignored. These were merely the means of concealment.

8. That phantasy is so intimately associated with the archaic theory of the mind, with the belief in the omnipotence of thoughts, means that there is no straight line running from phantasy, at least in its full-blown realization, to action. Neither in its occurrent nor in its dispositional realization is phantasy directly motivational in the way in which imagination, on the one hand, and desire, on the other, have been seen to be. One way of putting this would be to say that phantasy, rather than conjoining with belief to initiate action, assimilates itself to belief. Its informational content for the person is that the world already conforms to his wildest desires — though it must be added that this information is never found altogether convincing.

Nevertheless, it would be wrong to think that there is no characteristic outlet of phantasy into the external world. It is not the role of phantasy to detach the person from the reality he inhabits and to immure him in an inner reality of his own, along the lines of the powerfully charged memories that absorbed, if we are to believe their testimony, Dostoevsky and Rousseau. A general characterization of what phantasy does for the person in this respect is that, with variable efficacy, it remakes reality for him, and the instrument by which it does this is projection. It is through projection that phantasy discharges itself into the world. Phantasy, we might say, operates for the person rather like the great fables of chivalry did for Don Quixote, but not at the period when he read them day and night so that he was distracted from hunting and the care of his estate, but after he had put them down and had decided to embark on a career of knight-errantry or, as Cervantes puts it, but I would not, 'to translate his desires into action'.

We may distinguish between two forms of projection. The distinction that I have in mind is philosophically motivated, and it distinguishes between a simpler and a more complex form. The more complex form we shall have to consider in Lecture VII. It is, I believe, the source and origin of value. But in this lecture I shall introduce the simpler form, of which typical examples are when someone attributes to some other person or some thing a feeling or a mental state or a complex of mental states that are actually his own. A man hates his rival in love, he projects this hatred on to the rival, and now he is fated to think that his rival hates him. A man — the Rat Man, in point of fact — makes up prayers on behalf of a friend about whom he feels ambivalence: he then projects the hostile component of this ambivalence on to the environment, and so he comes to fear that there is an evil spirit lying in wait for him to start uttering the words 'May God protect him' and then it will insinuate the word 'not' into the prayer. The Rat Man is driven to increasingly ingenious devices to outwit his antagonist.

In such cases projection brings about changes in perception, thought, and belief — and, of course, consequential shifts in anxiety. The changes in perception, thought, and belief result in new ways of perceiving, thinking, and believing, old properties to be instantiated. However, still within the simpler form, there are cases of projection where the adjustment of the external world calls for more than its mere rearrangement in the mind. The world has to be physically rearranged. It is this that characteristically occurs when event-phantasy is projected. The event-phantasy is imposed on the world: it is 'acted out'. We have already come across cases where this happens. The Rat Man acted out a phantasy when he removed and then replaced the stone that he predicted would lie in the path of his lady's carriage. He acted out another phantasy in his nocturnal routine, when he provoked his father's ghost to return and surprise him first poring over his books, then poring over his genitals.

Why is phantasy acted out?

We need here to distinguish between extrinsic and intrinsic reasons, where the latter are internal to the role of phantasy and the former are not.

An extrinsic reason is that we have to do something. All our waking life, and some of our sleeping life, we have to do something — where something may, of course, include nothing provided it is undertaken as such — and so the relevant question becomes, Why on a given occasion do we act out a phantasy rather than act on a desire? And this leads us to the intrinsic reasons that there are for acting out a phantasy.

The fundamental intrinsic reason why we act out phantasies is in order to preserve them. Acting out a phantasy stands to that phantasy as the phantasy itself does to the desires it contains. Nor is this parallelism fortuitous. For though it is true, as I have been urging, that every disposition has its own reinforcement as part of its role, we should expect self-reinforcement or self-preservation to rank particularly high amongst the modifications that a disposition brings about when that disposition has the preservation of something else as the principal part of its role. As well as the general commitment to self-preservation, phantasy must preserve itself if it is to preserve desire. But how can acting out a phantasy serve to preserve it?

There are two distinct ways.

The first is that it can distract us from what we might otherwise do, which is to test the phantasy. The second is that it can serve to normalize the phantasy. It can, it is true, do all this only at a certain risk, which is the same risk as a desire runs when it is imagined satisfied. For, the phantasy acted out, the desire imagined satisfied, there is the possibility that the person will then react to what he has acted out, he will respond to the residual condition in which he finds himself, in such a way that the disposition will be on balance weakened. The internal observer will experience horror, or disgust, or boredom, or terror.

But it is important to see how, this counter-effect discounted, acting out a phantasy can normalize a phantasy. And the central device is this: that in running through the various actions that the phantasy imposes on him, the person will be required to find good reasons for these actions, but, more than this, he will be required to make it seem to himself as though he is acting on such reasons. He is required, as it were, to rationalize his actions from the inside, and it is to the effect of these successive rationalizations that we can look for the normalization of the phantasy.

In both the cases we have considered where the Rat Man's behaviour can be regarded as a case of acting out, we can observe this same cunning of phantasy. The Rat Man has an answer to the question why he should be working so late at night or up till the hour when, according to superstition, ghosts return; he has an answer to the question what his father, a worldly man, would have thought of his son's lapses into superstition: he was, indeed, anxious about the size of his penis and, if he was going to find reassurance, looking at it in a mirror would help. Or again, he can say what it is about the stone in the road that made it dangerous to a passing carriage, and he can also say why, on reflection, the danger must seem so remote, so improbable, that he could only be made to appear ridiculous if he was caught out paying it any practical attention. At each point in the story, Freud suggests, the Rat Man would have explanations of what he was doing that would add up to an overall account of his behaviour that was utterly convincing and false. Each time that he gives himself this account, which is each time he acts out the phantasy, the phantasy will seem a bit more normal to him, which in turn will make it a little more secure against the threat of criticism.

In the next lecture I shall take this point somewhat further. I have contended that, in preserving the phantasy, acting out also strengthens the disguise with which phantasy conceals the desires it contains. In this way acting out aids what may be called self-ignorance, or the tendency of the person to deny that he has certain desires that he has. But some phantasies not only dissimulate some desires, they simulate others, and they do both these two things in the same way: through the narrative that structures the phantasy. With such phantasies, when self-examination follows upon acting out, the person can, we shall see, be led beyond self-ignorance to self-error: he will start to lay claim to certain desires that he doesn't have.

The fundamental reason why we act out phantasies is, I have claimed, so as to preserve them. It is a response to anxiety. But this, as I have already indicated, is not the only reason. A subsidiary reason is to provide the desires that the phantasy contains with substitute-satisfaction. Removing the stone from the road is the Rat Man's thwarted attempt to give his lady the love and solicitude and affection that his other desires deny him the chance to demonstrate. Here we have the not purely inward way in which phantasy provides desire with substitute-satisfaction.

Acting out is brought into sharpest focus if we contrast it with action, and consider them in their different relations to desire. Let us first remind ourselves of the structural differences between the two phenomena. In action we are motivated by desire and belief, blended perhaps in intention, and in doing so we execute some bodily acts: in acting out we physically project on to the world a phantasy which contains certain desires, and, again, in doing so we execute some bodily acts. From these structural differences follow two broad differences in the way that desire fares in the two cases. The first difference is that the desires that the phantasy contains are never tested in the acting out of the phantasy. Acting out is never treated by the person as providing either confirmation or rejection of the view that these desires fit in with what he really wants. The second difference is that satisfying the desires that the phantasy contains through acting out the phantasy is not likely to provide the person with pleasure. No joy can be expected; at best, there will be relief. The two differences are, of course, closely related in that in the case of action the way in which a desire is tested, or confirmed or rejected as corresponding to what the person really wants, is in large part a matter of the pleasure that its satisfaction brings with it. In acting out, pleasure has been fully anticipated and fully discounted: the desire is not exposed to the fresh air of experience.

These two features of acting out are painstakingly illustrated in Sade's novel *Les 120 Journées de Sodome*. The four libertines, whose carefully arranged excesses make up the narrative of the book, have hit upon a device which we may think of as an externalization of the way their minds, and above all their desires, have come to be organized. Throughout their stay at the Château de Silling, the evening assembly or orgy is to be preceded by a lengthy storytelling entrusted, according to a carefully worked out programme, to one of four women, who will turn out to be amongst the few members of the little court fortunate enough to make the return journey to Paris. These are women who have led lives of furious debauchery, and they have been chosen solely for their experience, their eloquence, and their precise turn of mind. For their recitations, which are to analyze and itemize in mounting order of criminality the passions of man, are designed to exert total control over the imaginations of the four libertines. Each evening — such is the plan — the storytellers light a conflagration which the libertines with the aid of their retinue will extinguish. It is to be noted that the only objections that the libertines ever raise to the narration are when they feel that it, by neglecting some minute particular, has in turn left their desires suspended. The aim of the stories is in effect to allow no room for spontaneity, or the testing of desire. The universal sadism of their content is more than matched by the abject masochism that they demand from their hearers, and by the time we come to the culminating recitation, the so-called 'hell-passion', the same degree of regimentation has invaded, and taken over, the content of the story told. The rich nobleman, who is its protagonist, in imposing at each ceremony, as he calls it, the most protracted deaths upon his fifteen victims, prides himself upon being able to select for each patient the torture which is, 'according to his best belief', the most suitable for her, or the most voluptuous to inflict upon her. He is described by the storyteller as famous for his acuity and judgment in these matters, for his tact and discrimination. In other words, under the aegis of total sensuousness, a story, which is itself recounted so as to organize desire, reveals desire seemingly of the most unbridled or licentious kind as ultimately controlled by precise and irrelevant detail.

9. The question that needs to be asked is this: By the time that Freud had come to think that the domination under which the person could fall was not that of memory (as he had once thought) nor that of desire (as he next thought) but was that of phantasy, was he still talking about the tyranny of the past? The phantasies that can come to dominate a person's life have, of course, been formed at some earlier, some very much earlier, moment in his life, and persisted. But we need to distinguish between a tyranny that merely originated in the past and persisted, and the tyranny of the past. For the domination of phantasy to be, like the domination of memory, the tyranny of the past, it seems as though the past should enter in a substantive fashion into the explanation of why phantasy proves so dominant. Pastness should prove explanatory.

There are various ways in which this condition could be satisfied, but one way, a minimal way, is that occurrent event-phantasies that dominate the present should be, in the terminology of the last lecture, dependent mental phenomena: in other words, that, as they exert their influence over the present, they thereby preserve and transmit the influence of an earlier event in which the disposition that they manifest originated. This, we have seen, is true of the phantasies of internalization: is it also true of more complex event-phantasies? Or, to introduce a concession which involves no sacrifice of principle but would be realistic, do they, when they exert an influence over the present, preserve and transmit the influence of a cluster of events from which they derive through a disposition?

Occurrent event-phantasies that exert domination are, I believe, properly thought of as dependent mental phenomena, but not exactly along the lines that have thus far been proposed. When phantasy dominates the present, the past substantively enters into the explanation of the condition in which the person finds himself. And it does so twice over. The past helps to explain both the content of the phantasy and why it is dominant. The Rat Man's past, for instance, enters into the explanation not only of the elaborate nocturnal ritual in which he engages when he is working for his examination, but of why he engages, indeed is compelled to engage, in it and to what unsatisfactory effect. But the past that such explanations invoke — hence the past that exerts a tyranny over the present through phantasy — is not a past of events, it is a past of phases. Occurrent event-phantasies, as they come to dominate the life of the person, or (as we might think) as they come to deprive him of a life, preserve and transmit the influence of past phases from which they in consequence depend.

'Phase', in this context, means 'phase in psycho-sexual development'. And why past phases come to dominate the present life of the person, and why, when they do, their pastness is a crucial factor in the explanation of the person's present condition, are to be accounted for in terms of one and the same broad fact: that, as a given phase passes or is no longer in the ascendancy, the various mental phenomena that belong to this phase, and, in particular, the desires that were formed under its aegis, cease to be fully intelligible. They are no longer fully intelligible to the person who has them in the way that we should expect his desires to be: that is, in virtue of being desires whose formation has occurred within him.

I have already referred to unintelligibility as a mark of the desires that phantasy contains. But I have referred to other features as well. I have referred to the fact that such desires evade testing, that they lose their association with pleasure, and that they regularly are in conflict with one another. And the point that I now want to make is that, of these various features, unintelligibility is basic. If the other features do not owe everything to it, they owe their persistence to it: if it were not for unintelligibility, these other features might have been eroded, and so, for that matter, might the desires themselves.

But in order to grasp this point, we need to understand in just what way an archaic desire is condemned to unintelligibility. The unintelligibility is not primarily cognitive; it does not derive from the difficulty or the impossibility of retrieving the intentionality of the desire. At heart the unintelligibility of an archaic desire is affective, so that the person can no longer see what it is about the object of the desire that makes anyone — not just himself, but anyone with a similar psychology — want it. Around this affective core, concentric circles of incomprehension establish themselves.

The person can no longer tell what kind of pleasure he could hope for from the desire, were it satisfied. Nor has the person any proper appreciation of the confines of the desire, or of what substitutions can be made in the object, if satisfaction is still to be had or disappointment avoided. Nor will experience teach him. For though he can still derive unhappiness from some aspect of the desire being unsatisfied, he is incapable of deriving happiness from whatever part is satisfied. And this leads him to rerun time and time again an experiment that is bound to deliver no result.

It is in this way beyond the Rat Man's powers of historical imagination to have any conviction about what he wants of a parent who has become for him the patron of sexuality: practising it, hallowing it, holding it up for admiration, and also extending it his protection so that any attempt made by anyone else to help himself to even the smallest portion of it will be met with the direst punishment. And the loss of intelligibility means, equally, that the filial desires that the Rat Man has can neither give him pleasure nor be relinquished. They cannot be tested, in that neither pleasure nor disappointment will attach themselves in a conclusive fashion to their satisfaction — and there is a yet more radical sense in which they cannot be tested, in that the Rat Man can no longer recognize any course of action, any state of affairs, as their satisfaction. And unintelligibility of this order is the direct mark of pastness.

We can measure at once the changes in and the overall constancy of Freud's thinking as he moved beyond identifying memory, through considering desire, to settling on phantasy, as the agent of the past when we set beside one another the dictum of 1892 that we have already considered, 'Hysterics suffer mainly from reminiscences', and the dictum he enunciated in 1914, 'The patient repeats instead of remembering'. It is still the neurotic's past that makes him suffer, but what is pathogenic is no longer to remember that, it is to forget why. It is no longer to remember what he did or what happened to him: it is to forget why he desired this or why he believed that.

Some of the implications of this I shall return to at the beginning of Lecture VIII.

# VI  The Examined Life

1. Half-way through these lectures I return to the point at which I began. I return to the entry in Kierkegaard's *Journal* that I selected as their epigraph:

It is perfectly true, as philosophers say, that life must be understood backwards. But they forget the other proposition, that it must be lived forwards. And if one thinks over that proposition it becomes more and more evident that life can never really be understood in time simply because at no particular moment can I find the necessary resting-place from which to understand it — backwards.

2. I selected this passage because it served to introduce the topic of these lectures: what it is to lead the life of a person. However I return to it because, in identifying this topic, it also contrasts it with another: that of understanding life. The two processes are contrasted, and opposed. Kierkegaard is right. Living a life, understanding the life that one leads, are different, and there is a possibility of conflict between them. The attempt that a person makes to understand his life may interfere with his leading it.

Self-examination as a malign phenomenon is something to which I shall return at the end of this lecture, but that there is such a thing must show something about self-examination. How can it occur?

An answer to which common sense gives its imprimatur is that self-examination engaged in to excess detracts from life by distracting the person from living it. As he spends more and more of his energies in the investigation of his own thoughts and moods and feelings, he becomes so fascinated by the detail that self-examination brings to light that he has, first, little time, and, then, no taste, for the more strenuous pursuit of life. It is in such a posture that novels and journals of the first half of the nineteenth century depicted young men of an exaggerated sensibility and an analytic cast of mind: Adolphe, Armance, Dominique, Amiel. They are disabled by an excess of introspection.

Another answer is suggested by Kierkegaard's *Journal* entry. What is disabling about self-examination is the temporal direction in which the person who engages in it is required to face. To understand his life he must turn his back on the present and look into the past, whereas the leading of his life, living, requires him to turn his back on the past and confront the future.

In returning to self-examination as a malign phenomenon, I shall return to the question what makes it so, so now I shall only point out the obvious inadequacies of the two answers we have. The answer of common sense is characteristically superficial. The answer provided, I hesitate to say by Kierkegaard but by the Kierkegaard of the *Journal* entry, must be wrong because it is too sweeping: it has the consequence that self-examination is injurious as such. The thesis that I wish to advance and for which neither of these answers leaves room is that there is a benign form of self-examination, and that in its benign form self-examination has two characteristics, which are these: In the first place, it is an activity that is distinguishable from leading our lives but is not separable from it. It is not to be undertaken in the interstices of our lives, in what William James called 'holidays' that we try to take from them, but it must go on even as we lead them. And, secondly, though self-examination does indeed require us to look into the past, it is the only alternative to a more baneful relation to the past to which we are otherwise condemned. If we show ourselves unprepared to learn, or to try to learn, from the past in the way in which self-examination asks us to, we shall be forced to live in it.

3. But first a distinction, which may go some way towards explaining the disagreement I have with the sharp contrast that the *Journal* entry draws between living a life and understanding a life.

For, in talking of the way in which self-examination commits us to understand, or trying to understand, our lives, I do not have in mind that activity in which a person engages when he thinks of his life as something stretched out behind him and then tries to make sense of it in some overall way: an activity which in the first lecture I paired off with that in which a person engages when, once again thinking of his life as open to inspection, though this time reaching out ahead of him, he wills a plan, a project, to impose upon it. It goes without saying that a person committed to this form of understanding life can never attain it: it can fall only to those, like the population of Dante's Inferno, who live beyond the shades, with memory enhanced. For a living person even to try to understand his life in this overall way would involve him in the same sort of error that, I take it, Solon imputed to the man who thought himself happy.

In this latter case the error would be either to overlook the fact that happiness is a gestalt property or to be insensitive to what that involves. A man cannot say that he is happy just because he is happy now or has been so far — on that we would all agree. But neither would he be able to say whether he was happy if he had at his disposal information about all the remaining moments of his life and how many would be happy and how many unhappy. Of course he would need that information, but that information wouldn't suffice. For happiness is not aggregative. It requires perception, like the balance of a painting. It is only with his life complete, and then laid out for review, that a man's happiness can be determined: it is only then that he can be said to be happy, because it is only then that he can be seen as happy — though not, of course, by himself. Solon's maxim 'Call no man happy until he is dead' does not really deserve Aristotle's retort that then he is not happy either. Then he *is* happy — or unhappy as the case may be. Death prevents the happy man from seeing himself as happy, not from being so.

Some of the Ancients tried to weaken this conclusion by advancing the moment at which the happiness of a life is perceptible, and therefore the moment at which the happiness of a life is determined, by bringing it within the terms of the life itself, even if only by a split second. At the very moment of leaving life, both the happy and the unhappy can see which their life has been.

But from this position, it is an easy slide, though it is in effect a big step, to thinking that death is not just the moment at which a person's happiness is finally determined but the moment that uniquely determines it. This is in effect to reintroduce an aggregative view of happiness but to combine this with the rule that what happens at the last moment outweighs everything else put together: rather as though someone were to maintain that the value of a piece of music resides in the last measure, or of a meal in the last mouthful.

To return to the *Journal* entry: The opposition in which Kierkegaard here places understanding a life to living a life may well have something to do with his conceiving understanding of life in the synoptic way that I do not intend. For that certainly would require a resting-place of a kind that, I agree, is not available. Kierkegaard, in other words, may have in mind the understanding of what I have called the product. But I am thinking of understanding the process, for it is this that I take to be integral to the process itself, and this calls for no Archimedean standpoint.

4. The simplest way in which a person could conduct his life would be something like this: In each successive situation in which he finds himself, a pair composed of a desire and a belief manifests itself in a mental state, so that the intention to carry out a certain action is formed: and, on the next suitable occasion, if not there and then, this intention is acted on: and the action, carried out, gives the person nothing but pleasure. This is a picture of the unreflective life, and in this picture there is no place for decision, for procrastination, or for disappointment.

However this picture can fail to hold at various points, and then the life will be correspondingly disrupted. Let us look at these points in turn, and see what can go wrong.

In the first place, in some situation in which the person finds himself, no pair of desire and belief manifests itself in such a way as to cause an intention to form. Rather the person is required to make a decision if he is to form an intention. Secondly, an intention is formed: but suitable occasions come and go, and it is not acted on. The person procrastinates. Thirdly, an intention has been formed, furthermore it is acted on, but the action, having been carried out, gives the person something that runs counter to pleasure, even though he may on balance experience pleasure. The person is disappointed. In any one of these three eventualities the person is required to ask himself a question about his desires and beliefs — a question which would never have arisen in the course of the unreflective life. That in these circumstances he would ask himself this question is required not only by his situation but if he is to lead the life of a person. And this self-interrogation, once it has begun, has no natural termination.

5. A feature of the schematic picture I have just offered of the way in which the unreflective life becomes reflective is that at two of the three distinct points at which the person is now required to ask himself, for the first time, about his desires and his beliefs — that is to say, at the second and the third point — the question that he asks himself will naturally be of the form, Is *this* what I really desire? Do I really believe *that*? There will be a demonstrated desire or belief, a desire or belief picked out by a demonstrative, 'this desire', 'that belief', of which he asks himself whether it gives what he really wants or holds true. At neither point will the natural question for the person to ask himself be, What do I desire? What do I believe?

The explanation for this piece of linguistic practice lies on the surface. For at each of the two points, the background to the question is provided by an intention, which is identified by reference to the desire and the belief that in turn account for its formation. If the intention has been formed but the person who formed it either didn't act on it or found no satisfaction in doing so, then either the desire or the belief that prompted it is impugned. At least one or other didn't mean enough to the person, and this is the natural place for self-examination to begin.

But the more interesting feature of this schematic picture is that, if the person starts to ask about his desires and beliefs at the first of the three points at which the unreflective life may get disrupted, or in a situation which calls for an intention but where none is formed, then too the question that he puts to himself is likely to be raised in this very same form. It will ask of a demonstrated desire, a demonstrated belief, whether it gives what the person really wants or holds true. Even when there is no pair of desire and belief forceful enough to give rise to an intention, there are generally to be found both a desire and a belief which advance themselves as the likeliest candidates for filling this role.

If this is not always the case, and if in a situation that calls for intention and action, a person still finds himself asking himself, What do I desire? What do I believe? it is instructive to ask when and why this is so. And the answer seems to be that this form of self-questioning seems appropriate when the person is in a state of deep conflict, or when the conflict is so deep as to border on confusion. It turns out to be only *in extremis* that a person approaches his desires and beliefs with an open mind.

What does the fact that in normal circumstances self-examination begins with a particular desire, a particular belief, of which we ask whether it is ours, show? It shows something about the epistemology of mind, which in turn has consequences for the philosophy of mind. For how we find out about our mental phenomena is closely implicated with how these phenomena are structured in the mind.

Once, the unreflective life having been disturbed, we need to determine what it is that we desire or believe, there are two different methods upon which we can draw. On the one hand, we can acquire thoughts — and there is more than one way in which we can do this — that will inform us, fallibly, that we desire this or that we believe that. On the other hand, we look to see what beliefs or desires best fit in with the total corpus of mental states, mental dispositions, and actions and activities, mental and corporeal, that we are able to attribute to ourselves. There is, in other words, the *method of introspection* and the *method of interpretation*. That, in trying to determine what it is that we desire or believe, we standardly start off with a candidate desire or belief shows that there is the method of introspection, and, furthermore, that we use it in advance of the method of interpretation. Indeed, that there is this temporal priority of introspection over interpretation means that what we put to the corpus of our states, dispositions, activities, and actions is not an open question but the promptings of introspection. What we ask the corpus to decide is not what desire or belief, but whether the desire or belief indicated by introspection, fits in with it best. And that we have this method in reserve, or to supplement introspection, bears out the fallibility of introspection. The formula of self-examination is, Introspection proposes, interpretation disposes.

This twofold method of assigning desires and beliefs is replicated in the assignment of dispositions to others, which is also twofold, with the place of introspection now taken by the *method of intuition*. Intuition is, of course, filtered through culture and convention to a degree that seems implausible in the case of introspection, but that we have such a method is a significant mark of what it is to live as, hence to be, a person. But if it is a significant feature of being a person that we have such intuitions about others, it is a significant feature of our recognizing these others to be persons that we are ready to revise our intuitions in the light of interpretation. Philosophy does no service to the philosophy of mind by presenting persons as easier to gain knowledge of than they are.

A commitment to the method of intuition appears to set itself against behaviourism. Indeed it does. But that is not to say that intuition ignores behaviour. How could it? But it concentrates on certain kinds of behaviour, like intentional action and physiognomic expression, and it does not necessarily base its promptings on neatly demarcated stretches of behaviour.

I am, it will be appreciated, using all three terms, 'introspection', 'intuition', 'interpretation', as terms of art.

I shall consider, first, introspection, then, interpretation, in order to see what they are in themselves, and what they tell us about, or what implications they have for, the structure of the mind.

6. By introspection I mean the promptings that we derive from our mental states about our mental dispositions. These promptings are fallible, and there is more than one way in which they can arise. Introspection rests upon, hence an understanding of it has something to tell us about, the different relations that hold between mental states and mental dispositions. Let us look at this.

In Lecture II I considered the relation of manifestation. A disposition manifests itself in a mental state when it causes that mental state and the mental state furthers the role of the disposition. When the mental state furthers the role of the disposition in virtue of its phenomenology, it not only manifests, it also expresses, the disposition. Elation can manifest itself in finding, from time to time, things of no great consequence, like a seashell on a beach, just perfect. Fear of snakes can manifest itself in moments of terror on entering a forest that stretches away into the steamy delta. And it is to be noted that mental states that manifest dispositions regularly, through their occurrence, reinforce them. Senseless abuse of someone one loves can reinforce sadism. Terror on anticipating a snake writhing across the forest path can reinforce the fear of snakes. Nor is this reinforcement additional or adventitious to manifestation: for self-reinforcement can be seen as part of the role of a mental disposition.

Introspection exploits manifestation, and it can do so in two different ways. The first way presupposes that a disposition, in the natural course of events or through a happy accident, has manifested itself in a mental state. The person then notes the mental state, and draws a conclusion about the disposition: about what he really desires, or believes, or feels. He becomes aware of the terror he experiences on entering the wood, and he is led to recognize in himself an aversion that, let us say, up till then he had not confronted in himself. The second way requires mental activity, in that the person induces in himself a mental state in order to see which, out of a range of related dispositions, in that all of them are, say, directed on to the same object, it manifests. A person wonders what his relations with an old friend are, after so many difficulties have come between them, and he sets himself to imagine their meeting, and from the mental state that he induces he comes to learn what he still really feels about his friend. In each of these ways a person can become aware of a disposition that is backgrounded, as well as of one that is foregrounded, in the mental state which arises or is induced.

There is another relation besides manifestation in which mental states can stand to mental dispositions. I mentioned it briefly in Lecture II. Mental states may be reflective upon mental dispositions. Of this relation it can scarcely be said that introspection exploits it, for it is of necessity an introspective relation. When it holds, the mental state serves as a window on to the mental disposition.

The two distinct relations between mental states and mental dispositions that I have identified — mental states manifesting or expressing mental dispositions, mental states being reflective upon mental dispositions — give rise to two modes of introspection, though certainly the two modes are not themselves distinct. They are illustrated in the two following passages: Anna Karenina, dismounting from the train at Saint Petersburg, sees her husband waiting for her on the platform. 'Good heavens', she thinks, 'why are his ears like that?'—noticing the way the cartilage is pressed up against the brim of his round hat—and that perception brought home to her in a flash the hypocrisy, the pretence, with which she had invested their relations. In Bertrand Russell's *Autobiography* we read these two sentences:

I went out bicycling one afternoon, and suddenly as I was riding along a country road, I realized that I no longer loved Alys. I had had no idea until this moment that my love for her was even lessening.

In the case of Anna Karenina certain dispositions manifest themselves in a mental state. She considers this state and infers to the dispositions. But in the case of Russell there is a mental state, arising spontaneously, which is reflective upon his disposition. There is no inference here, the mental state informs him of his disposition.

To some philosophers the fact of mental states that are reflective upon mental dispositions seems totally puzzling. Such states would be puzzling if we assumed that they gave us incorrigible or infallible information, but we are not asked to believe this. Otherwise there is no inherent reason to find the relationship of a mental state to a mental disposition when it is reflective upon it any more, or less, mysterious than that when it manifests it. To find either relationship incomprehensible is simply to attempt to stand outside our own psychology. We stand outside our own psychology when, for instance, we insist that all introspection must really be interpretation.

7. I turn from introspection to interpretation.

By interpretation I mean the testing of some prompting of introspection against the corpus of our mental states, mental dispositions, and actions and activities, mental and corporeal. But the crucial element in this corpus is our dispositions. For if mental states and actions are also appealed to, this is primarily for the evidence that they provide for the dispositions that mental states manifest or that motivate actions. Philosophers have rightly stressed the weight that should be given to action in the interpretation of ourselves and of others, but this doesn't have to be taken as providing support for behaviourism: it can also, and rightly, be taken as recognition of the large part played by unconscious and preconscious motivation.

That interpretation, properly understood, has something to tell us about the structure of the mind derives from the constraints under which it operates. In all domains interpretation is possible only under constraints—constraints imposed upon the interpreter, and specifying conditions that interpretation of one and the same text, or one and the same legal system, or one and the same person, must satisfy. Constraints upon interpretation have two aims set them: one is to preserve the coherence of the interpretative activity, the other to make the activity cohere with known or assumed features of the interpretand. From these two aims it is natural to assume that we get two kinds of interpretative constraint, internal and external, of which the external constraints will be sensitive to, and therefore informative about, the nature of what is under interpretation.

If we apply this to interpretation as a method of self-knowledge or knowledge of others, it looks as though, if we consider the constraints that are externally set upon it, they will tell us something about the structure of the person. But there are two difficulties that confront us: the first concerns the very distinction between internal and external constraints in the domain of psychological interpretation, and the second, which is more serious, concerns the actual constraints that hold and what they are and what they tell us.

The distinction between internal and external constraints might initially seem not all that hard to apply in the domain of the person. Take consistency, which is anyhow likely to be a major constraint. Then we seem to be able to distinguish readily between a weak requirement that insists that a person should not be interpreted as, say, both believing or desiring that $p$ and not believing or not desiring that $p$, and some strong requirement that would insist that a person should not be interpreted as both believing or desiring that $p$ and believing or desiring that not-$p$. The weak requirement seems internally based, or designed to preserve the coherence of interpretation, whereas the strong requirement would be externally based, or designed to cohere with certain features of what persons are known or assumed to be like. More specifically, the strong consistency requirement would be designed to make interpretation respect the rationality of persons, so, if indeed it is a constraint upon the way we interpret ourselves and others, then it must be that we believe that persons are rational.

Some philosophers have denied that strong consistency is an external constraint in this sense. They have held that in interpreting persons we are necessarily committed to strong consistency, but this does not involve a belief in the rationality of persons per se. Alternatively they have maintained that strong consistency does involve a belief in rationality, but this belief is best regarded as some regard a belief in freedom or in intentionality as a feature of persons: that is, purely heuristically. The so-called belief is not really a belief, it is an entrenched way of treating people.

The view that we are necessarily committed to strong consistency, which in consequence tells us nothing about how persons are and has no psychological ground, is supported by two considerations which give alternative accounts of its ground. One is that, if we were to abandon this constraint, then our task as an interpreter would never get started. We would have no psychological corpus. For once we attributed inconsistent beliefs or desires, we would thereby license any kind of behaviour, and so from behaviour we would have no way of arguing back to motivating beliefs and desires. But this consideration, apart from its seeming neglect of introspection and intuition and its deference to behaviourism, assumes that, once inconsistency in belief and desire has set in, there is no possible ordering or structuring of belief and desire so that some might sort together, and others be kept apart, in the motivation of action. And this same assumption seems to be behind the other consideration in favour of strong consistency as a necessary constraint upon interpretation and not psychologically based. It is that the constraint is required just because it is beliefs, or just because it is desires, that we are assigning: it is the abstract features of belief and desire, not the psychology of persons, that force this commitment upon us. But could there not be both

inconsistency and yet rules or principles controlling the association of beliefs and desires — which is all that the nature of belief or
desire insists upon?

By contrast, it seems to me right to think that, if interpretation
of persons does operate under a constraint like that of strong
consistency, this must have a psychological ground. Its justification, if it has one, must be that it gets interpretation to cohere with
the known rationality of persons.

But at this point another objection will be raised. It is that the
constraint of strong consistency does not capture rationality, or
indeed any other feature that persons might plausibly be assumed
to have. The argument for this is different in the case of belief and
desire. In the case of belief the constraint is said to be too strong:
persons can and do hold inconsistent beliefs without prejudicing
their rationality. In the case of desires the constraint is said to be
inapplicable: there are no inconsistent desires.

I agree that strong consistency does not capture rationality,
though not necessarily for these reasons, but I should like to draw a
very radical conclusion from it. Instead of trying to devise in the
abstract constraints upon interpretation intended to capture rationality, what we should do is to examine the actual processes by
which persons do regulate, or try to regulate, their beliefs and
desires, and then argue back to the constraints. It is to such processes, which are in turn part of leading the life of a person, and not
to some idealized rationality, that the constraints upon interpretation must ultimately answer. And in doing so we should be prepared to find that the processes, and therefore the constraints that
cohere with them, differ markedly between the domains of belief
and desire.

8. Very roughly the actual situation seems to be as follows:

In the case of beliefs, a person aims to impose consistency upon
his beliefs. Furthermore, when he encounters inconsistent beliefs
in himself, he will prefer to hold those beliefs which are better
supported by such evidence as he either has or supposes to exist.
His aim, in other words, is to hold such beliefs as consort best with
reality. However he will not always succeed in this project, and
failure can attend it at two distinct places. In the first place, such

inconsistent beliefs as he has may not consciously get put together, and, if this is so, he will experience no need to do anything about them. Secondly, they may be consciously put together, and the inconsistency detected, but the belief that seems to the person to consort less well with reality may survive alongside that which seems to consort better. But, if this happens, then either the belief will be segregated or its intentionality will undergo a transformation. The fact is that in the case of beliefs there is an in-built mechanism in the psychology of the person that helps to secure rationality. This mechanism operates in such a way that, once inconsistency in a person's beliefs has been detected, then those beliefs which cohere less well with the evidence in his possession will, *ceteris paribus,* get deleted: support simply ebbs away. And *ceteris paribus* here means that the belief is not segregated, nor is its intentionality transformed. (It is, of course, the same mechanism that ensures that, as the balance of evidence in favour of a certain proposition accumulates, so *ceteris paribus* the degree of belief that the person affords it will rise: support simply flows towards it.)

The process is illustrated in the Rat Man case. After his father's death the Rat Man was so stunned that, while he accepted his father's death, he also continued to believe that his father was still alive. However the shock that he had received suspended for the time being the need for a coherent picture of the world in this regard: he did not consciously put together the two beliefs. Then about eighteen months later he had to put together the two beliefs, and both survived. Rationality now required of him that one of these beliefs — and it was the belief that his father was still alive — should be segregated, and it was only permitted to rejoin the rest of his beliefs when, as in the nocturnal ritual we examined, its intentionality had been disguised: it resurfaced as the belief that the father survived in the after-life as a potential *revenant.* And the Rat Man's rationality required of him, it is to be noted, not just that either one or other of the two inconsistent beliefs be segregated or disguised, but that it be the belief that he was not prepared to test or that cohered less well with the rest of the evidence in his possession.

In the case of desires it is different. A person does not even aim at imposing consistency upon his desires — though he will want the background beliefs in which his desires are grounded to be coherent. But the reason for this is not, as the earlier argument maintained, because consistency does not apply to desires. It does. And a person's desires could be inconsistent. He could, for instance, desire to kill a certain person and also desire not to kill that person — like Hamlet, or, presumably, any common murderer. That would be inconsistency. But, though consistency does apply to desires, it doesn't provide the realization of rationality in desire. It is possible for a person to be rational in desire while having desires that are inconsistent and whose inconsistency he recognizes. And he can be irrational in desire while having consistent desires. Rationality in desire is realized just in case desires satisfy a criterion that I shall call *co-existence*. 'Co-existence' is another term of art, and I shall say something about it in the next section. Here I shall observe only that it is a partially affective notion, and that its demands vary from person to person.

However, though co-existence is a different — indeed a different kind of — criterion from consistency, there is a parallelism, though only rough, between the application of co-existence to a person's desires and that of consistency to his beliefs. Non-co-existence of desire may go unnoticed, and it will do so if the non-co-existent desires are not consciously brought together. When they are brought together, one of these desires may be relinquished. However it may not, and both may continue to survive. And if this happens, then at least one of the desires will undergo — and here the parallel begins to fail — one of the following vicissitudes: it will be segregated, or it will have its intentionality transformed, or it will survive, unsegregated, untransformed, as a factor making for conscious conflict in the corpus of the person's desires.

Differences, as well as similarities, between the application of co-existence to desire and that of consistency to belief show up even in this abridged account. In the first place, there is no built-in mechanism to secure co-existence of desire as there is to secure consistency of belief. Secondly, what is actually secured in the case of belief is either consistency in belief or, at any rate, the appearance of consistency, but in the case of desire non-co-existent desires can live on to trouble even the surface of life. And, thirdly, of two non-co-existent desires there is no obvious way — which is not to say that there is no way — in which the desire that should be relinquished can be identified: whereas in the case of belief, it is generally clear which belief should go.

If we now turn back to interpretation, there seem to be three broad observations to be made.

In the first place, if we think it appropriate, as I have suggested that we should, to argue from the way persons try to regulate their beliefs and desires to the constraints that interpretation of the beliefs and desires of persons must satisfy, there is one very general conclusion that we can draw. And that is that it would be misguided for an interpreter to adopt what Robert Nozick has, in a quite different context, called a 'patterning' constraint or one that seeks to justify itself in terms of the pattern exhibited by the beliefs and desires that it assigns to individual persons. A patterning constraint upon the interpreter would be in place if, but only if, the persons whose beliefs and desires are under interpretation had already sought to impose such a pattern upon them. But, different though they are, neither the application of consistency to belief nor that of co-existence to desire is calculated to bring about such an upshot. It would only be if both were effective mechanisms of deletion that a patterning constraint upon the interpreter would be in order. Conspicuously they aren't.

Secondly, the constraints that are placed upon the interpretation of persons by the way in which they try to regulate their beliefs and desires amount in effect to this: that in interpreting persons we must be prepared to draw upon an account of how persons lead their lives that is, fundamentally, a genetic or developmental account. Hilary Putnam likes to quote a remark of Vico's to the effect that we should interpret persons in such a way as to preserve their humanity. My associated claim would be that we can do this only if we do it in the light of how persons acquire and maintain their humanity — where humanity is, of course, understood as the distinguishing mark not so much of humans as of persons.

Thirdly, it is possible to abandon the attempt to make the constraints upon interpretation of persons cohere with the way in which rationality actually operates within the psychology of persons. This is the course that decision theory takes, and there are contexts or causes in which it may pay. But it certainly seems something that is highly inadvisable when those whom we seek to interpret are ourselves.

9. What is the criterion of co-existence which rationality seeks to impose on the desires of a single person?

I shall approach this question through asking, What is conflict of desire, which co-existence seeks to redress? I say 'redress' advisedly. For another respect in which the application of co-existence and that of consistency differ is that the aim of co-existence is less total than that of consistency. Co-existence does not aim to eradicate conflict of desire as such. It aims to eradicate certain kinds of conflict and to reduce conflict as such.

What is conflict of desire?

Inconsistent desires, which we have seen to exist, provide the most perspicuous cases of desires in conflict. Inconsistent desires conflict because, even if it is possible for each desire to be satisfied singly, it is impossible that both should be satisfied. Hamlet's desires are in conflict because it is impossible both that Claudius should be killed and that he should not be killed. Furthermore, what brings the desires into conflict is true in all possible worlds. Taking a lead from inconsistent desires, we can identify further cases of conflict as those where, again, the desires cannot be jointly satisfied, though this is not true in all possible worlds. The obstacles to their co-satisfaction come from contingent features of this world and of worlds sufficiently akin to it. Examples of such conflict are provided by the desire to smoke heavily and the desire not to put one's health at risk, or the desire to see the buildings of Venice and the desire not to set foot off English soil. And beyond such desires are yet further cases of conflict which arise not because of the impossibility but because of the improbability of satisfying both desires, or perhaps only because of the improbability of satisfying them to an adequate degree. Examples of this kind of conflict are provided by the desire to be a famous actor and the desire to preserve one's privacy, or by the desire to gamble on horses and the desire to keep one's capital intact. And further along the same line are desires that are co-satisfiable in themselves, but where the actions that are needed to bring about their satisfaction are conjointly impossible or conjointly improbable. An example would be the desire to have a mastery of Hittite and the desire to be able to forge perfectly one of the great nineteenth-century masters: there is no conflict between these two skills or their exercise, but no one could find the time and the concentration to acquire both skills.

Each of these kinds of conflict arises because the desires collide on each and every occasion on which they motivate action. But we can also recognize pairs of desires that collide not on every occasion on which they motivate action but only on some occasions: but, if these occasions turn out to be sufficiently significant for the person, then the desires are thought of as in conflict. For Agamemnon there was a conflict between his desire to be a loving father and his desire to be a dedicated commander of his forces because of what transpired at Aulis.

The big question arises forcefully whether there is any conflict of desire that is not explicable in terms of the impossibility or improbability of co-satisfaction. This issue, it might be thought, could be resolved by an examination of cases. But this is an illusion, because the evidence turns out to be, for reasons worthy of consideration, peculiarly treacherous.

Consider the case of a man who, so he tells us, desires to be a farmer and also desires to be a poet. In each case he wants to be the real thing, he isn't interested in being a Sunday poet or a gentleman farmer. And he knows full well that there are people for whom it has proved perfectly possible to combine these two ambitions: to work as a farmer in the hours of daylight and to write in the evenings and then, the next morning, while out in the fields, to go over and over, testing, revising, rewriting, the lines that had been written the night before. For him however such an accommodation would be out of the question. Much though he would hate to relinquish either desire, he is convinced that he must give up one or the other because, as far as he is concerned, though not necessarily as far as they are concerned, they are in conflict. What kind of conflict could this be?

Now those who wish to claim that all conflict of desire is explicable in terms of co-satisfiability will contend that, if this is a genuine case of conflict — and why should it not be? — then it suffers from the man's under-description of his situation. In the case of at least one of the two desires, either amplify the description or append to it other desires that it brings in train, and then, though only then, the conflict will re-emerge as what it is: a problem in the co-satisfiability of what will be seen to be conjunctions of desires. So, the contention will go, the desire that the man has to be a farmer is not just the desire to farm, it is the desire to bury himself away on a farm remote from all contact with civilization, hence with poetry: or the desire to be a poet is an integral part of a whole set of desires which includes the desire to lead a life of freedom, without routine, a life given over to the study of the past and to the cultivation of the senses. On either redescription the difficulties of co-satisfiability will now explain the conflict — and, it will be further contended, the man, given this new account of his condition, would concur with it.

But suppose he does. Suppose he invariably does. What does this show? One answer would be that the man had always had the desires that satisfy the redescriptions, and now he acknowledges them. But there is another possible answer. And that is that the man accepts the redescription of his desires for the very same reason that people accept the claim that prompts the redescription, or that all conflict of desire can be explained in terms of failure of co-satisfiability. In other words, he accepts the redescription because it places conflict of desire in an acceptable light. It rationalizes conflict of desire by removing it from the person's mind and placing it in the real world: the conflict is displayed as a practical conflict. (In point of fact, if this is why the man accepts the redescription of his conflict, there are two distinct ways in which such rationalization could work. It could be that, when the man is given the redescription, or when it occurs to him, he comes to believe it even though it is not true, and that is why he acknowledges it. Or it could be that his being given the redescription, or its occurring to him, generates the desires which satisfy it, so that it is now true, and that is why he acknowledges it.)

However those who believe that desires can conflict for reasons not to do with co-satisfiability are required to provide an alternative explanation of how conflict arises, and there are two accounts that propose themselves, one which looks back to Lecture V, while the other looks forward to Lecture VII. The two accounts are compatible. The first account is that desires conflict just because they come out of different phases of psycho-sexual development, and they bear the marks of those phases stamped on them in the archaicism of their intentionality. In such cases, as we have already seen, a desire is likely to gain in persistence because it has lost in comprehensibility: it has become preserved in phantasy. The second account is that desires conflict just because they derive from different ideas that the person has about what he wants to be, or thinks he should be: they derive from what, when I come to them, I shall call 'ego-ideals'. The two accounts can be combined, for desires deriving from different developmental phases are likely to attach to different ego-ideals.

That conflict of desire can arise in ways that, though they give rise to, do not spring from, difficulties of co-satisfiability receives strong support not only from these general considerations about the nature of desire but also from special considerations about how conflict of desire is experienced, to which I now turn.

We might start with the familiar fact that, when our desires conflict, sometimes we are more certain of what our desires are for than of whether they really conflict, but sometimes, at any rate before rationalization sets in, we are more certain that our desires conflict than of what they are really for. A likely explanation is that, in the first case, we are waiting for experience to tell us what the consequences of our desires are, hence whether they are co-satisfiable, so, if the desires do conflict, this is where the conflict lies: whereas, in the second case, conflict between the desires lies in the desires themselves — it doesn't depend upon whether they are co-satisfiable — hence we know of it in advance of learning their consequences.

A look at the phenomenology of desire, which means, as we saw in Lecture III, the phenomenology of iconic imagination, lends further support to the view that there is a dual source for the conflict of desire. For within the orbit of iconic imagination, there are two distinct places at which conflict can be registered. One is inside the imaginative sequence, or in what is represented. Conflict shows up in the impossibility or the grave difficulty that the imaginative sequence has in representing the co-satisfaction — it need not, of course, be the simultaneous satisfaction, for few pairs of desires require that — of the two desires. But conflict of desire can also be registered outside the imaginative sequence but still within its orbit. And there are two ways in which this can happen. One way is in the response to, or the reaction against, what has been imagined: once desire has been represented as satisfied, the person will regret or repudiate the associated pleasure. The other external way in which conflict can be registered is in the relationship between the two imaginative projects: no sooner has the person imagined one desire satisfied than he will find himself imagining the other desire satisfied, and the two desires will compete for representation in fierce alternation. What I suggest is that, when the index of conflict is registered internally, then the desires conflict for reasons to do with co-satisfiability: but, when the conflict is registered externally, then it has its source in the nature or origin of the desires.

In the central dilemma of the Rat Man's life, we have a clear case of the second kind of conflict and of the vicissitudes it undergoes. The Rat Man's desire to be a dutiful son to his father and his desire to be a lover for the woman whom he admires — desires which other men, it is true, succeed in reconciling in their lives with some measure of success — enter into their titanic struggle because they originate in different phases of his development and never emancipate themselves from their origins. They correspond to an elementary distinction between the boy's desire to have, or be had by, the father and the boy's desire to be the father: the Rat Man's desire to be pliant to the most arbitrary injunctions that he can project upon his father comes out of the centre of the Oedipal situation, whereas his desire to assert his own rights to the sexuality that his father once enjoyed marks some kind of transcendence of the Oedipal situation. And, as the Rat Man in his early manhood struggles to come to terms with this conflict, which tears him in two, the desires themselves draw further apart and become aligned with differing ideas of what he wants to be or thinks he should be. Nevertheless, with his compulsive cast of mind the Rat Man experiences little difficulty in amplifying the two great desires of his life, or attaching to them ancillary desires so that the conflict can be made to appear — above all, to himself — as though it were rooted in the incompatibilities of the real world. He is adept at rationalization.

This analysis of conflict of desire requires to be taken a stage further. For if there are some desires that are in conflict because they cannot both be satisfied, and there are some desires that conflict because of the diversity of their nature or origin, there are also desires that conflict and the very fact that they do explains why they both exist. At least one of the desires is there in order to conflict with the other: it is a counter-desire, whose role is just to produce conflict of desire. I call such cases brute conflict. The very first case of conflict I considered, or that between inconsistent desires, seems to instantiate this phenomenon. For conflicts such as that between the desire to pay back a certain sum of money and the desire not to pay it back, conflicts which haunted the Rat Man in the days immediately following his hearing of the Chinese torture, are — on the assumption that the two inconsistent descriptions really capture the intentionality of the conflicting desires — best thought of as conflicts between a desire and a counter-desire, or even between two counter-desires. Of course, this will seem bizarre until we have some explanation of why counter-desires arise, and one account is that brute conflict aims to spread through the whole psychology of the person the sense of confusion that one specific and highly intense conflict generates. It seeks to normalize confusion.

10. If conflict of desire has this kind of complexity, what follows for the criterion of co-existence?

To begin with, the point remains cogent that what rationality cannot demand is the removal of conflict of desire as such. This is because there is in turn no conflict between what leads to, or makes rational, the formation of a desire and the fact that there are other desires of the person with which it runs into conflict. The latter doesn't bear on the former. This follows from the role of desire, and contrasts with belief, for there is a conflict between what leads to, or makes rational, the formation of a belief and the fact that it conflicts with other beliefs. The latter does bear on the former. This is ensured by the role of belief, for inconsistent beliefs cannot give rise to a picture of the world as it is.

However, if conflict of desire does not as such offend against rationality, there is one broad type of conflict that is offensive to rationality, and that is where the only thing that leads to the formation of at least one of the conflicting desires is that it conflicts with the other desire: in other words, brute conflict. However it is also observable — and, once again, the contrast is with belief — that just where conflict is most offensive to rationality, rationality is least effective as a mechanism of deletion. The recognition of a well-entrenched desire as a counter-desire does, as such, nothing even to attenuate it.

It might be argued that, if conflict of desire does not as such offend against rationality, the consequences of conflict mean that the removal of conflict is in all cases indicated by rationality. For rationality must favour maximising the satisfaction of desire, and the chances of attaining this would be enhanced if, in each case of conflict, one of the contending desires was given up. But the policy of maximising the satisfaction of desire at the expense of desire itself, like similar recipes for happiness or peace of mind proposed by some of the Ancients, overlooks the gross fact, referred to in Lecture II, that we have an attachment to our desires just because they are our desires — to which nothing comparable exists in the domain of belief. All such recipes require us to regard our desires as if they were impersonal desires: which some people manage to do, but not to their greater happiness.

But if there is only one type of conflict of desire that rationality condemns as such — and there it is ineffectual — are there not types of desire against which it sets itself, so that, if one of these desires is a party to conflict, rationality is committed to, or invariably favours, one particular resolution of the conflict? In the next lecture I shall consider aggressive desires in this light. Another contender would be desires that are incomprehensible to us, archaic desires, but, once again, as with counter-desires, if rationality condemns them, the condemnation does not delete them.

By contrast, in any conflict of desire and any attempt to impose co-existence upon it, there are at least two kinds of desire whose position is privileged. There are, on the one hand, desires that lie under the aegis of our conceptions of what we want to be or think we should be, our ego-ideals: their privilege is the product of culture. And there are, on the other hand, desires that relate directly to the body and whose satisfaction is the satisfaction of need: their privilege is natural. It is, in fact, the privilege that these latter desires enjoy that does more than anything else, more even than the close connection between our mental life and action, to make it true that the process of living as a person is what I at the beginning of Lecture II announced it to be: an embodied mental process. One distinctive way in which this privilege asserts itself is that, when a bodily desire, and particularly a sexual desire, finds itself in conflict at any rate with a counter-desire, the counter-desire seeks to become corporealized, or represented, misrepresented, as bodily. There are two routes along which this transformation can occur. The counter-desire can become corporealized in its intentionality, so that it turns itself into, for instance, the desire to avoid contagion, or to escape bodily punishment, or to gain a yet intenser form of pleasure. More subtly, the counter-desire can become corporealized in its subjectivity, so that, when it manifests itself in a mental state, it too is experienced as a bodily need: as when Rilke in his struggle to overcome masturbation experienced the desire to break himself of this habit as the need to retain within his body his creative energies.

Where this leaves the criterion of co-existence is that, unlike the criterion of consistency, it is at once personal and affective. What co-existence requires, though it may very well not have the authority to bring it about, is the reduction of conflict at least to a level that the person himself has discovered he can tolerate. The index of this limit is anxiety.

However it is also the part of rationality to place a premium on toleration itself, hence on a person's capacity to tolerate his own conflicting desires. But such toleration cannot be a piecemeal affair, and in this respect toleration of conflict differs from resolution of conflict, which proceeds conflict by conflict. Toleration requires the support of the person's changing conception of himself, and its progress depends on how the person represents his desires to himself and on how, in phantasy, he distributes them between the figures of his inner world, good and bad. Under the pressure of anxiety, externally or internally motivated, the level of inner tolerance is likely to be depressed, and once again the presence of desires in conflict will be found unbearable. A singular example is provided by the emotion of jealousy, understood not as the fear of the loss of love — the lover fears to lose the love of his beloved—but as hatred of the sharing of love—the lover is hostile to his beloved's love of another. For in many such cases, though they have no common structure, it is natural to think that the lover, having internalized the desires of his beloved, now experiences the discrepancy between her desires and his desires upon her as a conflict within his own desires: a conflict that, weakened by anxiety, he has no longer the strength to tolerate.

11. Interpretation, or the method of testing the promptings of either introspection or intuition against the corpus of a person's mental phenomena, takes place under constraints. These constraints have to cohere with the criterion a person employs in regulating the corpus of his mental phenomena, in particular his desires and beliefs. But it does not follow from this that we can in practice argue from the constraints upon interpretation to the criteria employed in resolving conflicts of belief or desire. For the former may turn out to be less accessible than the latter.

And so in the preceding discussion I reversed the order of inquiry, and I went direct for the criteria that a person requires his desires, his beliefs, to satisfy under pain of irrationality. And I contended that the criteria differ in the two cases. A person asks his beliefs to satisfy the criterion of consistency, and he asks his desires to satisfy the criterion of co-existence.

The question that now arises is, Can we now argue forwards from these criteria to the constraints upon interpretation? And, if we can, is it merely that the constraints upon interpretation should, or ought to, cohere with the criteria of rationality, or is there some built-in mechanism to ensure that they do?

There is a problem here. Even a brief look at the criteria by which persons regulate their internal conflicts suggests that they are so complex, in themselves and in their application, they they can be retrieved only through psychological inquiry. This is particularly true in the case of desires. But if this is so, surely we can make use of the actual criteria used in resolving conflicts only when we try to determine the desires of others: it seems implausible that we should be able to do so in determining our own desires. For appeal to the fruits of psychological inquiry in the course of self-examination would alienate us from ourselves at a moment in our lives which, if what I said at the beginning of this lecture is correct, is crucial to our leading them. But, if this is so, then, self-interpretation must accept different constraints from — that is, fewer than — the interpretation of others, and so a real gap opens up between the two.

Of course, self-interpretation and the interpretation of others do differ. They differ, for instance, in the material upon which interpretation works in the two cases: it is the difference between introspection and intuition. But I cannot believe that there is a further difference between them in the way in which information about our common psychology is made use of in the interpretative activity. I am therefore inclined to think that, both in the interpretation of others and in self-interpretation, we have available to us a certain amount of psychological theory which we draw upon. Specifically, we have available to us some fragment of a developmental account of our desires.

There are two major difficulties for such a view. The first concerns how we come by, or indeed whether we have, the knowledge that the view attributes to us. The second, to which I have already alluded, concerns what would be the effect of applying such knowledge in our own case.

That we do possess a fragmentary account of our own emotional development seems to fit in with the way in which that development occurs. For it is not an unmediated case of maturation — in the way in which much of our cognitive development is. Earlier desires give way to later desires, eased on by the fact that we find the earlier desires unappealing. We grow up, insofar as we do, partially by renouncing or relinquishing our desires, and it is therefore plausible to think that the periodic renunciations that have made us what we are have left behind knowledge of their order and occurrence as a kind of deposit.

As to the alienating effect that applying this knowledge to ourselves might be thought to have upon us, it needs to be pointed out that there are other cases where in self-examination we draw upon knowledge and no one claims that it has this baneful consequence. For instance, in introspection, if we think about ourselves verbally, we draw upon our knowledge of language. Is this alienating? The rejoinder that this is to confuse theoretical and practical knowledge, for it is only the interposition of theoretical knowledge that is injurious, begs the question. For what is the distinction between theoretical and practical knowledge but a distinction in the way in which knowledge is organized for use?

The empirical question remains, How large a fragment of developmental theory is likely to be available for a person to deploy in interpretation either of himself or of others, and is it likely to prove adequate? This, I believe, is very much a cultural question. There certainly will be forms of social order that make the means that nature has provided us with for understanding ourselves singularly hard of access, and in consequence we shall require science to retrieve these means for us. Relativistic social psychologies that talk of 'fictions of the self', which different societies are alleged to nurture, may be gesturing towards this truth.

I have talked of one clear difference between self-interpretation and the interpretation of others: one starts from the promptings of introspection, the other from the promptings of intuition. There is another clear difference which might be put by saying that, when we interpret ourselves, not only do we put knowledge to a practical use, but the activity in which we engage is itself a practical activity. In reconstructing his development, a person reactivates it. In this way there is a tendency to move from self-interpretation to self-assessment, from self-assessment to self-criticism, from self-criticism to self-change.

That self-interpretation is, or tends to be, a practical activity is a fact of immense importance for the way we lead our lives, and is also hard to state coherently. The point is sometimes made — by Spinoza, for instance, or by Proust — as though it set very severe limits upon the efficacy of self-knowledge. Our efforts to gain knowledge altering that about which we seek knowledge, we find ourselves with, for the most part, false beliefs. But to think of it in this way in turn assumes that what we are trying to understand — our mind and, more specifically, our dispositions — is something quite static, which precedes our attempts to understand it, which, accordingly, disturb it from the outside. But any such view must be wrong. The mind cannot be compared to a landscape, as, for instance, it is by Freud when, characterizing the psychoanalytic process, he wrote of the patient as like 'a traveller sitting next to the window of a railway carriage and describing to someone inside the carriage the changing views which you see outside'. If we are to persist with this image, then the mind cannot be situated entirely outside the train: its locus must include the changing experiences of the traveller as he peers out of the window, trying to make sense of what he sees and to relate it to what he expected of the land through which he is now passing.

12. Thus far, in considering how we understand, or try to understand, our lives even as we live them, I have respected two limitations, which it is now time to life. In the first place, I have considered this process only in a simple realization: that is, as the attempt to determine or establish what it is that we desire or feel or believe —nothing more complex than that. And, secondly, I have considered the process uniquely as something benign or as furthering the ancient maxim of enlightenment, 'Know thyself'. But at the very outset of this lecture I conceded the point to Kierkegaard, or at any rate to the Kierkegaard of the *Journal* entry, that self-understanding—and the point is of a piece with things that I have already said, as well as with further things that I shall find to say, about processes that normally perform a benign role in the way we lead our lives—can also operate to a malign effect and can impede us in our lives.

How is this to be explained?

At the beginning of this lecture I briefly considered two suggestions, both of which I dismissed. The suggestion that I now want to put forward has initially an air of paradox to it, and it is that a person's efforts to understand himself become malign insofar as they are undertaken in the cause of self-concealment. For, it will be asked, how could a person examine himself in order to know less about himself? But the air of paradox is dissolved when we consider two points. The first is that self-examination has no necessary connection with any particular motive: hence it does not have to be motivated by the desire for the growth of knowledge. All that it cannot do is, at any given point, to run counter to general constraints that such a desire would impose. And the second is that self-examination is a matter of degree: it can be engaged in up to a point. The formula according to which self-examination becomes malign is that a little self-knowledge comes to stand in the way of more.

However, in abandoning the second of the two limitations I have imposed upon myself, or in turning to consider the malign aspect of self-concealment, I have also, if not to relax, then to reinterpret, somewhat the first. I shall still not consider the determination of anything other than belief, desire, and emotion. (I shall not, for instance, consider the self-attribution of character, which I hold to be invariably evasive, since character has, as I see it, no roots in our psychology. Character traits belong at best to the shorthand of psychological description.) But in continuing to restrict myself to the determination of what we believe, or want, or feel, I shall now include cases where phantasy makes a crucial appearance on the scene. It can do so in one or other of two ways, which readily combine: either the disposition that we test has itself been transformed by phantasy, or the corpus of dispositions against which we test it contains phantasies prominently. For my claim is that, when self-examination engages with phantasy in either of these ways, there is a tendency for self-examination to place itself at the service of phantasy, and it is then that we have self-examination in its malign aspect.

Phantasy, as we saw in the last lecture, at once contains and conceals desires. It conceals what it contains, and it does this partly because of what it contains and partly because of how it contains it. It contains archaic, and therefore partly incomprehensible, desires, and it contains them enfolded in narrative. Phantasy has already discharged one part of its task, or containment, by the time it has constructed representations of the various desires that it amalgamates, and in order to discharge the other part of its task, or concealment, it invokes narrative to produce a story line. This story line will mask the archaic desires, which lend themselves to disguise because of their incomprehensibility. But, in concealing these desires, the narrative will be full of deceptive references to other desires, emotions, feelings, and all of a more evolved kind which the person probably lacks the maturity to entertain.

We now add the fact that, in order to perpetuate itself, phantasy is from time to time projected on to reality, bringing about sometimes internal changes in thought and perception, sometimes physical modifications of the external world. The world is changed when the phantasy is acted out.

In the last lecture we saw an example of acting out a phantasy and of how acting out helps a phantasy to conceal the desires that it contains, and thus to safeguard itself, when we considered the strange behaviour of the Rat Man on the day that his lady was about to leave him for a brief visit to her aunt. Let us look at this again.

Going for a walk in the country, Freud's patient observed a stone in the middle of the road and removed it, remembering that his lady was about to pass this way in a few hours' time and fearing that her carriage might come to grief against it. But, having done this, he then felt that he had made a fool of himself, and so returned and put the stone back in its original position. The phantasy contains, in the two actions that it narrates, the two emotions that the Rat Man had towards his lady: love and hate. The first action represents love, with great vividness, though pushed in the direction of solicitude, and for this reason it might be held to foreshadow, to some degree, the hate that the Rat Man also feels. But the hate itself is altogether masked. The second action represents it, it is true, but the story line of the narrative compels us to see this action as merely the critical repudiation of the first action.

So much by way of understanding the phantasy in itself or as it stands inscribed in the Rat Man's mind. But when the Rat Man comes to act out the phantasy, the disguise that has already been imposed on the Rat Man's hatred for his lady, hence on his ambivalence, is heightened. For, as the phantasy is acted out, the work of the internal dramatist requires the Rat Man to entertain a certain chain of thoughts, and in doing so, he is obliged first to find the removal of the stone appropriate, then to find it absurd, then to find that, all things considered, the replacement of the stone to where it originally lay is the most sensible thing to do. The Rat Man, it must be noted, does not merely allow these thoughts to occur. He thinks them, and acts on them. And in thinking them, and in acting on them, he makes it yet more difficult for himself to recognize the emotion that this sequence of thoughts is designed to conceal: hate. The second action, acted out, is now experienced as the phantasy represents it: it is experienced as merely the rectification of the first action. And so the Rat Man inculcates in himself a state of mind such that, if he were asked, either by himself or by others, whether he didn't also hate the woman whom he loved, whether his feelings weren't somewhat ambivalent, he would have to say, because he had no reason to say otherwise, No.

'If asked by himself.' It is then, at this very point, or by tacking itself on to phantasy and, in particular, on to phantasy acted out, that self-examination enrols itself in the service of phantasy and so advances the cause of self-concealment. It promotes self-ignorance.

However, the process can go further. Beyond self-ignorance there is self-error. In self-ignorance a person is unaware of, or denies, the beliefs, desires, and emotions that he has. In self-error a person attributes to himself beliefs, desires, and emotions that he does not have but, invariably, wishes that he did have. Self-examination, conspiring with phantasy, can promote self-error as well as self-ignorance. What happens, in brief, is that the person, trying to determine what he really believes, and, more particularly, what he really wants or really feels, borrows the terms in which to do so from the story line of the phantasy in which his real desires or emotions are concealed. Specifically, he borrows the terms from those deceiving references to desires and emotions that he cannot experience, in which the phantasy is so rich. It is this loan that ensures self-error.

A poignant example of self-examination fostering self-error is threaded through much of the central part of *A la Recherche du Temps Perdu*. There are many earlier moments in the novel, before I take up the story, when the Narrator has asked himself what he really feels about Albertine, and has had to recognize that for a number of reasons which he could cite he cannot reach a decision. Then one evening at Balbec he tells his mother that he has irrevocably decided not to marry Albertine, and that he will soon stop seeing her. A day or so later he is travelling in the little country train with Albertine, and, the rest of the company having alighted at Doncières, he has between Doncières and Parville to tell Albertine that he does not love her. Delicacy, as he puts it, requires it of him. The train approaches Parville, Albertine puts on her cloak, and then she discloses, inadvertently, that she is a close friend, like a daughter, like a sister, of Mademoiselle Vinteuil. Her remark transports him suddenly to that distant afternoon scene at Montjouvain, when, from behind a bush, through a window, he caught sight of the composer's daughter locked in a passionate, conspiratorial embrace with a girl friend. He stops Albertine from leaving the train, he begs her to come with him to Balbec, and he takes a room for her in the hotel in which he is staying. Now he knows three things: that she is a lesbian, that she is part of him, that he loves her. The next morning he tells his mother of his need to marry Albertine. He will not commit the imprudence of telling Albertine that he loves her, but just that fact, he is convinced, is what was revealed to him in that moment of unbearable pain. Later, with Albertine as his prisoner, he will reflect on his feelings and their symptoms and whether these show or don't show that he loves her or whether they show that he doesn't love her. But all these questions, with which he continues to vex himself, are unanswerable, though not for the reasons that he fastens on. They are unanswerable because the notion of love that he appears to be testing is not derived from his own psychological resources, and it does not correspond to anything that he can experience. It derives from the elaboration of the phantasy that contains and disguises the feelings that are indeed open to him: fear of the loss of love, hatred of the love whose loss he fears so much, and perhaps, by now, even some attachment to, some love of, the fear of loss. But so firmly has he projected this phantasy and its elaboration on to his life that he goes on asking himself whether he feels this one thing that he cannot feel, while he is condemned to repeating over and over again the few different things that he can feel. But each time he asks whether he does or doesn't love Albertine he entrenches himself deeper in the belief which the phantasy serves, and which then serves the phantasy: the belief that he is someone capable, in his own unhappy way, of love. The phantasy serves the belief in that the story line of the phantasy presupposes the belief: and the belief serves the phantasy in that it prevents the Narrator from testing the phantasy or uncovering the desires and emotions that it masks. And it is because of this belief, fostered by constant self-examination, that the Narrator is led, beyond the self-ignorance which is characteristic of the Rat Man, into self-error.

Some might think, This is only fiction. Out of deference to that scruple I move to the other end of the spectrum, and let me try to illustrate how self-understanding can obscure self-understanding, less of it prejudicing more, taking us once again beyond self-ignorance into self-error, by taking an example, chosen for its comparative simplicity, from my own experience of psychoanalysis.

One session I found myself saying that all my adult life I had found myself (as many do, I suppose) thinking of, and feeling about, certain men, men generally older but sometimes younger than myself, as though they were my father. So strong was this reaction of mine to them, I said, that very often, either in memory or in imagination, I found myself misrepresenting their looks, or their clothes, or their voice, so as to accord with certain visual or auditory images that I preserved of my father, and thus to heighten verisimilitude. That this was so I had long realized, but now I had another fragment, a new piece of self-knowledge, to add to it. I could not imagine how this advance had been so long deferred. For I now recognized that, whenever I reacted in this way to a man, I also felt distant from, or embarrassed with, the woman to whom the man was married in a way that the actual personalities involved could not account for. The explanation for this difficulty was, I now saw, obvious, and it was that each time I experienced this awkwardness, this embarrassment, this chill, I was merely reexperiencing, reenacting, if in a muted way, all the resistance that I felt in relation to my mother. This was the increment in self-knowledge. I finished. I waited for the interpretation. 'If you are right, then we have here an interesting piece of calculation. The calculation is this. "Your mother is just the woman to whom your father is married: that is all she is." '

This interpretation introduces several elements, which it relates or assumes related in certain ways. They are a desire, a phantasy, the projection of the phantasy, and a piece of self-examination undertaken in the wake of the projection and in the cause of self-error. The desire is one that we have already encountered, fleetingly, at the end of Lecture III: the archaic desire to have had another mother. The phantasy, which is related to the desire as at once containing and concealing it, has two dramatis personae: a man and a woman. The man is the man who is my father and the woman is the woman who is my mother. The man is my father in virtue, presumably, of some biological fact, and the woman is my mother in virtue of being married to this man — so the phantasy represents them. Now this phantasy contains the archaic desire in that it represents at least its partial satisfaction. For, according to the phantasy, the woman who is my mother is so for reasons other than those of biological fact: My mother is not really my mother. And if the phantasy does not represent the desire fully satisfied by having a third character, another woman who is, who is really, my mother, it at least leaves a space for such a person. And in containing the archaic desire the phantasy conceals it: it needs interpretation to detect it. As to the next two elements, the projection of the phantasy and the self-examination that is tacked on to it, in this particular case they are very intimately connected: so much so that it is plausible to believe that the projection of the phantasy is undertaken for the sake of self-examination, hence for the sake of self-error. The self-examination is, it is true, considerably deferred. But the only difference this makes is that, when the self-examination does occur, the self-error on which it terminates proves all the more irresistible: it broke upon me with the force of a revelation. What occasions the projection is the presence in my life of some man at once associated in my mind with my father and married: the personality of the woman is a matter of indifference. Having projected the phantasy, I then ask myself why I react to the woman as I do, and the answer, now familiar to us, dawns on me. Why I react as I do can only be because, the man being for me the equivalent of my father, the woman must be for me the equivalent of my mother. What else could she be, and how else could I feel about her?

The inference to the explanation of my feelings, or what I prided myself on as an increment in self-knowledge, not merely follows upon the projection of phantasy, it makes evident use of terms borrowed from the phantasy. Specifically it makes use of the equation, *my mother = the wife of my father.* In consequence, each time the inference is invoked, self-examination sides with the phantasy and the desire it contains against all attempts to subject it to scrutiny. My desire to have another mother remains unexamined so long as the thought 'My mother is just the wife of my father, she has no direct connection with me' remains inviolate. In hot pursuit of self-knowledge about a strange, unlikely occurrence of social embarrassment, I manage, each time I stumble, triumphantly, upon an answer, to immure myself deeper in self-error.

I have cited this interpretation for its comparative simplicity. But phantasy and the projection of phantasy are not themselves simple phenomena, and even in this schematic presentation we can see a hint of some further complexity that this particular situation carries. Significantly the phantasy fails to attribute to the woman any characteristic other than that of being married to my father. Hence the projection of the phantasy does not justify, though it explains, my response to the woman: I am embarrassed, but there is nothing that I am embarrassed by. This curious void in the picture suggests that, alongside the projective process that we have been considering, there is a supplementary piece of projection. Could it not be that, as well as projecting on to this unfortunate woman a role in a phantasy that I had about my mother, I also projected into her the blankness, the nothingness, the sense of absence that I felt in relation to my mother? The implications of this further process will concern us in my final lecture.

13. I distinguished in Lecture I between the person who leads a life, his leading of that life, and the life that he leads: or, as I put it, between a thing, a process, and a product. At the beginning of this lecture I reverted to these distinctions in order to make the point that what I was going to talk about was the examination of the process, not the product. The phrase 'the examined life' notwithstanding, I was not going to talk about the examination of the life that a person leads. At the end of the lecture I revert to these same distinctions, now to make the point that what I have not been talking about is the examination of the thing. The phrase 'self-examination' notwithstanding, I have not been talking about the examination of the person who leads the life. Nor have I been talking about the examination of the self or the metaphysical subject: I have been talking about a form of psychological inquiry, whereas that would have been metaphysical inquiry.

However, if it is right to distinguish between self-examination and examination of the self, or to assert that, when a person examines the way he leads his life, he is not conducting an inquiry into the metaphysical subject, it might seem that an adequate philosophical account of self-examination must tell us what the self is and what knowledge of the self is. The key consideration here would be that self-examination terminates on thoughts that the person has that refer to the self: the results of self-examination are characteristically conveyed by 'I' thoughts.

But why is this crucial? Equally the results of self-examination are conveyed by tensed thoughts. Does it follow that a philosophical account of self-examination must tell us what time is and what experience of time is?

This retort may seem obtuse, for, it might be argued, not only is reference to the self or the metaphysical subject ineliminable from reports of self-examination, but it is just such reference that makes these reports what they are, or secures them their introspective or self-interpretative character. But this cannot be right. For the use of 'I' in such reports is just the same as that in 'I am tall' or 'I am here', which do not record the findings of self-examination. What gives the reports their character is what is predicated of 'I'—and the circumstances in which the predication comes to be made.

# VII From Voices to Values: The Growth of the Moral Sense

1. Crucial to self-examination, crucial (in consequence) to the way in which we lead our lives, is the fact that we may bring our desires, emotions, and beliefs, our intentions and our aspirations, under a form of scrutiny that we think of as moral scrutiny. Just what moral scrutiny is, or what makes a form of scrutiny moral, I take to be one of the obscurest issues in human culture, and we should not close our minds to the thought that there is no one such thing. By which I do not simply mean that there is more than one sufficient condition for morality, but that the alleged unity of morality, or what makes the different conditions cohere, is a rationalization, a piece of secondary revision. A way characteristic of mid-twentieth-century philosophy of demarcating morality, which is through the terminology that morality employs, is illusory. Indeed, in their advocacy of this method contemporary philosophers have shown themselves to be, some unwittingly, some wittingly, accomplices of morality in its imperialising tendency, or its efforts to take over or dominate all attempts at self-scrutiny. For one of the means that morality uses to expand its frontiers is to claim total sovereignty over words in which it has only a part share. 'Duty', 'ought', 'virtue', 'good', spring to mind as examples.

2. There are two very broad ways of thinking about morality — each suggests how morality should be primarily thought of, and how it should be thought of derivatively — and which of these two broad ways we subscribe to will condition what we expect of morality and what we allow morality to expect of us.

On one view, morality is thought of primarily as a set of thoughts or propositions, which are true, and which are susceptible of formulation, though it may not be within our power to do so to any high degree of precision or completeness. On the other view, morality is thought of primarily as a part of the psychology of the person, or of how we live, including in its domain certain beliefs and emotions, certain thoughts and feelings, and a number of habits. To the first view is added the rider that inevitably people come across these propositions or such of them as circulate in their particular community: they assess them as best they can, some of them they will reject out of ignorance or prejudice or perversity, but they are likely to accept some and, when they do, they recruit these propositions into something that may then be thought of as *their* morality. To the second view is added the rider that all but inevitably people will get interested in that part of their psychology which is their morality, they will try to extract from the untidy mass of life in which they are implicated certain more or less general propositions, they will purify these propositions as best they can, and these propositions will be reconstructed as something that may then be thought of as morality *in the abstract.* The first view treats morality as like mathematics; the second view treats morality as like religion — that is, like religion as it appears to the infidel — or like art.

If we accept the second view, which recommends itself to me, though I shall not argue for it, then moral philosophy is pursued as moral psychology, but moral psychology too can be thought of in two different ways. This time the two ways aren't opposed, they are complementary: they generate two branches of the subject, though there are some who will say that one of these branches is of no specifically philosophical interest. So, on the one hand, moral psychology can be viewed as the study of those mental processes which are involved in moral deliberation, moral decision, and moral action. It studies moral reasoning, its nature and the defects to which it is susceptible. It is a synchronic study. On the other hand, moral psychology can be viewed as the study of the growth of the moral sentiments, moral beliefs, and moral habits in the typical life-history of the individual. It studies the moral sense as this develops from birth to death. It is a diachronic study, and, though it is this branch of moral psychology to which some deny philosophical interest, it is the one that I intend to take up in this lecture in the belief that it takes us deepest into the topic of morality.

3. I have referred to the growth of the moral sense from birth to death. I must guard against two misunderstandings that these words might encourage.

In the first place, though the history of the moral sense is long, it is not quite as long as the life-history of the individual within which it falls. The history of morality does not start literally at birth, for it is not a native phenomenon: rather, it arises in response to certain urges and impulses which it seeks to control and which are, accordingly, older than it. Commenting on a famous dictum of Kant's about the starry heavens and the moral law, Freud observed that, though conscience is indeed 'within us', it has not 'been there from the first', and in this respect he compared morality, to its disadvantage, with sexuality. We are born sexual but we are not born moral; though, of course, we may be born to be moral, and the teleology here could be variously based. Secondly, the history of the moral sense, once it does get under way, does not exhibit a simple nor a steady nor a straightforwardly upward growth: its history is chequered. And morality is probably best regarded as an emergent phenomenon: it is formed out of constituents pre-existent in the mind, but it cannot be understood solely in terms of them—which goes for much else in the psychology of the person.

4. Moral philosophy is the mirror that self-consciousness holds up to morality, and it tends to distort that which it reflects. It idealizes it. It gives it a cohesiveness or a clarity of contour that it lacks, and it exhibits it as uniformly benign, which it isn't. It gets away with this because it ignores or obscures the story of morality. Restored to its proper place in the life-history of the individual, morality does not self-evidently, or even evidently, have the features that moral philosophers have given it.

A return to the history of the moral sense can serve at once to provide a better idea of the nature and force of morality and also to fix the extension of the concept. The second half of the task may well have some surprises in store for us. For many beliefs that a person holds, many decisions that he reaches, many sentiments that he expresses, and which he certainly would think of as moral, may very well turn out not to be so, if the test is, as I am suggesting, whether the beliefs, the decisions, the sentiments, appropriately descend from the relevant part of his psychology. I personally don't shrink from the view that certain beliefs that a person has about, say, the proper distribution of goods in a society, and which he has got out of a book — perhaps a very good book — in which all the arguments are suasive for him, just may be no part of his morality, even though they are certainly beliefs of his, and even though they cannot be formulated outside the alleged 'language of morals'. It is their history that betrays them: it falls outside what diachronic moral psychology traces.

5. A crucial moment — the crucial moment — in the formation of a person's morality is the establishment of the superego.

The superego is an internal figure, or perhaps a group of such figures, singled out from the rest of the mind's dramatis personae or other internal figures by two criteria: by its history, and by the role that it plays in the life of the person. The superego aims to control the inner and the outer life of the person who houses it. In other words, the superego is characteristically phantasised as commanding, forbidding, cajoling, threatening, rewarding, punishing — and all this in the furtherance of norms that have no immediate or obvious instrumental justification. A feature of all internal figures, as we saw in Lecture IV, is, at any rate initially, the extreme and archaic nature of their actions and reactions, but what distinguishes the superego is the singleness of intention or purpose that is displayed in all the doings that phantasy ascribes to it.

But, we may ask, how does it come about that one internal figure, or one group of internal figures, is not merely phantasised as engaging in these regulatory or punitive activities, which also fall to the lot of other internal figures, but is phantasised exclusively as engaging in them? The answer lies in the origins of the superego: through, just as the superego differs not in kind but only in degree from other internal figures, so the circumstances in which it originates differ from those in which they originate not in nature but only in gravity. Introjection is a response to anxiety, and the introjection of the superego is the person's — or, let us be more specific and say the child's — response to the most severe anxiety-situation in which it finds itself. The only details of this situation that need concern us, or that belong to moral psychology, are these: The external figure that is the counterpart to the superego is a menacing rather than a menaced figure, it is a parent or someone upon whom the child is and feels utterly dependent, it is perceived as obstructing and threatening the child's sensual desires in the most terrifying fashion, and no small part of the explanation of why this figure is found so menacing is that the child has already projected on to it the aggressive impulses that the mere possibility of frustration ignites within him.

The two most general truths about the dominion of the super-ego — truths which are in the first instance truths about the phantasies of internalization in which the superego appears — derive from the circumstances in which the incorporative phantasy is entertained. In the first place, the dictates that the superego imposes on the infant are utterly alien to him in inception. They neither derive from nor do they trouble to mould themselves to the child's own needs and feelings. Indeed, it is often enough that the child should desire something for it to be forbidden him: equally, enough that something should be enjoined on him that he should experience compliance with it as something impossible. In this way the internal figure keeps up the hostility for the sake of which the counterpart external figure was incorporated. In Freud's phrase, in which one word does much work, the superego 'confronts' the ego. Secondly, the dominant response of the infant to the superego is terror: the superego controls the child by means of fear. In the phantasies of internalization in which the superego occurs, it appears as a figure set over and against the child, re-morselessly haranguing it, dictating to it, criticizing it, chastising it: in response the child imagines itself as experiencing terror, and the upshot of such phantasies is that the child is left terrorized. The structure of these phantasies observes a familar pattern. The super-ego is peripherally imagined threatening the child: the child cen-trally imagines itself threatened: and the internal audience, being empathic, ensures that, as a result of the phantasy, the child will find itself in the very condition in which it would have been left by those feelings which in the phantasy it imagined itself experiencing.

6. Morality inherits from the superego certain baneful features which are comprehensible enough in the light of its history and which it never altogether outgrows, though they can be remarkably attenuated. A more idealizing moral philosophy would not look at it like this, and would prefer to think of the features I have in mind as distinct from and inessential to morality. A genetic moral psychology challenges such assurance. Could we get the idealized version of morality free of all these failings?

First, then, there is the *asceticism* of morality, or the unwillingness of morality to take seriously the actual material on which it is exercised: the embodied person. Perfection, for instance, is considered as though it were a part of the genuine aspirations of morality. In the hands of certain thinkers, morality can come to pride itself on its asceticism, so that the content, even the motivation, of morality can be held to owe nothing to human nature. The obvious example here is the Kantian, if not Kant's own, singularly bleached view of morality, unstained by the demands of psychology. Secondly, there is *inwardness,* or the tendency of morality to disregard or to treat as irrelevant the distinction between the inner and the outer — between, on the one hand, thought or desire and, on the other hand, action, considered as objects of moral scrutiny. Such a distinction is held to correspond to no significant difference in moral responsibility. The *locus classicus* for inwardness is Christ's teaching about the woman taken in adultery, and it is not hard to make the connection between such thinking and the archaic theory of the mind. Morality condemns thoughts or desires as though they were omnipotent.

Both asceticism and inwardness reflect the close connection between the superego and introjection. Introjection is, as we have seen, a complex process, unfolding in two stages, and asceticism readily correlates with the first of these stages, inwardness with the second. Asceticism attests to the original incorporative phantasy, for the external figure that is taken into the child in the incorporative phantasy is the parent committed to the frustration of the child's natural desires. Inwardness attests to the later phantasies of internalization, for in these phantasies the internal figure (as it now is) is represented as having total access to the whole of the person it inhabits—mind as well as body, thought as well as deed. In point of fact, that the person is permanently exposed in this way to the scrutiny and censure of a figure whom it phantasises is a distinctive mark of the internality of that figure.

Thirdly, there is *delinquency*. Asceticism and inwardness are baneful features of morality that penetrate the content of action carried out under its aegis: delinquency is a baneful feature that corrupts the motivation of such action. The person who is burdened with a singularly harsh superego, remorseless and unremitting in its persecution, finds one way out of his predicament open to him. This is crime. And crime here means not just a course of action that society has proscribed, but one that the person concurs with society in thinking nefarious. In pursuing crime the person puts himself in the wrong in the eyes of many, including himself. What could possibly be the appeal of such a course of action to anyone—in particular to someone who already feels himself weighed down by an excessive sense of guilt? The answer is that crime has a twofold appeal: there are two ways in which it offers 'mental relief'. In the first place, part of the explanation of why guilt becomes intolerably oppressive is that it floats free. Attaching itself now to this action, now to that, attaching itself in turn to whatever at the time the person thinks or does or wants, it is attached, it follows, to nothing specific, to nothing as such. In this respect it resembles boredom, and one thing that crimes does is that it offers the person a specific object—the criminal act—on which to suspend his guilt. And, secondly, it promises him a way—through, that is, the punishment that the criminal act may be expected to bring in train—of purging his guilt. A further and more extreme form of delinquency is that where the person has projected the superego outwards into some figure of authority, and now experiences the commands of morality as doubly alien to him.

To describe the person whose guilt at once precedes and also motivates his misdeed, Freud borrowed one of the chapter-headings in *Thus Spake Zarathustra*. He called him 'the pale criminal': and a step beyond delinquency, beyond the pale criminal, is another malign feature of the motivation of morality for which Freud also had a phrase. The phrase is 'moral masochism'.

For an understanding of moral masochism, the crucial fact to recognize is that the superego is still heavily invested with the aura of sexuality that clung to the exteral figure from which the superego derives: the parent who is experienced as the interferer in the child's sensuous desires. The parent is felt to forbid the child's sexuality so as to keep it all to himself: he is, as we saw in the case of the Rat Man's father, the patron of sexuality. But once this sexuality is internalized along with the figure who claims to monopolise it, the terror by means of which the superego exercises its dominion is shot through with fierce erotic overtones. The bite of conscience, the *morsus conscientiae,* becomes a form of savage gratification, and the moral masochist is, like the pale criminal, swept up into behaviour that he condemns and swept up into it because he condemns it, but, unlike the pale criminal, he seeks in delinquency not a way of purging his guilt, but a means towards savouring or relishing it, an invitation to share in its savage pleasures.

Delinquency and moral masochism surely belong to morality, and, once we regard morality as a natural, if not a native, part of human psychology, to be theorised along with it, a parallel suggests itself. A theory of comedy would be inadequate if it gave no indication of why wit or comedy sometimes, under certain conditions, does not move to laughter. It is in this way that moral philosophy is incomplete if it avoids the question why it is that morality sometimes, or under certain conditions, can motivate what it denounces as its own infraction.

7. If the establishment of the superego is indeed a, or the, critical moment in the formation of the moral sense, there are two large questions that moral psychology has to answer. First, Is there a moral pre-history, or does the superego have antecedents, and if so, what are they? And, secondly, Is there moral evolution, or does the superego develop into anything, and, if so, how is this possible? In the absence of satisfactory answers to these questions, morality faces a challenge of remarkable gravity, which can be put very simply: Morality is from first to last, in its origins and throughout our lives, simply a price that we pay, and go on and on paying, for

relief from external fear. We are frightened in childhood, we interiorize the fear by substituting an internal for an external object, we placate the internal representative of the fear by the sacrifice of instinctual gratification, the gain in tranquillity outweighs even the crippling loss in satisfaction, but the sacrifice has nothing independently to recommend it. Morality is an internalized Danegeld. In *The Genealogy of Morals* Nietzsche considers some such hypothesis — indeed he comes very close to accepting it — and the question that moral psychology has to answer, if it is to justify its claim to be moral philosophy, is, Is this so? Or is morality entitled to a happier interpretation?

A happier interpretation of morality would be deserved if it could be shown that there are some needs, some desires, other than the avoidance of fear, and not shallow ones, that the establishment of the superego satisfies; or that there is some real advantage that derives from its persistence other than simply the avoidance of a recurrence of the original fear; or both.

I shall consider these two possibilities in turn: the first at somewhat greater length.

8. First, then, the pre-history of the superego, or whether there is some need or desire other than that which immediately accounts for the establishment of the superego that its continuation satisfies. At the outset we can surmise that any such need or desire would have to be for the control of impulse, and that the index of this need or desire would be anxiety.

In his earlier writings Freud thought that there was such a need, and it was the need for the control of sexuality, and he also found himself unable to explain it — why it arose or how it operated. He found himself unable to explain why it arose, since sexuality is not merely a source of pleasure but it offers the prototype of pleasure, and he found himself unable to explain how it operated, since, throughout this period of his intellectual development, anxiety, despite its natural place in such an explanation, was regarded by Freud as the transform of sexuality under repression — in other words, anxiety presupposed control of impulse and therefore could not account for it. Then in 1926 Freud changed his views. Anxiety became recognized as an original phenomenon, though closely connected with aggression, and from then onwards Freud seems to have thought that there was a primitive need for the control of impulse in the form of a need for the control of aggression. If there was also a felt need for the control of sexuality, this was a reflection of the way in which in the childish mind sexuality is fused with phantasies of greed, bodily plunder, and the interchange of ferocious satisfactions. I shall follow the later Freud to the extent of thinking that, if there is an independent need for the control of impulse, it is for the control of aggression. This is not, of course, to deny that morality frequently opposes itself to sexuality as such, but it is to cast doubt on whether, in doing so, it satisfies a prior, corresponding need.

It is, of course, a quite different issue whether, in the course of the individual's psycho-sexual development, specific forms of sexual desire and gratification, centred upon some zone of the body which they animate and idealize, are successively felt to require if not suppression, at least attenuation, and, if so, how this gets registered within his psychology. I have drawn attention to just such a process in Lecture V, but in its working out it does not look as though morality has more than an ancillary role to play. What morality does in such a case is to supplement with prohibition what the twin forces of disgust and incomprehension cannot achieve unaided.

So we have the question, What reason is there to think that the control of aggression is something for which the child has an original need or desire, which the superego independently satisfies? Or, more specifically, Does anxiety attach to aggression rather in the way in which pleasure attaches to desire?

In seeking an answer to this question, I shall return to the work of Melanie Klein, which I considered in Lecture IV.

Klein proposes two ways in which aggression and anxiety are linked, which she correlates with two types of anxiety. She calls them persecutory anxiety and depressive anxiety, each may be presumed to have its own phenomenology, and each is a signal of a specific set of dispositions. In the life-history of the individual, or in the story of infantile development, a cognitive achievement separates the two.

Of the two types, persecutory anxiety is the more primitive. The cognitive achievement that interposes itself between the two is the acquisition of the concept of a whole object or a whole person, for, whereas depressive anxiety requires such a concept, persecutory anxiety makes do with the concept of a part-object. A part-object is best thought of an an object insofar as it satisfies a highly simplified description or realizes one aspect of a whole object: though *ex hypothesi* it cannot be thought of in this way by the person in whose mind such objects, such concepts, have a monopoly. By contrast, a whole object is credited with a range of properties and with a history in the course of which these properties inevitably will undergo change. For instance — and the instance is crucial — a part-object will be either good or bad, it will be either loved or hated: a whole object will have its good aspect and its bad aspect, and, correspondingly, it will be loved at one moment and hated at another. The distinction between part-object concepts and whole-object concepts is framed in the perspective of the whole-object concept. But the difference which the distinction picks out is active in the mind that has not, as yet, the capacity to frame the distinction.

So long as the child is under the influence of persecutory anxiety, it has a motive to control its aggression, but not one that promises a happier interpretation of morality. For this motive is the fear of retaliation, of which persecutory anxiety is the signal. Nevertheless there are certain things worth noting about this phase, and about how persecutory anxiety operates.

The crucial feature of persecutory anxiety is that it is inextricably entwined with the aggressive impulses that arouse it. In other words, within a psychology that is dominated by aggression and persecutory anxiety, no premium would attach to such a device as Gyges' ring, which would secure invisibility for the offender. It might guarantee impunity, but it would not bring peace of mind. For in the mind of the aggressor, aggression cannot be insulated from the fear of retaliation by any kind of magical interference with the consciousness of the victim, and this is because it is in the very nature of aggression that the aggressor should credit the victim with certain thoughts — thoughts, that is, about what is happening to the victim. Aggression is not to be equated with mere expression, like a shriek or a gesture, which relieves tension and of which it just happens to be true that it has injurious consequences for those within range. Rather, aggression is the desire to inflict pain or destruction upon a figure perceived to be aggressive: that is the intentionality of aggression.

Indeed, to get the structure of aggression right so as to perceive how implicated it is with the fear of retaliation, we must appreciate that the perception of the figure as aggressive is not the initial condition for aggression, as we might at first think. The perception is not to be thought of as an external stimulus that causes aggression to be manifested, in some such way as the perception of a beggar might cause the manifestation of pity. The perception of the figure as aggressive is itself a manifestation of aggression. This perception is a mental state which is caused — partially caused, that is — by aggression and which, in virtue of its psychic force, lures the child into aggressive action.

If we now ask what the initial condition of aggression is, the answer seems to be a conjunction. The initial condition is the conjunction of an internal factor, which is the waxing of aggression, coming about for reasons perhaps beyond our grasp, and an external factor, which is a neutral perception, a mere awareness, of the figure. If, then, the perception of the figure as aggressive is, as I have just said, caused, or partially caused, by the aggression, that part of the perception which the aggression causes is the aggressive colouring. And in thus colouring the perception, aggression is projected. There is, then, a sequence, an elided sequence, of mental states of which the common element is that they all have a certain figure as their object. First, there is a mere awareness of this figure, and this awareness is, in conjunction with some internal modification of aggression itself, the initial condition: then this mental state serves as the vehicle for the projection of aggression, so that the figure comes to take on an aggressive colour: then the mental state, by now a perception of the figure as aggressive, manifests, indeed expresses, aggression — it expresses aggression in that it serves as a lure to aggressive action. All this might seem unduly complicated if it were not for the fact that, in manifesting itself in this way, aggression exhibits a pattern which it shares with a number of dispositions, that might be thought of as projective dispositions: other examples are scorn, boredom, greed, and sentimentality. They are all, it is to be noted, dispositions which are not cultivated, and with which no owner is happy. Soon we shall see, in the particular case of aggression, that the presence of projection in the orbit of manifestation suggests that there is a natural rejection or intolerance of aggression. The same, I suggest, goes, to some degree, for the other dispositions.

I have however exhibited the structure of aggression in order to show how implicated aggression is with the fear of retaliation. It is the element of projection that secures this link: for the child is familiar, from the inside, with what it projects. In projecting its own aggression on to a figure in the environment, the child thereby assigns to its victim two new mental phenomena, one of which is a disposition, and the other a mental state: the desire to retaliate, and the thought that what it is enduring, here and now, from the child, or the aggressive act, calls for retaliation. The child's projection of aggression consists in part of an enlargement of its victim's repertoire. And that the child has such a repertoire at its disposal to assign to its victim is part of its capacity to entertain aggression.

Having compared aggression to other projective dispositions, I should now add that these dispositions all have an aspect of aggression. And this they have in virtue of being projective. For the projection of unwanted aspects of oneself, corporealized under the archaic theory of the mind, is experienced by the person who discharges these parts of himself on to another as aggression. The great sentimentalists of fiction, the professional pitiers of Dickens and Dostoevsky, are correctly portrayed as in part the artificers of the sufferings they lament.

The connection thus spelt out between aggression and the fear of retaliation as it exists in the mind still dominated by persecutory anxiety will seem unnaturally cerebral, if it is for a moment thought that the child makes a series of inferential steps from how it sees a certain figure, through what it wants to do to this figure, to what it can reasonably fear from this figure. Naturalness is however restored to the connection if we think of it as forged in a sequential phantasy, which begins with the child's peripherally imagining a threatening figure in the environment and ends with its centrally imagining itself waiting for the retaliation to strike.

In point of fact, the intimate connection between aggression and persecutory anxiety is still not complete until a further layer is added. Thus far the child has been presented as having aggressive designs upon, and thereby fearing revenge from, an external figure. However, when the child begins to think or feel or act aggressively towards an external figure, the phantasies that generate anxiety may be counted upon to fluctuate between phantasies about external figures and phantasies about the corresponding internal figures, if there are such internal figures. In any such case, the internal figure comes to the aid of the external figure. And phantasies about internal figures are, just because of their internality, more potent in the production of anxiety, for two reasons: the first reason is the aggression that would have been projected on to the external counterpart and that it brings with it in the incorporative phantasy; the second reason is the special, and specially troubling, access that an internal figure has to the thoughts and feelings of whoever houses it.

However this last point might suggest that, so long as persecutory anxiety is dominant, not only is there, as I have conceded, no desire for the control of aggression that is independent of the fear of retaliation, but such desire as there is is derivative from fear of the superego. For, the argument would go, to invoke an internal figure in the explanation of this desire is just to invoke the superego: any internal figure that is apt to generate anxiety is, or at least is part of, the superego. It is, for the sake of later developments, impotant to see that this is not so.

There is probably no good reason for trying to make, as Freud thought he could, an absolute break between the superego and other internal figures. Rather, there is a spectrum of cases. However the superego lies at one end of this spectrum in that its responses — or the response of the cohort of internal figures that constitute it — to the impulses and actions of the child who houses it are excessively harsh, unrelenting, and, above all, insensitive to circumstance. By contrast, the phantasies that serve to bind persecutory anxiety to aggression and to intensify the fear of retaliation contain figures that are singularly reactive to circumstance: the figures they contain are quick to discern when they are under attack and are ready to respond to violence with violence — such is their repertoire. Insofar as the desire for the control of aggression depends upon such phantasies, it is not dependent upon the fear of the superego. And that is an advance.

In time however the child develops the concept of a whole object, and this cognitive achievement ushers in a whole new phase in its emotional development. Recognizing that the external figure whom it has attacked either in reality or in phantasy is the same as the figure whom it loves, the child now comes to feel a triad of emotions that had previously been beyond its range: the awareness of having damaged or wished to damage a loved person, or guilt; the fear of the loss of that person, and, in particular, fear of the loss of that person's love; and the urge to make reparation. These new emotions are certainly experienced in relation to persons in the environment, but, at the same time, they will be experienced towards the internal figures that are their counterparts. The new emotions are grounded in a parent emotion, which derives directly from the child's awareness of a whole object and its recognition of its own fluctuating or ambivalent impulses. This emotion is called depression, and its signal is depressive anxiety. Depressive anxiety is, like persecutory anxiety, increasingly bound to aggression through sequential phantasy.

It is not to be expected that the child will be able to tolerate in a steady fashion the new recognition and the depression that it brings in train. Insofar as it finds the burden too heavy, it will revert either to the highly primitive defence of splitting, once again keeping the loved and the hated aspects of the figure apart in its mind, or to the more evolved manic defence in which hate and harm are denied. But these defences slackening — if they do, and as they do — depressive anxiety comes to the fore, and depression, and the emotions into which it decomposes, become more firmly established as dispositions in the child's mind. And these dispositions certainly establish a need and a desire for the control of aggression that have nothing to do with the fear of retaliation.

There is a difficulty in this account, which might most forcefully be put like this: Granted that with the onset of depressive anxiety the child recognizes that it loves and hates the same figure, why does this provide any kind of motivation for it to control hate and to cultivate love? Why shouldn't the child prefer hate to love?

Part of the answer lies in the fear that persecutory anxiety generates and the prospect of its recurrence. But that is not the whole story. There are further aspects to it, and aspects that take us beyond fear.

A large part of the answer lies in a difference, an asymmetry, between love and hate. Hate presumed a certain perception or a certain characterization of its object: the object must be seen or thought of as hateful, though it does not have to be objectively hateful. As we have seen, aggression, which is in itself objectless or free-floating hate, has first to be projected on to an object so as to make that object seem hateful before it can be picked out for attack: until the projection has been effected, and the perception of the object modified, hate seems not to be justified. Love, by contrast, presumes no special perception or characterization of its object. Love is not deserved. The love of a person for an object is fundamentally a response to a certain relation in which the person stands, and knows that he stands, to that object. In the most archaic situation of all, love is anaclitic: it is a response — a response, not *the* response, for in these same circumstances envy is another likely response — to the relation of total dependence. In later life, love is the response to whatever relation of mutuality it is with which the person tries to displace that of total dependence. This asymmetry between love and hate has the consequence, crucial to our lives, that, if love sometimes has the power to dissolve the perception or characterization on which hate depends, it is not then required to replace it with another perception of its own, which hate, or more precisely, aggression, could then falsify.

One error, fostered by religion, is to think that love requires a conception of the loved one as perfect. In point of fact the conception of something as perfect, or all-good, and the conception of something as all-bad have much in common: they share an emotional source, in aggression. The difference between them is comparatively superficial. Idealization is a reaction-formation against, and so a surface transformation of, the picture of its object that hate requires. It reflects no underlying change of disposition.

There would however appear to be at work another, and profounder, reason why, when confronted with the fact that the figure whom it loves it also hates, the child will tend to privilege love over hate. (I say 'tend', for the privilege relates to love and hate per se: but quantitative considerations enter into the matter, as do concomitant factors, and they can tip the balance the other way.) This reason derives not from the relative favour in which love and hate are held, though it affects this, but from the absolute disfavour that attaches, and must attach, to hate. There is, in other words, a native incapacity to tolerate aggression, of which we have already seen some evidence in the fact that aggression is, in a special way, a projective phenomenon. As aggression mounts within the person, it is projected on to some external figure, who thereby becomes an object of hatred and consequently the victim, or the likely victim, of attack. Furthermore, it is only when an external figure has had aggression projected on to him, has been made hateful, that he is attacked. If we think of projection as an attempt to rid oneself of somthing unwanted, the very frequency of aggression testifies to our intolerance of it.

A difficult question is how the intolerance of aggression is registered within us. It may be assumed to do so through a kind of pain or unease to which aggression gives rise: that is to say, through subjectivity. And since aggression is a disposition, and therefore in itself without subjectivity, intolerance must be registered through the mental states that manifest aggression. And the most convincing account seems to be that aggression registers itself as intolerable, not through any internal feature of these mental states, but through some response or reaction to them. This reaction, as we have had occasion to see in other contexts, falls outside the confines of the mental state, but it has subjectivity. The reaction leads the person to think of his aggression as dangerous to himself, and to do so even before he begins to feel guilty about it.

It will be recognized that what I have just said about the intolerability of aggression is closely connected with what I said in the last lecture about conflict of desire insofar as it does not derive from the failure of co-satisfiability.

9. If love does not require or presuppose any particular perception or characterization of its object, it has a tendency — no more than that, for, again, there are countervailing forces at work — to generate a perception or characterization, a special kind of perception

or characterization, of its object. This is the tendency to see or think of the object as good or as of value. The conception of something as good or of value is the result of projection.

Projection takes two different forms: simple and complex. In Lecture V I mentioned this, and spoke only of one form, the simple form. The simple form of projection is exemplified very clearly in the formation of paranoia. A person, let us say, finds himself unable to tolerate his hostile impulses towards another: the feeling generates excessive anxiety in him: in consequence, as a defence against the anxiety, he imputes to the other the very feelings that he himself has. Momentarily, at any rate, the anxiety lifts. On the level of judgment, projection (in this form) can be represented by the speaker's applying to someone or something else a predicate that he himself satisfies. When he projects his hostility on to someone else, he asserts that this person is hostile, which is just what he is himself. 'I hate him' becomes 'He hates me'. Further examples of this simple form of projection would be where we project the past on to the present, or phantasy on to reality, in ways which ultimately uphold the tyranny of the past. What can be projected is, it will be observed, either a mental disposition or a state, though it is usually a disposition.

Then there is the complex form of projection. Here too something inner is projected on to the outer world, but there are two important differences. In the first place, the outer world has to collude much more substantively with the inner world. There has to be a real match or correspondence between them, which is not always the case with the simple form of projection. It is not, for instance, the case with the paranoiac's projection: almost anyone can turn out to be the paranoiac's enemy, as we learn from Suetonius or the worse stretches of our own experience. Secondly, when the disposition or state is projected on to that part of the outer world which is seen or thought to correspond to it, what is imputed to the outer world is not that very disposition or state but something that corresponds to it. On the level of judgment, this can be represented by the speaker's applying to someone or something else either an old predicate that in its literal application he himself satisfies but that he now uses metaphorically or a new predicate introduced into the language specifically for the purpose of projection. In this way complex projection breaks into two kinds. I shall give examples of each.

Examples of the first kind, or projection where metaphor is involved, are provided by the physiognomic perception of nature and of art. Looking out over an estuary and the salt-marshes through which it winds its way to the sea and a broken tower on some high ground, or looking at Constable's *Hadleigh Castle,* which depicts a landscape with much this character, and in each case touched by melancholy, I respond by judging the scene itself to be melancholy – that is, metaphorically melancholy. These two examples of metaphorical predication differ in that, in the case of nature, the projection does not submit itself to a standard of correctness but is merely constrained by the look of the landscape, whereas, in the case of art, projection submits itself to a standard provided by the achievement — the achievement, not just the intention — of the artist. Examples of the second kind, where novel predication is brought into play, are provided by the assignment of value. That this is what the assignment of value is — projection of a complex form, which on the level of judgment is represented by the application of a new predicate introduced for this very purpose — is the central claim of this section.

If this claim is right, then evidently with complex projection cases of the second kind play a much more significant role in our lives than cases of the first kind. Value is very important. However cases of the first kind, just because they explicitly involve metaphor, give us the stronger insight into the form of projection that they exemplify. This is because, even in situations where metaphor doesn't occur in the judgment that represents the projection, and its place is taken by novel predication, there is always at work the very thing that lies behind and is captured in metaphor: the symbolic, the emblematic, the awareness of match observed and the elaboration of match invented. For, as we have seen, it is sensitivity to match that triggers off complex projection, and it is this fact that in turn differentiates complex from simple projection.

It remains only to say what it is that is projected in the ascription of value: and so my further claim about value would be that it originates in the projection of archaic bliss, of love satisfied.

I have introduced value at this stage in my argument—that is, while still engaged with the pre-history of the superego and whether it satisfies a need or desire independent of fear—despite the fact that value clearly has a bigger role to play in the late development of the superego, and I have done so for three distinct reasons.

In the first place, I wanted to record the point, which to my way of thinking is the central contribution that moral psychology has to make to moral philosophy, that morality—that is, morality in the narrow sense, which I take (stipulatively) to be that which has obligation as its core—and value have fundamentally different sources. One (morality) derives from introjection, the other (value) derives from projection. One is in its origins largely defensive and largely coercive, the other is neither. One tries to guard against fear, the other to perpetuate love. These are all exaggerations, but worth making.

But, secondly, and thirdly, I have introduced value because there are two discrete points in my account of depressive anxiety where that account can only benefit from insertion of the notion of the good. The account can only gain in plausibility by associating depressive anxiety with the most primitive perception of value—at, as I say, two points.

One point is where I invoked the asymmetry of love and hate, or that hate presumes a particular conception of its object which love can dissolve but that love presumes no corresponding picture for hate to dispute, and did so in order to explain the preference for love over hate once, or so long as, the concept of the whole object is firmly established. For this point can be deepened if we allow ourselves the further developmental premise that much early hate is envy, or that, when aggression attaches itself to an object, the child conceives that object as envy requires it to do. For envy is a special variant of hatred: it is hatred of something conceived of as good, and hatred of it in large part because it is good. If we wonder how it could be that something conceived of as good could be hated in large part just for that reason, the answer lies in a constellation of dispositions upon which envy rests: for instance, the belief that the good object may vanish or be lost, or the belief that the good object may fail to go on producing satisfaction, or the feeling that a good object engineers a humiliating dependence upon it. Now, if this characterization of envy is correct, and it is the case that envy does indeed permeate hatred at an early stage, then not merely is there no conception of the object that love presumes only for hate to destroy, but a great deal of hate only confirms the conception of the object that love generates. Envy, in other words, confirms the picture of the loved object as good. To adapt La Rochefoucauld's famous maxim, envy is the homage that hate pays to love. Of course, this is not to deny that envy in manifesting itself can reinforce itself; it is only to assert that, in doing so, it undermines its own rationale.

The other discrete point in the account of depressive anxiety where value can profitably be inserted is the outcome of depressive anxiety or what depressive anxiety motivates: namely, reparative action. For if we are to understand what reparative action is, we must borrow from the moral psychology of value. The moral psychology of obligation unaided will not help us. And that is because when, under the influence of depressive anxiety, the child, the person, is motivated to repair the damage that he has done, the operative desire is not, or is not generally, the desire literally to restore the world to the state it was in before the damage was done. The desire is rather to bring about a state of affairs that corresponds to, or matches, the undoing of what was done: reparative action is emblematic of repair. And this is why it has always seemed appropriate to the better class of moral philosophers to connect morality, at least initially, with the practices and beliefs of particular communities. For what the community does is to fix, or pin down, the otherwise unregulated discernment of match or correspondence. The metaphors of reparation, which is what reparative action sets itself to satisfy, come to the moral agent, even before that is what he is, encoded in *sittlichkeit* or custom. Even if the agent remakes these correspondences, reinvents them, which is what he will want to do if he is in any way a critic of his society and its ways, they provide him with the initial exemplars of match. And this whole corpus of match, metaphor, invention, emblem, custom, criticism, upon which value rests, stands initially in sharp contrast to the literalism, the legalism, that impose themselves on the injunctions and prohibitions that issue from the superego — until they in turn begin to fall under the softening influence of value, a point to which I now turn.

10. For I now take up the second large question that, I said, moral psychology has to answer. Is there moral evolution, or does the superego develop into anything, and, if it does, how is this possible?

Development of the superego, or development beyond the superego, is to be explained in terms of a cognitive achievement, the emergence of new dispositions, and the vicissitudes of internal figures. In Lecture IV, in the course of discussing introjection, I remarked on what I called a 'grade' within internalization. There are figures that are merely internalized, and there are figures that are internalized and with which the person identifies: and I connected this grade with the different modes of imagination in which phantasies about the internalized figure are cast. A merely internalized figure will invariably be imagined acentrally or (more plausibly) peripherally; by contrast, a figure with whom the person identifies tends to be centrally imagined. And if I may now draw from that lecture another distinction that I employed in the course of it — that between a merely indicative criterion and a creative criterion — the shift from peripherally imagining to centrally imagining some internalized figure furnishes a criterion of identification that is not merely indicative but is also creative. For with centrally imagining we get a new type of internal audience, a change in psychic force, and appropriately different consequences as far as the beliefs, desires, and emotions of the person are concerned. Centrally imagining an internal figure creates, or helps to create, the identification that it indicates.

My suggestion, then, is that the development of, or development beyond, the superego is best understood in this way: that the internal figure, or the group of internal figures, whose phantasised activities regulate the thoughts, feelings, and conduct of the person start off life as merely internalized figures — they 'confront' the ego — but, gradually, or at some rate depending on the circumstances, they come to be figures with whom the person is able to identify.

How does this change come about, and what follows from it?

Two questions with a single answer. For the conditions that make identification possible are altogether continuous with the consequences that identification brings in train. What makes identification possible are the following: the diminution of persecutory anxiety; the narrowing of the gap between the internal figure and its external counterpart; and the increasing acceptability of the attitudes, judgments, and reactions, of the internal figure. The repertoire becomes congenial.

One way of describing this development would be to take substantively what Freud claimed to be a purely terminological change in his account of morality. In the essay on narcissism he used, in order to pick out the watching, scrutinizing, criticising agency in the mind, the term 'ego-ideal'. Later in *The Ego and the Id*, when he put forward the structural theory of the mind, he expressed a preference for the term 'superego', but he disclaimed any appreciable difference in what the terms conveyed. However the two terms do not to the intuitive ear, to the ear that has not been theoretically conditioned, suggest the same thing. Suppose that we attend to these intuitions: we then have a way of describing the evolution of the moral sense as the growth of the superego into the ego-ideal. A preoccupation with what a person should do gets overlaid by a concern about how he should be. The concept of the whole object, which provided the necessary condition for the emergence of depressive anxiety or guilt, has now been extended by the person from others to himself. From awareness that it is a whole object that his aggression has been directed against, the person advances to the further awareness that it is out of a whole object that his aggression springs. The realization that the object he now hates is the same as the object he once loved is now paralleled by the realization that he who now loves the object is the very same person as he who once hated it.

But once this stage has been reached, it suggests a further development in the moral sentiments. And that is that the sentiment of guilt is now supplemented by a new sentiment, which specifically relates not to actions and how far they fall short of the person's internal prescriptions, but to the condition of the person himself and how far it meets or disappoints the ego-ideal. This sentiment might then be thought of as shame. Perhaps we can come to think of shame as standing to the ego-ideal in the same way as guilt does to the superego.

Perhaps: but, if we do, we must observe three major reservations.

In the first place, if we are to think of shame as the prime moral sentiment of evolved morality, of morality beyond the superego, it must be conceived to be just as much an interiorized sentiment as guilt is. We must, in other words, free ourselves of certain misconceptions about the contrast between shame and guilt which popularising anthropology has wished upon us. To have the requisite motivational force to activate something that we can acknowledge as morality broadly conceived, shame must be experienced in relation to an internal figure. So we can suppose that shame makes itself felt in the following way: A person centrally imagines himself feeling ashamed as he appears disgraced before a figure whom he tends to, or whom he otherwise would, imagine centrally, and as a result of this, he finds himself in the condition in which the experience of shame might have been expected to leave him. There are two mandatory features of this phantasy. It must contain a figure whom the person otherwise centrally imagines: that is, it must contain someone with whom the person identifies. And it must represent the person as appearing before this figure, whose gaze rests on him. And this is because the essence of shame, or what is reverberatory about it throughout the psychology, lies in the look, in the disparaging or reproving regard, whereas the essence of guilt lies in the voice, in the spoken command or rebuke.

Secondly, if shame does adhere to the ego-ideal and play a crucial part in its functioning, it must not be concluded that shame ever supersedes guilt any more than the superego is ever replaced by the ego-ideal. For not merely is it famously the case that in what are often called the moral crises in a person's life there is a powerful regression to the most daunting, the most persecutory, the least reactive, of his internal figures, but, even when the ordinary tenor of life is undisturbed, there will still be two distinct places where there will be a continuing demand for the superego. Within the domain of self-regarding concerns, the superego will be needed to generate obligations that are instrumentally required by the ego-ideal. Someone who has decided to become a poet will still stand in need of an inner discipline to regulate his energies. And then, however liberally the domain of the self-regarding concerns is interpreted, there will always be tasks and problems in life that are purely other-regarding, and in this context the precepts and prohibitions of the superego, softened and attenuated though they may be, will continue to seem appropriate.

And, thirdly, just as any account of the morality of the superego is one-sided if it does not find room for the various defects and deformities from which this morality is inseparable, so any account of the morality of the ego-ideal must make reference to the ways in which it too lends itself to depravity. The morality of the ego-ideal can readily become pressed into the service of narcissism. Let me explain.

We have already seen that one reaction that a person may make to the perception of goodness in the world, and, above all, to his sense of dependence upon this goodness, is envy, or the desire to destroy this goodness. Envy is largely prompted by the fear of loss, the fear of disappointment. But envy brings in train the fear of retaliation, and one reaction that a person may make to envy is to deny that there is anything good in the external world or to assert his own complete independence of anything outside himself. He is now, as he sees it, the source of all value that he needs, and he can thus come to think of himself as totally secure from loss, harm, or disappointment. This retreat into himself, accompanied by a massive overestimation of his own resources, is narcissism, and it is not difficult to see how the morality of the ego-ideal can become the vehicle of narcissism. In the plays of Corneille, where the hero's *magnanimité* is his cult of a self swollen by self-love, we witness a corruption of morality parallel to, and as profound as, delinquency or moral masochism.

11. Morality broadly conceived is an amalgam of morality narrowly conceived and the sense of value: it is morality constructed at once upon obligation and upon goodness.

Before I close, I should like to say something about the part that recognition of the composite character of evolved morality, as I have sketched it, plays in the thinking of one of the greatest moral philosophers, John Stuart Mill. What are often treated as weaknesses in Mill's thought derive from his recognition that obligation and value have different sources, and somehow or other they have to be integrated. Mill said he was, and as much as any intelligent person can be he was, a Utilitarian. That is to say, he held that Utilitarianism provided the content for morality narrowly conceived: what each person ought to do is to maximize utility. This I call Utilitarianism proper. But the question that then arises is, What is utility? and it is a crucial fact not only in Mill's intellectual development but (as we know from the *Autobiography*) in his emotional life generally that he thought that this question went deep. After his crisis in early manhood he was not going to settle for any easy answer.

Mill's view is that each person has his own conception of utility. What accounts for the differences between different people's conceptions is presumably something to do with their different constitutional make-up, their different upbringings, and their different cultural allegiances, but nevertheless all these different conceptions agree in this: that they are conceptions of *utility*. They are different person's realizations or appraisals of one and the same value. In virtue of what is this so?

There are, I think, three common struts on which Mill allows conceptions of utility to rest. In the first place, everyone's conception of utility goes back — along some route that, presumably, the subject that Mill in the *System of Logic* called 'ethology', or the science of the development of human character, would eventually clarify — to certain original or primitive experiences of pleasure. Conceptions of utility conceptualize not pleasurable sensations, but the descendant of pleasurable sensation, and it is this developmental link that legitimates them. Secondly, each person's conception of utility is expressed by employment of the very same concept, 'utility' or 'happiness': this concept is that for which every native speaker reaches in trying to fix or record that which he wants to see maximized in his own and everyone else's case. And, thirdly, it is characteristic that the concept is applied, the descendant of original or primitive pleasure identified, not straight off, but only after a process of trial and error, punctuated by what Mill called, in a famous phrase to be taken literally, 'experiments of living'. Once this process has been crowned by the application of the concept 'utility', with due attention paid to its ancestry, the person has arrived at his conception of utility, and from now onwards this conception must be taken into account in their deliberative calculations by those other members of the same community whose actions are likely to impinge on him. What they ought to do in regard to him is now mediated by what he would like, or would prefer, to happen. For Mill, judgments of obligation aggregate not utility impersonally conceived but utility as this is fixed in different persons' conceptions of it, reached through the evidence of their own lives.

Utility is for Mill — so I suggest — a value which fits the general characterization I have proposed for value. Each person arrives at his conception of utility by projecting on to some tried and tested way of life a certain inner state of mind. Utility is emblematic of bliss.

Now what is of present interest for me about Mill is that, in emending classical Utilitarianism in this way, he at once gave recognition to the two sources of evolved morality, and sought to integrate them.

The first and most obvious way in which Mill sought to integrate obligation and value was by insisting that the obligations of each person derive, at least in part, from the evaluations of others. But this is not all there is to his project, and its most original aspect lay in a layering or hierarchy of morality.

Mill, I claim, never swerved from Utilitarianism proper: that is, he never entertained any interpretation of what obligation is other than the maximization of utility. But his interpretation of what utility is, and its connection with individual conceptions of utility, led him to introduce something which is prior in incidence, though not prior conceptually, to Utilitarianism proper, and which I therefore call preliminary Utilitarianism. Just as Utilitarianism proper is committed to the advance of utility, so preliminary Utilitarianism is committed to the advancement of people's conceptions of utility. Preliminary Utilitarianism enjoins whatever conditions are necessary for, or conducive to, people forming such conceptions. It urges upon us those social conditions in which people are likeliest to be able to devise and test and maintain their own conceptions of utility, and in which they can most readily come to respect other people's. Of necessity, preliminary Utilitarianism has in all this to make do without the authority of obligation, at any rate in its basic form.

Utilitarianism proper and preliminary Utilitarianism are bound to clash. Mill perceived this, and one of the most innovatory aspects of his moral philosophy is that he thought that, when they did clash, then, if the loss in utility is not too great, the claims of preliminary Utilitarianism should be preferred. For better than most things is that persons should develop their conceptions of utility. Only when they have done so, which in turn requires that they should enter into the maturity of their faculties, does Utilitarianism proper become really compelling.

It is failure to recognize what was at work in Mill's reasoning that has led his critics to accuse him of inconsistency when in fact he was guilty of nothing worse than subtlety. The two spectacular cases where Mill's reasoning has been misunderstood, or where his preferment of preliminary Utilitarianism over Utilitarianism proper has been misinterpreted, are the following: where in chapter 2 of *Liberty* he argues the case for liberty of opinion and speech beyond any possibility of benefit to truth, and where in chapter 4 he denies state protection to the susceptibility to mental pain of the morally outraged. In both cases utility has almost certainly something to lose from the implementation of Mill's liberalism, but conceptions of utility, or people's attempts to work out for themselves how they choose to live, have much to gain. And it was this that weighed with Mill. It was to such lengths that Mill went to keep in balance the claims of obligation and value.

12. The evolution of morality as the transition from the dominion of the superego to the cultivation of the ego-ideal does justice to the only two fundamental intuitions that I have about morality. The first is that morality, if it is anything at all, is an achievement: it isn't something that can be learnt or inherited. The second intuition is that, whatever may be the content of obligation, obligation itself is primarily self-directed. It is self-directed, though it may be other-regarding. For it expresses itself in a thought that a person has about what *he* ought to do: though he may well, and appropriately, think that what he ought to do is something for the benefit of others. It is also true that a person may well have

thoughts about what others ought to do, but my conviction is that either these thoughts do not express obligations or they require some circuitous interpretation. For they have no clear root in our psychology. Often they aren't in place, and then they represent the presumptuousness, the arrogance, for which morality is such a traditional medium of expression.

I have found in this account no room for the view that morality is ultimate or overruling. I see no reason to believe it. After all, no one would dispute the total commitment to his art of a painter just because he occasionally took time off to get drunk or to go to a smart dinner-party, and did so without claiming that it would make his art either more profound or truer to life. I see no reason why morality should ask more.

# VIII The Overcoming of the Past and Our Concern for the Future

1. In Lecture V, in tracing Freud's changing views about the pathogenic factor in mental disturbance as they shifted from memory and inculpated first desire, then phantasy, I asked the question whether, provided only that the hold that this factor exerted over the present was firm enough, it remained right to think of it as the tyranny of the past. For we have need to distinguish between the tyranny of the past and the tyranny of something that began in the past and has persisted.

A crucial consideration is, I suggested, how, at each shift in Freud's thinking, the pathogenic factor and its hold over the present are to be explained, and whether the past substantively enters into this explanation: that is, whether pastness is an explanatory factor. And at least in the case of the dominance of phantasy, this condition is satisfied. It is satisfied in that we substantively invoke the past both to explain why phantasy is as it is and to explain why it dominates the present: though the past that is now invoked is not (as in the case of dominant memory) a past of events, it is a past of phases — of phases, that is, in psycho-sexual development. And that the past invoked is of this nature makes it more perspicuous that pastness enters into the explanation. For the explanation goes like this: Dominant phantasies are as they are because they contain desires that belong to past phases, and it is because the desires that such phantasies contain do belong to past phases that the phantasies are dominant. But desires that belong to past phases are not simply desires that happened to arise in past phases, they are desires that have the pastness of such phases stamped all over them. They are archaic desires, and the key characteristic of archaic desires is unintelligibility. The unintelligibility of archaic desires, or the way they lie beyond the reach of the person's historical imagination, at once betrays their origins in the past and explains their persistence into the present. Unintelligibility is transmitted by these desires to the phantasies that contain them, where it is compounded. Phantasies are, then, doubly unintelligible: for the desires they contain, and for the way they conceal these desires. Unintelligibility tends to make phantasies tyrannical, because the desires they contain cannot be tested: and it also makes it right to think of this as the tyranny of the past.

What the Rat Man wants of his father, or, for that matter, what Proust's Narrator wants of his mother, are things that neither can any longer understand. They lack, above all, affective understanding of their desires. Each, for just this reason, is locked into a phantasy or phantasies which he over and over again projects on to the world, sometimes in ways that result in nothing worse than grave misperceptions of himself and of those around him, and sometimes in ways that amount to arbitrary and unhappy interventions in the real world.

2. One test, then, of whether the dominance of phantasy, if firm enough, can be regarded as the tyranny of the past is whether the past substantively enters into the explanation of phantasy and its dominance in the present. But now a complementary test proposes itself, and that is whether the past substantively contributes to the remission of phantasy and its dominance. We can, in other words, supplement the test of explanation with the test of therapy.

But to think that these two tests will give us the same answer is to assume that, if there is a new aetiology, there will be a new therapy. And this is the very assumption that psychoanalysis itself makes. It holds that aetiology and therapy should move in tandem because it equates the therapeutic with some operation upon the pathogenic. We have observed this association to be operative in Freud's thinking from the beginning. When he regarded memory as the pathogenic factor, therapy was for him the retrieval and dissolution of memories, or, to put it another way, the recovery and forgetting of remembered events. Hence, as the pathogenic gets reidentified, so does the therapeutic.

But it is important to appreciate that this association of aetiology and therapy was not based on any simplistic view of the nature of cure as such, or the crude equation of cure with the reversal of cause. Freud would have had no difficulty in recognizing that there are many cases in which the undoing of a process that caused a certain pathological condition is neither necessary nor sufficient for its cure. Freud associated aetiology and therapy in the way in which he did because of a conviction to which he remained wedded that no psychological change could be deep or lasting unless in the course of it the person gained insight into what Freud called 'the play of mental forces'. By this phrase Freud meant both those forces which sustained the illness and those which were contributing to the cure. No therapeutic method could retain Freud's support for long once it could be shown of it that it denied the patient such illumination.

I have then used the awkward and uncommunicative phrase 'the remission of phantasy' to pick out whatever therapy it is that goes along with the identification of phantasy as the pathogenic factor, only provided that, whatever other features this therapy has, it satisfies the formula that within the mind, or psychologically, the therapeutic is some operation upon the pathogenic. But what other features does it possess?

An initial question to be got out of the way — though, as the Wolf Man case illustrates, Freud himself experienced great difficulty with it — is prompted by the method that prevailed when memory was regarded as pathogenic. Is there, once phantasy is regarded as pathogenic, any therapeutic significance to the recovery of what might most generally be called traumatic events?

Certainly there are two ways in which the recovery of events might still be held to be valuable. If the event recovered was the event in which the dominant phantasy originated, then recovery of the event would demonstrate the phase to which the phantasy belonged and hence the kind of archaic desire that it contained. And if the event recovered was one on which a dominant phantasy had been projected, then its recovery could be expected to show the content of the phantasy or what specific archaic desires it contained.

But in both cases the value that still attaches to recovery is purely derivative, and there are various considerations that could bring this value in further doubt. If it is true that phantasies, like other dispositions, originate in events, is there for each phantasy an identifiable event or set of events to which it can be traced? And if projection of phantasy is always on to actual events, does it matter what the phantasy is projected on to, or is what is projected the only issue of therapeutic significance? What worried Freud about this whole issue is instructive. If therapy abandoned the search for historical events, would this mean the sacrifice of the account of psycho-sexual development in which he had invested so much time, energy, and reputation? The true answer is that it would not involve such a sacrifice if the developmental account could be made to predict the content of successive phantasies, so that phantasies and the anxieties and beliefs as well as desires they contained could be ordered in a phase-specific fashion.

However, if, with phantasy established as the pathogenic factor, therapy no longer had a commitment to the recovery of events as such, it still remained committed to those values which, when memory was viewed as pathogenic, the recovery of events was held to realize. In other words, the commitment remained to a method that guaranteed the patient insight into his mental progress, and, more specifically, that allowed him to gain detailed information about, and also to re-establish the feelings and emotions he originally associated with, the pathological condition from which he suffered. It was this commitment that ultimately led Freud to regard a method which he came upon inadvertently and for some time viewed with grave suspicion as indispensable to psychoanalytic treatment.

When in November 1882 Breuer first told the young Freud of a remarkable treatment he had carried out some years earlier in which a hysterical female patient had found herself 'talking away' her symptoms, and thus set him on the track of psychoanalysis, he also let it be known that the treatment had come to an end in an abrupt and altogether unsatisfactory fashion. Gradually over the years, though not fully until 1895, Freud pieced together the 'untoward event', as he called it, on which the treatment of Anna O., for it was she, had terminated. One day Anna O. had summoned Breuer to her house and told him that she was pregnant, and by him. The pregnancy was, of course, hysterical. Breuer broke off the treatment. Over the years Freud came to see this event in a changing light. In the postscript to the Dora case he referred to the patient's eroticized tie to the analyst as 'the greatest obstacle to psychoanalysis'—though also as 'its most powerful ally', and, as his estimate rose of what the transference had to offer, so his idea of what it actually was enlarged. Starting from a view which the facts suggested, that the transference was simply a case of falling in love, and in a particularly foolish fashion, Freud came to think that what happens in the transference is that the patient reactivates his most fundamental attachments, anxieties, and conflicts, this time around the person of the analyst: and, once Freud had come to think of it in this way, and saw the therapeutic advantages it offered, he defined psychoanalysis as an investigation that took as its starting point two sets of facts—the facts of resistance and the facts of transference.

3. I return to the first session of the Rat Man's analysis in order to look more minutely at what went on within it. We are able to do this because of Freud's general guidance, but we have to do so without benefit of anything in particular that he says about this hour.

Freud, as we have seen, expressed himself pleased with the amount of material that was forthcoming. He was right. The Rat Man begins by telling Freud how dependent he had always been upon the interest taken in him, and the opinion held of him, by other men. It was crucial to his self-esteem. He makes it clear that he would treasure Freud's high estimate of him. Then, as Freud puts it, 'without any apparent transition' he sets about trying to secure it. He starts to talk to Freud about those things which he must have thought were just what Freud would particularly have liked to hear. In other words, he treats Freud just as he would still most like to treat his father. But how does he do this? He does this by telling Freud his sexual thoughts, his sexual experiences, his early interest in touching and inspecting the genitals of young women: in his sixth year he would wait with mounting eagerness for the moment when his governess, a young good-looking woman, would press out the abscesses on her buttocks. In order to win Freud over he tells him the very things that, if Freud had indeed been his father, would have most displeased him. Then, having done this, with another seeming change of topic, he tells Freud that, as a young boy, he used to think that his father knew his sexual thoughts because he had spoken them out loud without intending to, and that only harm could come to his father from this knowledge: for instance, his father might die. He brings the session to an end by leaving in Freud's mind confusion on the one subject on which he most wishes to be and to remain confused himself. He plants his own confusion in Freud's mind, we might say. He rids himself of a burden, but in such a way as to immobilize the person whom he has wooed and provoked, whom he has provoked through the way he has chosen to woo him. Freud's notes on the case indicate that the Rat Man was more successful in this stratagem than the text of the case-history concedes. Freud's notes on the first session conclude with the words 'His father is dead'—then in brackets he adds 'When?'

Here we see in a particularly evident fashion all the attitudes that the Rat Man had towards his father. (The only departure from total clarity is the ellipsis when the Rat Man expresses the fear which he used to have that, if his father knew of his sexual wishes, he would die. For the Rat Man omits the three beliefs that the fear assumes true: that the father will fly into a rage on learning of his son's thoughts, that the Rat Man will then wish his father dead, and that his wishes are omnipotent.) It is in virtue of this capacity to produce such a vivid reconstruction of the patient's pathology that the transference could lay claim to realize the values to which psychoanalytic therapy was committed: detailed information and the re-establishment of emotion. All that was needed was that the patient should take full cognizance of what was presented before his very eyes. He had to learn to listen to himself.

But it is here that the difficulties—specifically two difficulties —begin.

In the first place, the transference, as it is illustrated in the Rat Man's case, has evident overlap with acting out. But, if acting out confronts the person with information about his own condition, it is information of which he cannot make use. It is inaccessible to him. For, as we saw in Lecture V, acting out subserves the role of phantasy or preserves the desires it contains, by, above all, preserving them from scrutiny. Nor is this simply the result of the person being distracted or unaware. For, as we saw in Lecture VI, when self-examination follows hard upon acting out, the effect is compounded and self-examination too is pressed into the service of phantasy. The person's desires as these are contained in the phantasy are again preserved from scrutiny, and, by way of diversion, the person is led, or likely to be led, into examining himself for desires which he no longer has, or perhaps never had, the capacity to form. How, then, can the transference overcome the consequences of acting out? Secondly, if it is true that acting out confronts the person with information about his condition of which, or so it turns out, he cannot make use, there seems to be no way, even in principle, by which it could restore to him the feelings and emotions originally associated with the desires that the phantasy contains, for, above all, these desires are affectively unintelligible. They are, as I have put it, beyond the reach of the person's historical imagination in a very special way.

The theory of psychotherapy attempts to answer these questions in that it proposes empirical changes conducive to psychic change. It suggests conditions under which acting out a phantasy can be a prelude to recovering the desires it contains, and it suggests conditions under which recovering the desires that a phantasy contains can be a prelude to restoring to them affective intelligibility. In these suggestions the part of the analyst and the place of interpretation are carefully specified. The detail of technique is none of my concern. I want only to make one general point about the nature of the remission of phantasy. It is an analogy.

4. The analogy for the process of working through of phantasy that suggests itself is with our understanding of a work of art, in particular of a painting or a piece of music. The analogy is with the critical task or process properly conceived.

I start with this last phrase, or the contrast between the proper and the improper or prevailing conception of the critical task or process.

Improperly conceived, understanding a work of art consists in, first, attending carefully to the work of art: then, in conjunction with whatever is held to be relevant background information, acquiring beliefs about the work: and, finally, using these beliefs as evidence, arguing to the fullest possible statement of what the work means or is. On this conception the salient features of criticism, which as a process unfolds in three stages, are, one, perception of the work, two, the subsequent formation of beliefs about it, and, three, inference from these beliefs to a conclusion, which may be regarded as the best available interpretation of the work.

This conception may be contrasted with another conception, which I believe to be correct, and which totally restructures the process. There are now two, not three, stages to the critical task. The first consists in gaining beliefs about the work of art, and this we may do by any means to hand. Perception is one way of arriving at such beliefs, but it certainly is not mandatory. There is scholarship, and hearsay, and the consideration of parallel cases, and there is no good reason to privilege in principle one of these sources above the others. However, where perception is indeed mandatory is at the second stage, when we draw upon all the information that we have collected, not though as evidence for a conclusion, but as background information to perception. For understanding the work is a matter of perceiving it in the light of everything that we have come to believe about it. Subsequently we may, or we may not, as we see fit, try to formulate or set down something of what we have taken the work to mean or to be, but this would be a record of the interpretative process, not part of the process itself. If, for some reason or another, we fail to write up our findings, this would not call in question the way in which we have discharged the critical task. Understanding a work of art, we may say, is experiential or by acquaintance, not inferential or by description. It is a further consequence of this that, however far we go with setting down what, as we see it, the work means or is, this can never be complete, just because experience, hence our experience of the work, can never be exhausted. And if the work is such as to repay the effort, we shall anyhow want to go back to it over and over again in order to renew, and probably to revise, what we learnt about it through experience.

There are, of course, limits to the analogy between coming to understand a work of art and working through a phantasy. The most obvious difference is that the patient works through a phantasy of which he is, whereas the critic attempts to understand a work of art of which he is not, the author. A further difference is that the work of art is made to be, whereas the phantasy is not made to be, indeed is made not to be, interpreted.

However the crucial similarity is that, within both processes, there is a fundamental division between, on the one hand, the accumulation of information, which is preparatory to the act of understanding, and, on the other hand, the act of understanding itself. The act of understanding is not the result of an inferential leap to a further or synoptic piece of information. The act of understanding is not propositional at all, and therefore we neither need to have, nor are we debarred by lacking, means at our disposal with which to record the meaning either of the work of art or of the phantasy.

To return to the case of phantasy: If we now wonder how we can ever come to understand a phantasy that we cannot articulate, the answer lies in the fact that the desires that the phantasy contains once were intelligible to us: they were once our desires. And if we next wonder why, having understood the phantasy, we do not need to articulate it, the answer lies in the fact that the desires that are now intelligible to us are also desires of which we have, at any rate for the most part, no further need. They are not desires that, in the circumstances of adult life, offer promise of pleasure.

A misunderstanding should be guarded against. It would not be correct to think that, within working through, the distinction between the information that needs to be secured before a phantasy can be understood and what we experientially grasp when the phantasy is understood corresponds directly to the distinction between intentionality and subjectivity. It may, for instance, be necessary to obtain information about the subjectivity of the phantasy before it can be grasped, and, again, there may be some part of the intentionality of the phantasy that the person can no longer be informed of and that he must grasp experientially.

5. I have talked of the overcoming of the past as this might be achieved through the psychoanalytic process, in which an interpretation originates with the analyst and then is brought to bear by the patient upon, in that it informs a certain kind of experience of, that which exerts the tyranny of the past over him: notably a phantasy. But I do not wish to give the impression that this result

cannot be attained outside the psychoanalytic process or that, if it is, it relies upon some different mental mechanism. On the contrary, working through is something that patterns itself, strongly or weakly, over much of life, and there are two areas which are particularly propitious for it: creativity, and sexual experience. In both cases archaic phantasy affirms itself and is then projected outward, and the artist and the lover enjoy unparalleled opportunities for judging how much of what is projected satisfies the demands of truth in belief or of co-existence of desire. It is therefore no coincidence that in both art and love the greatest single obstacle to self-examination, or the force that works most strenuously to distort ourselves to ourselves, should be much in evidence: I refer to idealization.

I hope that I have said enough to answer the question raised at the beginning of this lecture and to make the point that pastness is as much involved in the remission as in the explanation of phantasy. On both counts, the powerful hold of phantasy can be equated with the tyranny of the past.

6. And now suppose that someone does indeed manage to liberate himself from the tyranny of the past. What is he to do? Where should he turn? How is he to live?

An answer proposes itself: He should live in the present. He should do just what up till now had been the one thing that he was unable to do. It would only be a fool who, having liberated himself from the burden of the past, assumed that of the future.

In one of Nestroy's plays there is a character who has long wanted to do something for the future. Every time the desire occurs to him, a voice inside him asks: 'And what has posterity done for me?'

For Gottlieb Herb this voice is the voice of prudence, and a question to ask is, With what principle does this voice speak? Two principles suggest themselves, though there are other hybrid or intervening principles.

The first principle, which could be called that of *living for the present,* requires concern solely for present persons and their states. It enjoins indifference to all states of persons who are not yet born, and perhaps also of persons born but not yet leading adult lives. Such a principle clearly justifies indifference to posterity.

An objection to this principle, at any rate as that with which the voice of prudence speaks, is that a person might very well recognize, even as he considers the principle, that sooner or later he will come to regret his adherence to it because of his growing attachment to persons who as yet count as posterity: this regret will prove painful for him; and, since this regret is amongst the things which, even as he entertains the principle, should be of moment to him, being a future state of a present person, the principle recommends its rejection.

A second principle, which might be called that of *living narrowly for the present,* requires concern solely for present states of persons. It enjoins indifference to all future states of persons, and it does so impartially for the future states of future persons and the future states of present persons. This principle clearly justifies indifference to posterity, and does so even if the person committed to it believes that this indifference, through causing pain to posterity, will eventually cause him regret, and this regret will be painful for him. For the principle gives him now no more reason to avoid the pain that he will experience than to prevent the pain that posterity will experience.

The second principle, then, avoids the objection to the first principle, but the very aspect of it that allows it to do so exposes it to a further and fatal objection. (There is more than one fatal objection to it, but I shall consider only one.) For the new principle requires that the person who subscribes to it should disregard his own future states, though not as such. The principle establishes a democracy of future states: and all future states, no matter whose they are, are to be disregarded. But the fact that the principle asks the person to disregard his future states, even if only *inter alia,* means that the principle ignores or denies a constitutive feature of what it is to lead the life of a person. This feature is a relation in which a person must stand to his future, or to what he believes his future to be. This relation I call *self-concern.*

How are we to understand self-concern?

7. I am told that something good, something bad, will happen to someone I know. 'Something' here means either a mental state or a partly mental state, and it happens to someone when the mental state that it either is or includes is his, or he enters into it. Of course

good things and bad things can befall persons which neither are nor include mental states, but I omit these from consideration.

So I am told something like the following: Someone whom I know will to-night meet a friend whom he loves and misses. Someone whom I know will tomorrow morning wake up blind. Then I learn that this someone, the someone whom I know and to whom this will happen, is me.

There is a characteristic — characteristic, I insist, not invariable — way in which I shall respond to such a lesson. This response I call 'the tremor'. The tremor is a characteristic but not an invariable response to such a piece of news, and it is a response that is not even to be anticipated unless a further condition is assumed satisfied. This is an epistemic condition, and it is a condition which, for all its importance within self-knowledge, is neglected in conventional epistemology. It is a condition upon beliefs, and I shall call it 'acceptance'.

So — to run through the story again — I am told that someone whom I know will tomorrow morning wake up blind: then I am told that the someone is me. Now I shall tend not to believe this: told it, I shan't learn it. Suppose however I do believe what I have been told. Then I shall tend not to accept it. I shall reject it, and, if I do, it is not to be anticipated that I shall respond with the tremor. However, if I do believe the terrible news and accept it, then the characteristic response would be the tremor. (Another pattern of response, another way the story might unfold, is this: Initially I believe what I am told. I accept what I believe. I respond with the tremor. But then, just because I have responded in this way, or in revulsion to the tremor, I reject the news, I cease to accept it: and a step beyond this might be that, not merely do I cease to accept the news, I also cease to believe it.)

The tremor is a part of our natural sensibility, and we may think of it as a sensible index of self-concern.

8. I am told that something good, something bad, will happen to someone whom I know. Then I learn who the someone is. It isn't me this time, it's a friend. The news is likely to affect me, and this response, which I shall call 'the impact', is to be distinguished, and non-arbitrarily, from the tremor.

What do I mean by 'non-arbitrarily'?

It would be an arbitrary way of making the distinction if there was a response that I had when, having been told that something good, alternatively something bad, would happen to someone I know, I then learnt who it was to whom it would happen, and I simply called this response 'the tremor' when the person turned out to be me and called it 'the impact' when it wasn't me, and who the person was — that is, me in the one case, someone other than me in the other case — was the only difference on which the distinction was made: so that, shuffling the characters around, I might equally have called this very same response 'the smemor' when the person to whom the something good, something bad, would happen turned out to be Karl Smith, and called it 'the impact' when it wasn't Karl Smith — when it was anyone other than him, including me. In other words, the distinction between the tremor and the impact would be arbitrary so long as it corresponded to no difference in the way in which we live our lives — and I want to compare, to contrast, the tremor and the impact, as they occur in our lives, to show that this is not the case.

But there is a prior point to be made. The impact — and here the tremor and the impact differ — comes in two forms: a generalized form and a particularized form.

When the impact comes in its generalized form, it simply registers the fact that *an* answer has been given to the question, To whom will this happen? The generalized impact records, or is a sensible index of, the passage, the effected passage, from ignorance to belief. It is a response to the fact that curiosity has been satisfied, not to the way in which it has been. By contrast, though the impact in its particularized form registers the fact that an answer has been given to the question, And to whom will this happen? it does not simply register this. It does more. It also registers the particular answer that has been given. The impact in its particularized form, though not in its generalized form, is sensitive to the identity of the person to whom the something good, the something bad, will happen.

The impact in its particularized form comes more sharply into focus if we make the following supposition: that, having been told, say, that someone whom I know will tomorrow wake up blind, I ask who this will be, I am told that it will be Charles, a friend, and then this is corrected, it will not be Charles but it will be George, an enemy. Now if it seems reasonable to think that, on each occasion when I am given news of who it is, I respond in a way that simply registers the fact that I have been told something, or in a uniform way, it surely also seems reasonable to think that, when I am given the first piece of news, which turns out to be incorrect, and, again, when I am given the second piece of news, which turns out to be correct, I shall, on each of these two occasions, respond in a way that registers the very piece of news I have been told, or that I shall respond in a differential way.

It is worth dwelling on the impact in its particularized form for a moment or two longer. If this turns out to be something of a digression, it is a digression that has broad consequences for the philosophy of mind.

The particularized impact is differentiated in more than one way. It is differentiated in its intentionality or thought-content. For my response to learning who it is to whom the something good, the something bad, will happen will contain the thought of that particular individual — of, in my examples, Charles or George. And it is just this differentiation that makes it, or is definitive of its being, the particularized impact. But in consequence of its being differentiated in this way, it is also differentiated in another way. It is differentiated in its subjectivity, or what it is like for a person to be in that state. For as the thought of the particular individual to whom the something good, something bad, will happen is brought into contact with the good news, the bad news, so I shall invariably experience some appropriate affect. This affect will colour the impact.

The impact in its particularized form has inevitably a very complex phenomenology. And this is likely to be enough to lead philosophers of one tradition to deny that it has a phenomenology at all. This is because such philosophers have been trained to think of phenomenology as always a very simple affair. For them pain or grief are central cases of phenomenology, and the interest of the particularized impact for the philosophy of mind is that it can help to liberate philosophy from this prejudice. However in this connection it is worth considering, alongside the particularized impact, the impact in its general form. For though this has indeed a very simple phenomenology, these same philosophers are likely to discount it too, since it is a phenomenology without affectivity. The paragon of phenomenology within the analytic tradition is a phenomenology that is at once simple and affective, and a study of the impact in both its forms should help to dispel first one, then the other, component of this illusion. This ends the digression.

With the impact thus detailed, I return to the question whether, and, if so, how, the impact and the tremor differ.

The impact in its generalized form clearly differs from the tremor, just because the impact in its generalized form is a mere response to a cognitive increment as such. By contrast, when I learn that it is I who will tomorrow wake up blind, then, though the tremor that I experience is a response to a cognitive increment, it is certainly not a response to a cognitive increment as such. It is not simply the index of curiosity satisfied.

But does what distinguishes the tremor from the impact in its generalized form assimilate it to the impact in its particularized form? There is a temptation to think so, but it is one to be resisted.

Both the tremor and the impact in its particularized form are sensitive to the identity of the person, news of whom provokes the response. But the identity of the person enters into the two responses in very different ways. We can begin to see this by supposing an extension to the situation I last supposed. So let us now suppose that, having been told that someone I know will tomorrow wake up blind, and, asking who it will be, I am told, successively, that it will be Charles, my friend, that it will be George, my enemy, then that it will be me. In each case I respond to the news in a way that reflects the identity of the person. But in the first two cases the identity of the person — first of Charles, then of George — is reflected in the response in a way that involves an attitude on my part to the person. My attitude to the person modifies the response. By an attitude to a person I mean at once my conception of that person or my picture of what he is like, and the favour, disfavour, or indifference with which I consequently regard him. I mean the materials out of which I would construct a repertoire for him. However, in the third case, in order for the identity of the person — that is, of me — to be reflected in my response, there is normally no involvement of an attitude. Characteristically, no attitude of mine to myself modifies the tremor. In pathological cases, it is true, the tremor may be mediated by the way I conceive myself and the favour, disfavour, or indifference in which I hold myself: so, I am holy, and therefore this misfortune is a welcome trial, or I am evil, and therefore this misfortune is a just punishment. But, in cases that remain this side of the pathological, self-concern suffices, and self-concern neither is nor includes an attitude towards myself.

I shall go on to pursue this last point, but first I must guard against a misunderstanding of what I have just said. In saying that in the case of others my response to news of good or bad things that will befall them, or the particularized impact, is mediated by my attitude towards them, I am not suggesting that, having been told that someone I know will tomorrow wake up blind, then, if I learn that it is a friend to whom this will happen, I shall be appalled by the news, whereas, if I learn that it is an enemy, I shall be delighted. All I am saying is that how I take the news will depend on the nature of the news and my attitude towards the person, and that my attitude towards a person will include such things as whether I regard him as a friend or an enemy. But just how I take, say, bad news about an enemy is a further question: whether the news about him saddens me, or whether I find it sweet, or whether (as the Old Testament counsels) it leads me to try to alleviate his misfortune so as to make it even worse for him, to heap coals of fire upon his head, allows of no automatic answer. It is a matter of how far the civilizing process has gone.

(If this seems out of line with what I said about the predictable responses of the sympathetic audience in Lecture III, I intended those responses to be of an elementary kind. This seemed to me in keeping with the Dionysian appeal that the theatre, for all its attempts to outgrow it, can never completely disavow. What I have called the civilizing process may be regarded as the infiltration of empathy into sympathy.)

9. So far I have been trying to illuminate the tremor, or the response that I characteristically have to learning, and accepting, that some news I have been told is true of me, by contrasting it with the impact or the response that I characteristically have to

learning, and accepting, that such news is true of someone whom I know who is other than me. But light can also be thrown on the tremor by contrasting it with certain other responses that I may have to learning and accepting that some news is true of me, where these responses, unlike the tremor, do involve an attitude on my part. In this respect these responses resemble the particularized impact. But there is a difference: a big difference. For with the particularized impact the attitude is an attitude about the person concerned, or of whom the news is true. By contrast, with these new responses the attitude is not one that I have towards myself: it is, perhaps, an attitude that I have towards life or towards the way in which I lead my life. Furthermore, these attitudes do not simply mediate the response as the attitudes that I have towards others mediate the particularized impact. They motivate it. In their absence there would be no reason for the response in question. Indeed, these other responses can be defined by means of the attitudes that give rise to them. In consequence I shall pass straight to the attitudes themselves and leave the responses to reconstruct themselves.

All these attitudes, it must be pointed out, are optional. They are attitudes that we as persons may, but need not, adopt. If we adopt them, they will presumably find a place in the ego-ideal, though some of them are so shot through with aggression that they are bound to destabilize the ego-ideal. And that they are optional is one reason why we should not think of them as presupposed or involved in self-concern, which, I have claimed, without arguing for the claim, is not optional, but is, rather, constitutive of what it is to lead the life of a person. However I shall not rely on this claim, but shall look, one by one, at these attitudes and consider their connection or otherwise with self-concern.

The first such attitude is *egoism*.

Egoism is primarily an attitude that a person has towards his desires, though derivatively it is an attitude that he has towards certain of his future states: namely, those states which result from the satisfaction or frustration of his desires and which in anticipation are associated with pleasure or pain. The attitude that egoism requires of a person towards his desires, or towards those of his states which directly depend upon them, is to believe that they are more important, at least within certain broad limits, than the desires of others, or the states dependent upon them. One consequence is that the egoist always has, at any rate within those same limits, a conclusive reason for trying to frustrate the desires of others so as to secure the satisfaction of his own desires. A person would undoubtedly be crazy if he was prepared to bring about the destruction of the whole world in order to avoid the discomfort of a pricked finger, but, within the bounds of day-to-day satisfaction and frustration, egoism would call upon him to seek out his satisfaction — or, more strictly, the satisfaction of his desires — at the price of another's frustration.

This is the place to observe that egoism (at any rate as I understand it) does not involve selfishness, nor for that matter does selfishness involve egoism. Selfishness is a property of a person's desires and derivatively of the person in virtue of his desires: it holds of his desires because of what those desires are directed towards. Egoism, by contrast, is an attitude that a person may adopt towards his desires and their fruition, and there is no specific object that egoism presupposes his desires to be directed towards. To spell it out: A person's desires are selfish insofar as they are directed towards his well-being, his good name, his mental or bodily health as such and to the neglect of anyone else's well-being, good name, mental or bodily health, and the person is selfish insofar as he is motivated by such desires. Selfishness determines roughly how, or along what route, a person seeks satisfaction. Egoism is indifferent to how he does so, but it places a special importance upon his doing so. Indeed, it is one of life's ironies that there are few people who are quite so egotistical, or quite so insistent upon the satisfaction of their desires, as the unselfish, or those who desire supremely the well-being of others as they envisage it.

Self-concern does not involve egoism. Self-concern involves the thought that, for instance, my future states are important to me in a way that yours aren't or couldn't be: but not the thought that my future states are more important to me, let alone the thought that they are more important, than yours are or could be. Furthermore, self-concern implies the thought that your future states are important to you in the very way in which my future states are important to me. And to someone who thinks that there is a residual question whether the importance to me of my future states is or isn't more important — not to me, but absolutely — than the importance to you of your future states, self-concern, properly understood, is likely to retort that there is not necessarily, perhaps that there is not usually, an answer to this question. If I am very old and frail and you are very young and healthy, or if I am a poet of genius and you are a cretin, then, maybe, but only maybe, there is an answer. But when there is an answer, the answer is certainly not provided by self-concern unaided.

To think that self-concern presupposes egoism is on a par with thinking that, because I insure my property and not yours against fire, this shows that, if there were a fire, I should prefer your property to burn down to mine doing so. Self-concern does not presuppose egoism. Nor does it eliminate it.

The second attitude that I want to consider is that of *finding life worth living.*

For a person to find life worth living, as I use the phrase, is for him to think that his life, as it stretches ahead of him, promises a tolerable balance between pleasure and pain. How pleasure and pain are to be gauged, and what counts as a tolerable balance between them, are further questions, and, as far as finding life worth living is concerned, they certainly do not require that anything like a Benthamite interpretation is placed on them.

Self-concern does not involve finding life worth living. It does not do so in either of two ways that might suggest themselves. My concern for some particular future state of mine is not concern whether that state will or will not make, or contribute to making, my life worth living. Nor does my concern for any such state depend on or presuppose my already finding my life worth living. Those are the two ways in which self-concern might involve finding life worth living, and in neither does it.

And one and the same case can be employed to show that both these ways of connecting self-concern and finding life worth living fail. The case is that of the rational suicide, and to appreciate it we do not have to believe that anyone ever actually kills himself on rational grounds.

Now if we think of the rational suicide as a person who kills himself just because he finds his life in prospect not worth living, then we may inquire whether, and, if so, how, self-concern enters into the deliberative process by which he arrives at such an estimate of his future. And the answer seems to be that it does in this way: The person, in surveying his individual states and coming to find them good, bad, or terrible, as the case may be, has, in each case, not only to believe that this is how they will be, he has also to accept it; in other words, he must get himself into the situation in which, had he had the states described to him, then been told that they would be his, he would, characteristically, have experienced the tremor. And this is equivalent to saying that they must already fall within the scope of self-concern. It would, for instance, much alter the character of Sade's novel if we were to read that one of the young prisoners in the Château de Silling who were awaiting, with ribbons in their hair, first the pillage, then the destruction, of their bodies, had decided to anticipate the sombre events that were to unfold in the banquet-room and the torture-chamber of the castle, and had attempted suicide. For the pliance of the victims to the phantasies of their masters is presented as being at this stage so absolute that there seems no room left in their psychology for what such a decision presupposes: self-concern. The grief, terror, despair, of which they are still capable, and which their tormentors require of them, seem not to reach into the future.

However, if the rational suicide is required to feel concern for his future states before these states can provide him with good reason for suicide — that is, before he can decide on the basis of them that life is no longer worth living — nevertheless it is also true that the concern he feels, or his acceptance of his future states as what they are, cannot by itself settle for him the question whether his life is worth living. To answer that question, values must be consulted that go beyond self-concern. Such values are required, on the one hand, to decide what is to be regarded as pleasure or pain, and, on the other hand, to assess what is a tolerable balance between them.

From all this it follows that self-concern does not involve finding life worth living in either of the two ways proposed. It cannot be that a person's self-concern is dependent upon his already finding life worth living: for his future states have to be the object of his self-concern for them to lead him to find life worth or not worth living. But equally it cannot be that a person's concern for his future states is concern whether they will or will not make life worth living: for he can feel such concern and still be quite uncertain even how we would set about determining whether life is or is not worth living.

The third attitude that I want to consider is that of *finding life worth while.*

I distinguish, then, between finding life worth living and finding life worth while. As we have seen, a person's finding his life worth living is a matter of the balance of pleasure and pain that it promises him. By contrast, his finding his life worth while is, as I use the phrase, a matter of the opportunities it promises him for the satisfaction of those desires or plans of his which he thinks important. And his life becomes for him more worth while if his future states turn out to be not only sufficient conditions, or parts of sufficient conditions, for the realization of what he values, but also necessary conditions so that, if he died, his major projects would go unfulfilled. Someone might find life worth living but not worth while: this was presumably the fate of Napoleon on St. Helena. And someone might find life worth while but not worth living: such was the fate sought out by some of the early Saints, or is that endured by someone who spies for a foreign power that he admires and lives in constant danger of detection.

Self-concern does not involve finding life worth while: it does not involve it in either of the two ways that proposed themselves in connection with finding life worth living. My concern for some particular future state of mine is not concern whether that state will or will not make, or contribute to making, my life worth while. Nor does my concern for any such state depend upon, or presuppose, my already finding my life worth while. And once again, a single consideration suffices to show that the involvement does not hold either way.

The crucial consideration is this: Self-concern does not require that a person should already have the capacity to form desires or plans, furthermore desires or plans that he thinks important, whereas such a capacity is presupposed both by his trying to find out whether, and by his believing that, life is, alternatively that it is not, worth while.

I am ready to concede that, in the absence of desire, self-concern would not exist. But that is not to assert the priority of desire over self-concern. Rather, in the absence of self-concern, the role of desire would be under pressure. Now, perhaps, if self-concern did not exist, it would be harder for certain kinds of desire or for desires with certain kinds of object to get formed: but that is not the point that I am making. My point relates not to the formation of desire but to its motivational force. And this goes back to the mechanism that I discussed in Lecture III whereby desire characteristically acquires motivational force within the psychology of the person. The mechanism unfolds in three stages: one, a person tends to imagine what he desires; two, imagining what he desires tends to please him; and, three, just this pleasure lures him to act or gives the desire motivational force. This sequence of stages ensures what I have called the truth in psychological hedonism. Now the transition from the imagined pleasure to actual pleasure does not, as far as I can see, rest upon self-concern. But the absence of self-concern, the person's indifference to his own future states, could block the transition by raising the question 'What does it matter to me here and now that I would be pleased if I were to do this or if that were to happen?' And to the extent to which the transition is consistently blocked, desire would either lack motivational force or have to find it elsewhere than in the imagination. Either the role of desire would shift, or the way in which it is fulfilled would change, and either way round we should be outside the psychology of the person. We should be dealing with a different way in which we would live. That is why we can no more have desire without self-concern than self-concern without desire.

If, then, we think of desire and self-concern as coeval, both the proposed ways of connecting self-concern with finding life worth while fail. Self-concern neither presupposes finding life worth while nor is it the concern whether life will or won't be worth while. For either way round, this would require the priority of a person's capacity to form desires and plans over his concern for his future states.

And there is an additional reason for thinking that a person's concern for his future states cannot be concern whether those states will or will not make or contribute to making life worth while, and this reason deserves attention. It is that the equation would make self-concern derivative in a way that cannot be right. What the equation would do is to convert the importance or value to a person of his future states — that is, the importance or value that they have in virtue of being his future states — into an instrumental importance or value. A person would set store by such states as means to the end of getting his desires satisfied or his plans implemented: and, correspondingly, should those states cease to hold out this promise, should their instrumental value be diminished, then, as a rational creature, he would be required to withdraw his interest from them.

Such a picture, however strong its philosophical motivation may be, can never be anything but ridiculous. It enraged Montaigne:

> We are great fools. 'He has spent his life in idleness', we say, and 'I have done nothing to-day'. What! have you not lived? That is not only the fundamental, but the most noble of your occupations.

In point of fact, I too think that self-concern is derivative. But I do not think that the importance or value to a person of his future states is instrumental. That is not the way in which self-concern is derivative. I shall return to this point in section 11.

10. I now want to consider an alternative account of self-concern that a philosopher has proposed to me. According to this account, self-concern presupposes self-love. Self-love is a necessary and a sufficient condition for a person's feeling concern for those future states of his which he both believes in and accepts — though this account does not have to maintain that self-love suffices to produce self-concern in a creature that lacks whatever dispositions or states are necessary for that creature's leading the life of a person.

Strictly speaking, there is no inconsistency between this new account of self-concern and what I have been explicitly urging. For I have been urging that self-concern does not involve an attitude that a person has towards himself. And self-love does not involve such an attitude: if, that is to say, self-love is modelled on love. For love, I have contended, does not involve an attitude which the person has towards his beloved, though love may, indeed certainly will, bring such attitudes in train. Love neither is nor includes an attitude: it is an emotion inspired by a relation, and the presumption integral to the account under consideration is that what goes for love goes for self-love. However, if the new account does not offend against the letter, it offends against the spirit, of what I have been saying in that it grounds self-concern in a local part of the psychology of the person. Furthermore, I find the account objectionable for more substantive reasons: for the distorted picture it offers of several reflexive emotions.

There are two distinct cases which seem to favour the view that self-concern presupposes self-love. The first is that of the lover whose love of his beloved induces in him a relation to her future states that replicates that in which self-concern places him towards his future states. The second is that of the utterly dejected man whose descent into self-contempt or self-hatred induces the loss of self-concern. Very roughly, the first case suggests that self-love is a sufficient condition of self-concern, the second that it is a necessary condition.

I start with the first case, and for the lover's relation to the future states of his beloved I shall use the phrase 'lover's concern'. Lover's concern, it must be emphasised, is not the same as love: it is a consequence, a likely consequence, of love, which can sometimes work against love.

Now there is indeed an analogy between self-concern and lover's concern, but it does not support the view that self-concern derives from self-love. For it is an imperfect analogy, and just where it gives out is that lover's concern involves an attitude on the lover's part towards the beloved. In fact it involves two attitudes. Both these attitudes are attitudes that love may be expected to bring in train, and both are analogues — perfect analogues, this time — to reflexive attitudes that we have already examined and decided are not involved in self-concern. Lover's concern involves one attitude to his beloved that is the analogue of egoism and another that is the analogue of selfishness. Lover's concern combines the view that the desires of the beloved and their fruition are more important than the desires of others and their fruition, and the view that her welfare should be advanced ahead of that of anyone else.

If lover's concern were the perfect analogue to self-concern, then a lover's concern for the future states of his beloved would, if I am right about self-concern, just be a matter of her future states being important to him in a way in which they could be only to her and not to him. But that lover's concern isn't merely this — in fact, it isn't this at all — can be seen in two ways. In the first place, the lover does not — does not even try to — attune his concern for his beloved so as to echo her self-concern. His concern for her will make him solicitous for her even when, or particularly when, she, without any loss of self-concern, shows herself ready to sacrifice herself for a cause or a person. Secondly, though the lover may very well respect the concern that another lover has for *his* beloved, he will not be inclined to respect the imperatives or dictates of that concern. He will behave as though he believed himself to be the only lover in the world. He will act as though what love had done to him was to open his eyes to something to which everyone else was still blind: that is, the supreme importance of the person he happens to love.

None of this means that the lover will not in certain circumstances let other considerations — money, fairness, an ideological commitment, or the imperious demands of love itself — outweigh his concern for his beloved, or that he will not be prompted to place other outcomes above her desires or her advantage. No view that aims to be convincing can eliminate this possibility. We are not all Antiochus. But my point remains that, so long as love induces lover's concern, it does so through attitudes which serve to make lover's concern no analogue to self-concern. Hence the case that self-concern is motivated by self-love is not served by a consideration of what concerns a lover.

But must it be that love generates concern for the beloved only through the mediation of attitudes? Could there not be a form of lover's concern that was a perfect analogue to self-concern and thereby gave us reason to believe that self-love was involved in self-concern? No demonstrative argument against such a possibility can be given, but what the preceding discussion should have shown is the difficulty of imagining a form of concern that is for the future states of another and is not either motivationally much stronger or motivationally considerably weaker than that which a person has for his own future states. And this may be taken to reflect a more general fact, which might be put by saying that the stake we may come to have in others will either go beyond or fall short of, not that which we actually happen to have, but that part of it which, so long as we live as persons, we can't but have, in ourselves.

I now turn to the second case: that of the utterly dejected man who rages against himself and is seemingly without self-concern. The support that he gives to the view that self-concern derives from self-love comes from thinking that the fact that he both lacks self-concern and feels self-hatred is no coincidence. The withdrawal of self-love, which is implicit in self-hatred, explains his lack of self-concern.

Any such argument contains two assumptions. The first assumption concerns how a state like lack of self-concern is to be explained. It is to be explained by reference to the absence of some factor which, when there is self-concern, is present, and whose presence is important. It is not to be explained by reference to the presence of some factor which, when there is self-concern, is absent, but whose absence is not specifically significant. Explanatorily, lack of self-concern is less like polio, which is explained by reference to the presence of a virus, and the explanation tells us nothing about health except that healthy people don't have this virus; and more like scurvy, which is explained by reference to a vitamin deficiency, and the explanation tells us something about the importance to our health that vitamin C has. The second assumption is that self-hatred and self-love are contrary phenomena, or emotions that may be placed on a single scale or spectrum. Both assumptions I believe to be erroneous.

The error to the first assumption cannot, of course, be conclusively shown prior to producing a satisfactory explanation of self-concern, to which I shall turn in the next section. But that there is a presumption against thinking that self-concern depends upon a single, identifiable factor, such as self-love would be, arises from the difficulty of trying to think of a creature that was without this factor, and therefore, on this hypothesis, lacking in self-concern, then evolving into a creature that exhibited self-concern through the development or the implantation of this factor. Indeed, under closer scrutiny, cases that are presented for the purposes of discussion as cases in which there is a lack of self-concern, like that of the utterly dejected man, turn out not properly to deserve that description. They are cases where self-concern is neutralized rather than absent. The utterly dejected man, we might think, is unmoved by his future states and is so for just the very reason that the self-concerned man is concerned about them — that is to say, because they are his future states: just as the 'pale criminal' is unmoved by the sufferings of his victim and is so for just the very reason that the sensitive man will be sensitive to them — that is to say, because they are the sufferings of a victim. In each case there is a pattern of acknowledgment and rejection, not just indifference.

The error to the second assumption really consists in thinking that self-love and self-hatred are love and hatred directed by a person on to himself: he becomes his own beloved or his own enemy, with the consequence that insofar as he experiences self-hatred, self-love must be in abeyance, and vice versa. But in point of fact, both self-love and self-hatred have a highly complex structure which position them in no clear relationship to one another. The point can be made by looking just at self-love.

If self-love were modelled on love, then a person's self-love would be a response on his part to a relation, a perceived relation, in which he stands to himself. There is no such relation. Self-love, or narcissism, which we have already considered in connection with distortions of evolved morality, seems better thought of as a reaction against a relation, a perceived relation, in which a person stands to others. That relation is one of total dependence upon them, and self-love is a denial that anything outside the person has value or could justify dependence. Self-love then is an alternative to love, but not a variant of it. It is also an alternative to envy, to which it bears a closer resemblance. These considerations seem to me to sever, at one and the same time, both the proposed negative connection between self-love and self-hatred, according to which what the man who hates himself lacks is self-love, and the proposed positive connection between self-love and self-concern, according to which what the man who is concerned about his future states feels is self-love.

11. Self-concern, I have contended, is derivative: but not in a way that would make it dependent on some local part of the psychology of the person being as it is. From what does it derive?

Self-concern, is my claim, derives from the process of living as a person. It is dependent upon the whole of the psychology of the person functioning as it does.

Self-concern, I have already claimed, is constitutive—that is, partly constitutive—of this process. Now in claiming that it is derivative from the process, what I have in mind is that we do better to try to understand self-concern through the process of living as a person than vice versa.

Let us take those mental or partly mental states which make up the rest of my life. Of them it will be successively true that they are future states of mine, that they are present states of mine, and that they are past states of mine. That is a metaphysical fact, deriving from the nature of time, and it requires only that I am an animate creature. If I am additionally a person, further metaphysical facts hold, deriving from the nature of living as a person. They are that, when these states are present states of mine, I enter into them: when they are past states of mine, or I have entered into them, I lie under their influence: and so long as they are future states of mine, or I shall enter into them, I am self-concerned for them. Self-concern derives from what it is to live as a person in three ways: first, self-concern is correlative with those relations in which I stand, respectively, to present states of mine and to past states of mine, and do so in each case just because they are states of mine; secondly, the three relations—that is, self-concern, entry into the present, and influence of the past—must all be understood together; and, thirdly, of these three relations, the most significant is that in which I stand to my present mental states, or that of entering into them.

To this scheme it might be objected that the relations of self-concern and the influence of the past cannot be correlative because they are so evidently heterogeneous. But then it is no part of my claim to assert that the two relations are homogeneous. Who could think that they are? The way in which we stand to our past and the way in which we stand to our future are not mirror images of one another, for what they reflect is, amongst other things, the metaphysical asymmetry of past and future. It is, then, only with due weight given to this asymmetry, or *mutatis mutandis,* that the relations of influence of the past and self-concern correlate. That is my claim, and that is what the objection must dispute. The objection, then, must be that the relations are unduly heterogeneous, and there are two different arguments on which it can rest.

Of the two arguments one is more general, the other more specific. The first argument claims that the relations differ in their nature or in the kind of relation that they exemplify. The second argument offers a relation in which we stand to past events in our lives which, it claims, clearly pairs itself off with self-concern, and this makes the scheme I have proposed implausible.

The first of the two arguments is that the relation of the influence of the past is a causal relation, and is not epistemic, whereas the relation of self-concern is an epistemic relation, and is not causal. If I lie under the influence of some event that has happened to me, this is something that that event has brought about, and it is not required that I have any beliefs about the event for this influence to hold. By contrast, if I am concerned about some event that will happen to me, it is required that I have a belief about the event, and the concern is not something that the event itself has brought about.

Beyond a doubt the two relations do differ in the causal condition: but that is precisely what the asymmetry between past and future predicts. If however we turn to the epistemic condition, the opposition between the two relations is grossly exaggerated by the present argument.

On the one hand, it is not true that, within the life of a person, the influence of the past is without an epistemic condition. For, as we have seen, the causal influence of an event upon the later life of the person to whom it occurs is characteristically exerted through mental states, specifically through mental states that convey information about the event or belief-states. The familiar claim that memory is a source of belief is false if belief means disposition, but it is true if belief means mental state. Admittedly we do not have to have particular beliefs about all the particular events under whose influence we lie: for the beliefs can get amalgamated. But so too can the influence — as Hume had the insight to see.

On the other hand, though it is true that I cannot be self-concerned about some particular event that will happen to me unless I have a belief about it, not all self-concern is directed on to particular events. Sometimes it is directed on to areas of the future, and when it is—and this parallels the situation with the influence of the past—it is only a very diffuse epistemic condition that self-concern is required to meet. Indeed, self-concern characteristically runs ahead of particular beliefs about our future in two very important ways. Conceptually self-concern for particular future events is comprehensible only as an application of a general concern for the future. And in practice it is often this general concern for his future that leads the person to find out about the particular events that will make up his life—and for which he will then feel more particularized self-concern. To employ for a moment an analogy which I have already rejected for full-time use: Self-concern in its general form is rather like the condition that St. Augustine attributes to himself as a young man arriving in Carthage—in love, but with no one in particular whom he loves, and spurred on by this to find someone to love.

The second argument against the claim that self-concern and influence of the past are correlative relations is that self-concern more plausibly pairs itself off with some more specific relation to the past. Suggested correlatives to self-concern are remorse, or pride, or regret.

This argument, it will be appreciated, assumes a different understanding of the nature or structure of self-concern from what I have given it. For the suggested correlatives—remorse, pride, regret—involve attitudes on the person's part towards his life, which I have claimed is alien to self-concern. However there is something that makes the letter though not the spirit of this suggestion plausible. A sizeable part of what pride, regret, remorse are, apart from the specific attitudes to the past that they involve, is acknowledgment, perhaps even acceptance, of the influence that some event in our past has had over us. It is because of this influence, in addition to its specific characteristics, that we feel pride, or remorse, or regret, over the event. It is then a possibility that it is precisely this aspect of these suggested correlatives to self-concern that gives them such plausibility as they have. It is because they attest to the influence of the past that they might be held to be correlative to self-concern: therefore their plausibility as correlatives does nothing to upset the view that the real correlative to self-concern is the influence of the past.

But ultimately to appreciate the force of the view that self-concern and the influence of the past are correlatives, or that self-concern is derivative from what it is to live as a person, is a matter of seeing how the three relations to future, present, and past mental states hang together, and how they do so under the aegis of that relation in which we stand to our present states. The key idea here, which is ultimate, is that entering into our present states acquaints us with phenomenology. There is no other source through which we gain access to it, and it is then the thought that each one of us has that this acquaintance has already been effected through his past states, his and no one else's, and will again be effected through his future states, his and no one else's, that underlies the influence that the one has over us and the concern we have for the other.

But what entry into the present does for us must not be traduced. It isn't that we merely acquire from the present, like Cherubino from his torments, a certain concept which we then go on to apply to our past and our future states. The phenomenology of past and future states is not just something that we infer to be the case. It inheres in the present. There are two ways in which it is continually brought home to us. One is through ourselves and what we are. For entering into present states, we do so as persisting creatures who will enter into future states and have entered into past states. The other way is through the mental states themselves and what they are like. For amongst present mental states are included memories of past states and what I shall, in the next lecture, call previsagements of future states, which through their own phenomenology exhibit, rather than merely provide evidence for, the phenomenology of the states they represent.

# IX Cutting the Thread: Death, Madness, and the Loss of Friendship

1. Death, madness, and the loss of friendship are naturally thought of as the three great misfortunes of life beside which that of not having been born pales into, literally, insignificance.

2. In a course of lectures devoted to the process of living, the topic of death, which has a natural right of entry, has two entrances to make, in two distinct guises. It may be expected to figure as phenomenon, and it may be expected to figure as thought. The phenomenon, or death itself, belongs to these lectures, because it is death that brings to an end the process of living. Without introducing death we should not have a complete picture of what it is to live as a person. The thought of death belongs in these lectures, because the thought of death, or that we are mortal, along with all the feelings that associate themselves to it in the psychology of persons, exerts a large and creeping influence over the process of living. Without introducing the thought of death, we should not have a complete picture of how persons live.

3. I made in Lecture I a claim about death. The claim could be re-expressed in the following way: Suppose that we listen to a number of stories, each of which professes to tell us in the minutest detail the life of one person. These stories are constructed according to a special narrative convention which permits only two kinds of element into the recitation: descriptions of events of the kind that make up the lives of persons, though no reference to the individual person is allowed into these descriptions, and a specification of the relations that hold between these events. Some of

these stories are inauthentic in that they erroneously include events from the lives of more than one person, though not only do they describe the events totally accurately, they also specify quite truthfully how these events are related to the other events in the same story. We are then set the task of sorting out the authentic from the inauthentic stories. The assumption is that we should be able to accept certain stories on the grounds that events related in the way they specify must belong to a single life, and to reject others on the grounds that events related in the way they specify could not belong to the same life. And the rule governing how we carry out the task is that we employ solely intuitions that we have which will enable us to react, at each point in the recitation at which a relation is specified, with either a nod or a shake of the head. We are not to introduce non-relational information, such as general principles — even if they are general principles about relations, which, in conjunction with the relations in the narrative, could allow us to infer a judgment on the stories.

My claim was that, if we cling to the rule, and limit ourselves to our intuitions, the task set us cannot be carried out. There will not be decisive results. And this is because there is no relation such that its failure to hold between some event securely ascribed to a person's life and any later event can elicit from us the immediate response, 'So he died', entailing that nothing that follows in the narrative could possibly be ascribed by us to his, to that person's, life.

I did not deny that, when a person dies, there will be no future event related to any of the events making up his life as they are all related just to one another. I conceded that there may be a unity-relation for persons. But what I did deny is that there is a relation such that its failure to hold in this way can intimate to us with the force of intuition that, at this very point, at the point of relational failure, death has intervened. The situation is not with our lives as it is with a chain where the absence of a link compels us to recognize that we have come to the end of the chain. And what I deny has, though what I concede has not, metaphysical importance. It is fatal for the relational theory of a person's life. It shows that a life is not essentially relational: because, if relational theory were true, then we would have intuitions of the kind that such thought-experiments as I have been considering assume.

In point of fact, I also made the claim against relational theory more simply by arguing that, even if it is true that, when a person dies, unity-relatedness is broken, we cannot invoke the latter fact to explain the former. But I have reverted to the argument expressed in terms of intuition in order now to make a stronger claim, not just that we have no intuitions about death based on relations, but that we have no intuitions about death. There is, in other words, nothing that we can, as in a thought-experiment, imagine happening to a person such that, as the immediate result of matching what we would say to what we have imagined, we would be forced to recognize that what we have imagined is death.

Once again it is important to get clear about the rule that governs such a thought-experiment. We must concentrate exclusively on the event that we imagine befalling the person. We must not imagine it under the general description 'whatever it is that brings a person's life to an end', nor must we introduce ancillary information. For I am not denying that there are general propositions that, brought into conjunction with what we have imagined, will assure us that what we have imagined is death. I am, in other words, not denying, or casting doubt on, knowledge of death. What I am denying is that we have knowledge of death based on intuition. And, once again, what I deny has metaphysical importance, though, undoubtedly, in this case, what I concede also has metaphysical importance.

That death in this way eludes our intuitions alerts us to something very important about death as we bring it into connection with our lives. It is that the concept of death in its application to persons is a hybrid or impure concept.

Let me explain. We might imagine the concept of death developing in the following way: The concept of death — that is, the concept of death of a person — starts with a core sense. This core sense is of that which terminates the process of living as a person. Death, insofar as it means just this, is a pure concept. But, since the process of living goes on, necessarily goes on, not just in a body, but in a body of a special kind, or that identified by reference to a person-species, it is only to be anticipated that the concept of death will be affected by this. So the concept collects and makes part of its sense the conditions under which the dissolution of such a body or the failure of its vital functions occurs. Death, as it absorbs these conditions into itself, becomes an impure concept. Heart-death and brain-death are different attempts to make precise this impure concept. One significant difference between the pure and the impure concept is that in its pure conceptualization death marks, whereas in its impure conceptualization death explains, the end of a person's life: The pure concept furnishes a merely indicative, the impure concept a creative, criterion of death.

It is a feature of an impure concept that it gives rise to few or no intuitions.

The question can be raised, Why should we use the impure concept of death? We have it. But would it not greatly facilitate our inquiries about death if we were to employ the pure concept, for that would then allow us to treat as an open question an issue such as whether we must die when the faculties on which we have depended fail? Use of the pure concept would not foreclose on the question whether the death of the body must be the death of the person.

Appeal to the pure concept of death can throw light on the impure concept that we have. But this does not justify the conclusion that there is such a concept available for immediate use with which we could coherently describe some possible world, or speculate about this world. If someone now claimed that I have already said enough about the concept to ensure that it is indeed available, I would point out that, though there certainly are at least two ways in which the pure concept could be used, neither, I fear, would be to the satisfaction of its advocates.

One possibility is that we might use such a concept in a totally abstract or uninterpreted way, not concerning ourselves with what it would be like for what we seemingly suppose to be realized. In using it, we would be concerned exclusively with not entangling ourselves in inconsistency or self-contradiction, and every dispute that we brought to a determinate conclusion we would do so stipulatively. Whatever was held to follow from, or be compatible with, someone's dying would be determined solely by the way we had defined death, and we should refuse to allow anything to count as a test of or check upon these findings. In other words, our use of the pure concept of death would be absolutely along the lines in which, as we saw in Lecture IV, the concept of Q-memory is employed by philosophers. The other possibility is that we should not use the concept in this abstract way, we should indeed be prepared to say what it would be like for what we supposed to be realized, but this could, I contend, turn out to be at the cost of incomprehensibility. For the concept would, for instance, permit us to conceive of the last hours of a person in his corporeal form in a way that parodied the condition of metamorphosed Actaeon. The mind could remain intact, fully alert, but gradually, out of defer-ence to corporeal decay, dissociate itself from the various activities that it had controlled. It would be like a pilot bored by his ship. Eventually it would withdraw into itself altogether, and then wait either until it was moved or until it moved itself — no indication being given of how either would come about — to another body, which would house it and such of its dispositions as it managed to salvage and bring with it.

Presumably, the suggestion that the interests of inquiry would be better served if we did use the pure concept of death envisages a third possibility: that is, that we should use the concept other than stipulatively but so as to talk sense, not absurdity, about persons of a kind that we know in a world that we try to conceive. If there is this third possibility, or if there is a pure concept waiting to be used in a way that is at once concrete and intelligible, the onus of proof seems by now to lie on those who think that there is. And in shouldering it, they would have to produce a concept that, in an overall way, allowed them to talk about persons who had led lives of the kind I have sought to characterize but have this peculiarity to them: that they and their bodies die apart. And this leads to a further point. Anyone who lays claim to the pure concept of the death of the person, which carries with it no implications for the body, must also supply a pure concept of the death of the body, which carries with it no implications for the person.

Until then we must think that we die when our bodies die, and we must find this a misfortune.

4. In the last lecture I introduced a condition upon beliefs, which I called acceptance. There are things that I believe but do not accept. I reject them. Sometimes rejection is overcome, or I overcome it, and then I begin to accept what previously I had rejected. But

sometimes rejection is so strong that I cease to believe what I have found it impossible to accept.

Rejection is supremely the interferer with self-concern. By this I mean that, though it can interfere both with self-concern and with the influence of the past, there is this difference: in the case of the influence of the past, rejection combines with other interfering factors of an affective kind such as phantasy, and its contribution cannot always be singled out, but, in the case of self-concern, it works on its own and the work it does is apparent. And that there is this particular disparity between the future and the past shows up in the outcome. For when the influence of the past is interfered with, it is distorted: and this suggests that many factors have been at work and to varying effect. But when self-concern is interfered with, it is merely attenuated: or that is the normal outcome, and this suggests that just one factor has been at work, and that that factor is cognitive in nature. Rejection has dimmed the prospect of the future.

To talk of acceptance or rejection as cognitive factors is not to deny that in their genesis, or guiding their operation, other affective factors will be at work.

I do not intend to say what acceptance is, but I shall say something about how it operates. Acceptance manifests itself in a certain kind of mental state, a certain kind of iconic mental state, which I call previsagement. States of previsagement sharpen our concern for our future.

Characteristically I previsage events or sequences of events that I believe will happen. When I do so, I represent these events to myself, and I represent them as, or more or less as, I believe that they will be. I can previsage events centrally or accentrally, but, when the event is an event in my life, I must previsage it centrally, and I must previsage it with myself as the protagonist. When I previsage an event in my life, I shall tend to previsage myself not only doing what I believe I shall do, but also thinking, feeling, or experiencing, what I believe I shall think, feel, or experience. I shall do so liberally and systematically. And if I do previsage myself thinking, feeling, experiencing, as well as doing, what I believe I shall, then I shall tend to find myself in the very condition in which these thoughts, feelings, and experiences are likely to leave me.

Previsagement is clearly akin to two kinds of mental state that have been given a great deal of attention in these lectures: iconic imagination and event-memory. All three are iconic. Roughly speaking, previsagement lies in between the other two. It occupies an intermediate position, which is best thought of as a departure from event-memory in the direction of iconic imagination. In other words, event-memory provides the natural point of comparison, but the comparison is imperfect. The three kinds of mental state may be compared and contrasted in their relations to disposition and in their phenomenology.

First, then, in relation to disposition: Previsagement is like event-memory in that it invariably, or on each occurrence, manifests a disposition, and that disposition is, or includes, belief. By contrast, iconic imagination only sometimes manifests a disposition, and that disposition is desire. However previsagement, unlike event-memory, is not a dependent mental phenomenon, and so is not caused by that which the belief it manifests is about: that is, the future. In this respect it approximates to iconic imagination. Secondly, phenomenology: Previsagement is like event-memory in that, when a person centrally previsages an event, it must be himself whom he centrally previsages. (Indeed, if he previsages an event that will be part of his own life, he must centrally previsage himself.) By contrast, iconic imagination allows a person, within certain limits, to centrally imagine anyone he chooses. However previsagement is unlike event-memory in that a person can previsage an event that will not form part of his life. So again it approximates to iconic imagination.

That previsagement in these two respects departs from event-memory in the direction of iconic imagination reflects two distinctive features of the way in which previsagement sharpens our concern for the future: features which have no parallel in the way in which event-memory keeps us under the influence of our past. The first difference is that our future has no direct natural or causal hold over us: the hold that it has arises out of our thoughts, even if it is natural for us to have these thoughts. And the second difference is that our concern for our future invariably goes hand in hand with our concern for the future as such. The fact that previsagement is not a dependent phenomenon reflects the first of these differences: the fact that previsagement can be directed on to events that will not be, as well as on to events that will be, parts of our life reflects the second.

5. Of all the beliefs that we have about the future, about our future, the hardest to accept is that we shall die. And here previsagement does not serve us well: for we cannot previsage our own death. We can previsage ourselves dying, but only where this means the preliminary to death, a period which might be, for all that previsagement teaches us, indefinitely continued. We cannot previsage the moment of death.

This claim differs from the claim that I made a short while back: that we have no intuitions about death. For in saying that we have no intuitions about death, or that there is nothing that we can imagine happening to a person which must bring his life to an end, I made the claim not just narrowly for an iconic form of imagination, but for supposition.

It is inviting to think that the two claims derive from different perspectives. That we cannot previsage death captures the first-person view on the issue. As we project ourselves imaginatively into the future, there seems no barrier that we can represent to ourselves that we cannot also represent ourselves surmounting. That we have no intuition about death captures the third-person or impersonal view of the matter. As we take up a neutral standpoint, there seems no event that we can suppose and of which we must suppose that it is death. A striking difference between the two claims is that the first can be exploited to support immortality, but the second cannot be. For from the fact that there is nothing that we can suppose of which we must also suppose that it is death, it does not follow that we can suppose that death does not exist, or that we might live for ever. That we have no intuitions about death, deriving as it does from the impure character of the concept of death, implies that the phenomenon it conceptualises, or what death is, is a matter for inquiry to determine. But it does not leave open the possibility that the inquiry could show that there is no such thing as death. By contrast, that we cannot previsage our own death lends itself to the view that death does not exist, or that we are immortal.

6. That death is a misfortune is compatible with, hence is not controverted by, any of three considerations, which are also essential to the place that the thought of death occupies in the way we lead our lives. These considerations are: first, that life without death would be a meaningless kind of existence for a person, or that we just couldn't live like that, whatever might be true for, say, angels; secondly, that circumstances can arise in a person's life when death is preferable, or we would rather die; and, thirdly, that death is not something that a person endures or suffers, like a painful illness or the death of a lover, but that, in Epicurus' striking phrase, 'When death comes, we no longer are'.

I have ordered these considerations according to the directness with which they challenge the view that death is a misfortune, but none overturn it. What the first consideration points out is that immortality too would be a misfortune. To this the second consideration adds that this is not merely the fruit of abstract reflection, but is how the absence of death could come to be experienced by a person on a specific occasion: death could be welcome. And the third consideration has it that death is not an event of the kind that we should look upon as a misfortune: it ought not to detain us. If none of these considerations upsets the view that death is a misfortune, they should deepen our understanding of how we must think about it.

7. Let us then look at these three considerations in turn.

First, that immortality would be, at least for a person, a meaningless kind of existence.

That life would be meaningless without death is made true by whatever attenuation it is that life would undergo if the thought of death were removed from it — or were reduced to an improbability. And it is natural to think that the point at which deathlessness would most strikingly affect the character of life is at the moment of choice. Many of the reasons that we currently have for choosing this rather than that would be removed, and similarly the reasons that we currently have for experiencing satisfaction at or remorse over the choices that we have made would be transformed. Questions whether we should do this rather than that would rewrite themselves as questions whether we should do this before or after that, and answers to these new questions would be found by considering not the intensity of our wants or the ends to which they are directed, but the favourable opportunities that the present provides. Weather reports would gain an immense importance in our lives. Of course, the change that I am talking about would not happen immediately upon the removal of death: it would be ushered in only once a culture appropriate to immortality had established itself.

But, we must ask, What is the value of choice that this change endangers?

In the last lecture, in discussing what our attitude to the future might be once we had liberated ourselves from the tyranny of the past, I made no reference to a notion that has immensely appealed to some philosophers in this context: that is, the notion of the project, or the one big choice wherein a person appropriates to himself his future. In not doing so, I was influenced by three considerations. The first is that I am uncertain whether most persons are capable of stamping these self-imposed patterns upon their lives, or whether on the surface — on the level, that is, of character and behaviour, which is all that choice can control — our natures are not too inconstant for them to take. Secondly, it does not seem to me that whatever value choice may have in our lives is done justice to by rolling it up into one overarching decision. One big choice is, after all, only one choice better than no choice. If choice has a value, it appears to depend upon the irradiation of choice throughout our lives. And so to the third consideration, which is the most relevant here. I do not believe, as supporters of the notion of the project appear to, that the value of choice lies in the act or moment of choice, which, on the view that I reject, is credited with introducing freedom into our lives. Choice is valuable, as I see it, for what leads up to or surrounds it: the consideration of alternatives, the matching of them against our inclinations and aspirations, the testing of them in imaginary situations, identification with what is chosen, and, in this whole process, the introduction of spontaneity, and the appeal to phenomenology at many different points. To lose all this would be to lose something.

But I do not see that, even if it is true that immortality would be a misfortune, this does anything to show that death is less of a misfortune than we thought. All that it does show is that immortality is not the answer to death, and that perhaps, of the two, death is a misfortune that accommodates itself better to the way we live.

Secondly, that sometimes death is preferable to life.

That there are circumstances in which we would prefer to die rather than to live is, again, compatible with death being a misfortune because these are circumstances in which life has become a yet greater misfortune. In deciding that we would rather die than live, we set one misfortune against another: one with the thought of which we have always lived against another that is new to us. Indeed, it might be argued that, in such circumstances, it isn't that we choose to die rather than to live, for what we choose is to die sooner rather than to die later. We make our choice against the background of certain death, so that, if a third possibility were unexpectedly offered us, that of living for ever in the condition we are in, and not just living in this condition for a while and then having to die, it is compatible with our decision and with what has led us to make it that we should accept this new offer. We might settle for living as we are for ever — although it remains true that just what we should be doing if we accepted this new, this indefinite, lease of life is far from clear. However what is certainly clear is that in preferring, in particular circumstances, dying to living, we are not, explicitly or implicitly, denying that death is a misfortune.

Indeed, what this consideration brings out is that, if the fact that death is a misfortune is in some way dependent on the way we view it, it is a view that goes deep: it is not, or so it seems, sensitive to circumstance. For death remains a misfortune even when life is no longer worth living. By contrast, our attitude to life and whether it is worth living is sensitive to circumstance and depends on the course life takes. Struck down, or so I am told, by an illness that offers only the prospect of unendurable pain, I find life a misfortune: and then learning that, after all, this is not the case, that the diagnosis was in error, I no longer find life a misfortune, it is worth living. But all the while, with a greater constancy, on which poets have often commented, death intimates itself a misfortune.

Thirdly, that death is not something that we should regard as a misfortune.

The argument, associated with the name of Epicurus, that we should not regard death as a misfortune goes as follows: Death could be a misfortune only if it were an experience of ours, and a painful experience; but it is not an experience of ours, and those who view it as a misfortune must therefore make the simple error of bringing it (in their minds) forward in time and placing it within, rather than on the confines of, life.

To meet this argument, and establish the compatibility of death's not being an experience in our lives and yet being a misfortune, philosophers have resorted to the expedient of showing that there are other things which are not experiences in our lives and yet which we regard, rightly regard, as misfortunes. They have accumulated examples of such things, and these examples fall under two broad headings. In the first place, there are those things which become misfortunes for a person because they involve frustration of some desire of his, directed on to some object outside himself. So, for instance, the destruction by fire of a man's life-work will be a misfortune for him, even after his death, if he desired fame — for this desire is now frustrated. Secondly, there are those things which become misfortunes for a person and which may indeed involve frustration of his desires, but this is not why they are misfortunes for him. They are misfortunes because of something of which they rob either him or his life. That Oscar Wilde fell in love with Lord Alfred Douglas was a misfortune for him because Douglas manipulated Wilde's love for him so as to bring about his humiliation: and that Wilde also sought his own humiliation in no way diminishes the misfortune — and that Wilde finished up in prison certainly increased this misfortune but did not produce it.

However it is one thing to discover other examples of misfortunes that aren't painful experiences, or that, if they are, aren't misfortunes for this reason, and quite another thing to go on to assimilate death to some one such example, or to think that death is a misfortune for the very same reason that this example is. And this second step, the assimilation, should be resisted. It should be resisted for two reasons: the first general, the second more specific. The first is that, if death is a misfortune, it is surely a misfortune *sui generis*. And the second is that any such assimilation seems to move the misfortune of death in the wrong direction: towards the objective. It makes death an instrumental misfortune, or a misfortune that is to be regretted for its consequences, and, at the same time, a misfortune of the kind that is at least as apparent to the observer as to the sufferer.

Lucretius, in reproducing Epicurus' argument, adds that, just as death cannot be a misfortune because of the painful sensation that it is, it cannot be so because of the pleasurable sensations it deprives us of. The additional consideration is less convincing. Indeed, Lucretius' thought seems to bring us closer to seeing why death is a misfortune — provided it does not suggest that, if each of us had some finite number of additional pleasurable sensations, he would no longer regret death.

Let us survey what we have so far learnt. That death is a misfortune is not because we would be better off if we lived for ever: for immortality too would be a misfortune. Nor is it because life is so good when death comes to remove it: for death is a misfortune even when life is bad. Nor is it because of some specific thing that death does to us: for death is not painful in itself. But it may have something to do with some unspecific thing that death does to us: and this unspecific thing is likely to be even less specific than Lucretius suggests. It is not that death deprives us of some particular pleasure, or even of pleasure. What it deprives us of is something more fundamental than pleasure: it deprives us of that thing which we gain access to when, as persisting creatures, we enter into our present mental states and which, from then onwards, we associate in some special way with our past mental states and our future mental states. It deprives us of phenomenology, and, having once tasted phenomenology, we develop a longing for it which we cannot give up: not even when the desire for the cessation of pain, for extinction, grows stronger.

8. In a late essay, which is based upon an autobiographical theme and is entitled 'A Disturbance of Memory on the Acropolis', Freud compares and contrasts two ways in which we may fend off something that we are unable to accept. They are exercises in rejection,

of an extremely powerful sort, and they come about through reiterated mental activity. The vehicle of such mental activity is phantasy. The two terms that Freud uses for these ways of dealing with the intolerable are 'derealization' and 'depersonalization'.

Derealization and depersonalization are mirror-images of one another. They are mirror-images of one another in what they bring about, and the phantasies that are their vehicles are mirror-images of one another in their content. In derealization we deny a part of the world: in depersonalization we deny a part of ourselves. In denying a part of the world, we come to regard it as dependent upon our thoughts and feelings: that is how we come to phantasise it. In denying a part of ourselves, we come to regard it as independent of our thoughts and feelings: that is how we come to phantasise it. Derealization, the denial, the lived denial, of some part of the world, in effect denies it a life of its own. Depersonalization, the denial, the lived denial, of some part of ourselves, in effect denies us a life altogether of our own.

Both derealization and depersonalization, carried far enough, lead to madness. Of the two, depersonalization is the more radical. It is the more radical in that, whereas derealization induces a depleted or erroneous picture of the world, depersonalization induces a confused or incoherent picture of the world. In point of fact the two processes are invariably complicitous.

It is in what I said in Lecture IV about the inner world that the materials for understanding depersonalization are to be found. For the course of depersonalization is marked out by changes that occur in the ways in which internal figures are phantasised. In the first place, for an increasingly large number of inner figures, the repertoires that the person assigns to them become alien to him. They become increasingly alien to him. Secondly, as this occurs, so the number of inner figures whom the person centrally imagines, or with whom he identifies, diminishes. He phantasises more and more figures peripherally. These two transformations interact and reinforce each other. And as they gain momentum, a third transformation joins in. Inner figures whom the person now phantasises as alien in outlook or attitude and as peripheral in standing he starts to imagine, in increasing numbers, as outside himself.

The psychic mechanism on which depersonalization rests is

projective identification, and, as even this partial account of what it achieves makes clear, projective identification goes well beyond what we have so far considered under the heading of projection. We owe our knowledge of projective identification to Melanie Klein, and it will be useful to consider some of its distinctive features.

In the first place, then, it is distinctive of projective identification that the person who wishes to rid himself of some part of his psychology that he can no longer tolerate, whether this be a thought, or an emotion, or, most plausibly, a sequence or cycle of thoughts or emotions, will first associate the unwanted element with an inner figure. This inner figure, which may be a whole object or a part-object, he will then phantasise as expelled into the outer world. Secondly, in parallel with the general pattern exhibited by introjection, having phantasised the expulsion of this figure, he will then be disposed to phantasise it as continuing to exist in the outer world. But it is distinctive of projective identification that this figure is also phantasised as retaining the marks of internality. Of these marks the most ominous, at least as far as the aftermath of projective identification is concerned, is the special immediate access that the figure retains to the mental processes, to the thoughts and feelings, of the person who once housed it. Add to this mark those of immutability, deathlessness, and insensitivity to circumstance, and it becomes clear how figures expelled through projective identification form an environment of persisting, looming presences. Thirdly — and here we see the influence of the archaic theory of the mind under whose aegis projective identification tends to be invoked — not merely are these expelled figures phantasised as being outside, or beyond the confines of, the person who has projected them, but there is somewhere, some specific place, where they are phantasised as being. They are lodged in — that is, inside — someone else, someone whom the person loves or, more likely, hates.

This last point is of considerable significance when we come to reckon the range of advantages that even massive projective identification has to offer those who resort to it. The expulsion of thoughts and feelings that are found intolerable will evidently bring relief, if of a short-lived kind, and such relief must be regarded as the primary aim of projective identification. But because of the means by which this primary aim is realized, a secondary aim comes to attach itself to the process. The unwanted mental phenomena being projected in the guise of inner figures, the insertion, in phantasy, of these inner figures into a parent, a lover, an enemy, can be experienced as a way of attacking, or humiliating, above all of controlling, this person. Once again, this is a short-lived satisfaction, since the delusions of power that projective identification fosters are likely to arouse massive fear of retaliation from these lurking figures.

Projective identification, though not in this florid realization, has already been briefly anticipated in these lectures — indeed, at two separate points. One point, to which I have nothing to add, was at the end of Lecture VI when, in discussing an incident out of my own analysis, I suggested that we could see, alongside the projection of a phantasy on to certain women, the projection into these women of certain feelings which the phantasy itself denies. The other point was in Lecture VII, when I made a passing reference to a form of pale criminality more extreme than anything that Freud contemplated. In this realization the guilt-ridden person turns to crime not just to placate his superego but also to disown it. Through delinquency, or a course of action that he concurs with society in thinking criminal, he aims to bring down upon himself punishment that matches the guilt that he already, that he independently, feels — so much is the essence of pale criminality. But the person we are now considering precedes this by first projecting into the institution or authority that will punish him the superego who has instilled the guilt in him. Once he has done this, then the punishment will be consoling twice over. The pain that it imposes upon him will, with varying degrees of efficacy, allow him to purge his guilt, but the fact that the pain is imposed, that it is inflicted from without, will help to sustain the thought — no matter that it is ultimately incoherent in itself — that a persecuting inner figure, from whose vexations he has suffered so deeply, is now outside him. Each move that the external agencies of civil repression take against him, harsh and painful though it may be, confirms the message of inner liberation with which projective identification deceives him: that he is now unburdened of his superego, that he is a conscienceless agent. It is just this phantasy of the criminal law and its enforcement as a projected superego, as conscience expelled into the outer world, that Rousseau attempted to normalize in the central doctrines of the *Social Contract.*

Projective identification brings in train characteristic tribulations. In considering, as I shall do next, the malign consequences of projective identification, it is crucial that we do not lose sight of the benign consequences. It is they, after all, that provide the motivation for which it is undertaken. Indeed, when projective identification is undertaken, it is not just that the short-term advantages are felt to outweigh the long-term disadvantages and are thus motivationally effective. Rather, the long-term disadvantages count for nothing: they are not even put into the balance. This is because projective identification is invariably an unconscious process, and unconscious processes work to a certain rule, which Freud called the Pleasure Principle. The rule is that the processes always select better states of affairs over present states of affairs even if these better states of affairs inevitably lead to states of affairs that are worse than the present. In this respect unconscious processes behave in just the way in which Jon Elster has pointed out evolutionary processes behave, and both thereby diverge from processes of rationality, which would never countenance such selections. The unconscious and evolution are incapable of waiting.

The undesirable consequences of projective identification for the person who resorts to it, at any rate on a massive scale, lie in the way in which the world must present itself to him. They lie in the picture of the world that depersonalization induces, and we are now in a position to see two of its graver aspects.

On the one hand, the person is cut off from himself. He is deprived of awareness of certain of his dispositions — that is to say, of those which he has projected into others. It is not impossible — indeed, in certain cases it is to be expected — that he will continue to manifest these dispositions, but, if he does so, he will manifest them without benefit of any internal representation of them. The upshot is that he will stand to certain parts of his psychology — furthermore, parts of his psychology which, it can be inferred from his desperate attempts to rid himself of them, have a strong and distressing significance for him—in the relationship that behaviourism takes as standard. His knowledge of them will be exclusively inferential.

And, on the other hand, the person finds himself surrounded by others—that is, those into whom he has projected his unwanted dispositions—of whom the phantasies that he entertains force him to believe that they have some very special knowledge of him. They know his most painful secrets, and they have come by this knowledge just as he might have been expected to come by it: not inferentially, not by testimony, but by immediate access.

If we put together these two aspects of the world as it presents itself in the wake of depersonalization, then it may be said to contain others who know, or appear to know, the person in the same way as, and better than, he knows himself. And about this world he is also obliged to have two further thoughts: it is a world somehow of his making, and it is a world of which ultimately sense cannot be made. He has brought this world into being by means of phantasies whose content is in the end incoherent in that they depict inner figures as inhabiting the outer world.

We can observe this phenomenon instantiated in the case of the Rat Man who, as we have seen, found himself stuck with the idea that his parents knew his thoughts. Furthermore they knew his thoughts, or so he seems to have felt, specifically in the area of a desire of his which regularly motivated him but which also completely baffled him: that is to say, the desire to inspect the naked bodies, and particularly the genitals, of young girls. The Rat Man tried to justify his belief about his parents by supposing that he spoke his thoughts out loud in their presence. This supposition is clearly a rationalization, but it also records with remarkable fidelity how the Rat Man may be believed to have experienced the actual course of events: that is, that the Rat Man had phantasised lodging in his father and mother an inquiring, peering, searching part of himself, which retained the characteristics of an inner figure. Attempting to rid himself of his scopophilia, he had resorted to projective identification, and the consequence was that he believed that his parents had direct knowledge of certain desires of his, which he could no longer understand, but which did not cease to move him.

To grasp the full predicament in which depersonalization results, it is necessary not only to recognize the two principal
thoughts under which the person's phantasies compel him to perceive the world, but also to be aware how they fit together to such
devasting effect. That others know him better than he knows
himself is bad: that others know him in the same way as he knows
himself is bad. But combine the two thoughts, and it emerges that
the person in trying to rid himself of intolerable thoughts and
feelings has laid himself totally at the mercy of an alien, hostile
world. Instead of losing parts of his psychology, he has only lost
awareness of them: and this awareness he has lost to others, who
now possess it, and who thereby gain unlimited power over him.
He is Caliban to their Prospero. But in trying to explain how this
came about, he has to fall back on thoughts which he owes to
phantasy and which cannot be intelligibly stated.

9. Such a person as I have described, being mad, lacks friends: his
madness will have lost him the friends we presume him to have
had. He combines, it would seem, two of life's three great misfortunes, their combination is no coincidence, and his predicament
provides us with a chance to look at once at the nature of madness
and at the nature, and the value, of friendship. Extreme situations,
I shall find reason to claim, not only test friendship, they test
accounts of what friendship is.

Our sufferer lacks friends, because he cannot be one. But at the
same time he needs friends, because he suffers. We must ask, What
needs can such a person have that friends can satisfy? and, In what
way can friends satisfy these needs? What is it, in sum, to be a
friend to someone who is himself incapable of friendship?

My answer to these questions is of startling simplicity. What a
friend can do for our sufferer is to be a certain kind of person,
which happens to be the very kind of person that our sufferer
cannot be. To be a friend to our sufferer is to be someone capable of
friendship, and capable of friendship to him.

To appreciate this answer, its force as well as its simplicity,
requires an account of friendship. The essence of friendship lies, I
suggest, in the exercise of a capacity to perceive, a willingness to
respect, and a desire to understand, the differences between per-

sons. Friendship lies in a response to the singularity of persons, and a person's friendship extends only as far as such singularity engages him. But, if ordinarily it goes without saying, in the present context it must be emphasised, that this sensitivity to differences makes no contribution to friendship unless it is combined with the grasp, the practical grasp, of a fundamental distinction: the distinction that each person has to make between himself and others. If a person loses his practical grasp of this distinction, and, say, treats another as himself, friendship has been discarded.

This is not to deny that there are, in and out of friendship, responses that are equally appropriate as responses to ourselves and as responses to another. Humour is an example. More significantly, there are responses that are equally inappropriate as responses to ourselves and as responses to another. On and off through these lectures I have made this point about idealization, and to idealization can be added peremptory or placatory attitudes. However there are certain responses that a person may appropriately have to himself but which it would be inappropriate for him to have to others. The crucial case of this sort for the understanding of friendship is that which I discussed at the end of Lecture VII, or the response that is customarily expressed by saying that someone or other morally ought to do this or has an obligation to do or refrain from doing that. Such a response, I have contended, is sometimes appropriate as a self-addressed response: there can be a warrant for it in our psychology. But it is invariably inappropriate as a response addressed to others: it lacks any psychological warrant. It is of the essence of friendship that it requires us to abandon the beguiling satisfactions of moralism.

This account of friendship clearly justifies the remark that I made earlier that it belongs to our sufferer's predicament that he cannot be a friend. The very characteristics upon which friendship rests are those of which depersonalization divests a person: sensitivity to the singularity of persons, an active sense of the distinction between oneself and others, and tolerance both of others and of oneself. By contrast, depersonalization breeds, on a massive scale, intolerance, confusion, insensitivity, and their mutal reinforcement.

However it is clearly one thing to show that a friend is just what our sufferer cannot be, either to others or to himself, so that, if he were to become a friend, this would be proof that he had somehow or other overcome his predicament: and it is quite another matter to think that having a friend, or being with someone who is just what he cannot be, is a means towards this end. How can this be justified?

To set the matter in perspective, I should like briefly to turn to two traditional views of friendship, which run counter to mine. What both these views propose is evidently something of which our sufferer cannot avail himself, and, in saying that extreme situations test accounts of friendship, part of what I had in mind is that our sufferer, through his suffering, through his madness, acquires an insight into the way in which people treat him which ought not to be ignored if we want to know what friendship is.

One traditional view of friendship is that friendship is an alliance for the sake of the good, or that the friend is the critic, supremely the moral critic. The other is that friendship is that affective relation to another which otherwise a person stands in only to himself. Both views have a long history, and even so untroubled a thinker as Montaigne was inclined to look on both with favour. But what is wrong with them becomes, I believe, much clearer when we reflect how it is that someone inspired by them could only multiply the troubles that our sufferer already endures. Regaled with criticism or exhortation about how he should or should not behave, finding his most intimate thoughts and emotions appropriated as though they were a mere extension of another, told in either case that such treatment only reflects the consideration and affection in which he is held, our sufferer is bound to find in such professions of friendship confirmation of his worst persecutory fears. So there is, he must think, after all, someone in the world who does know him better than, and just as, he knows himself. Such a perception of the world is undoubtedly mad. But in entertaining it our sufferer is responding to someone in whom he senses that the intolerance and the confusion so rampant in himself are already stirring.

But if friendship modelled on these traditional views has nothing to offer our sufferer, what reason is there to think that the view that I have proposed is better favoured? Even if there are many things that someone can do in the name of friendship which are pernicious, why is the answer to be sought not in doing something but in merely being something? What utility attaches to such a course?

The answer to this question comes out of the answer to a larger question: How can we help one another? What use are we to each other?

Let us set aside the alleviation of physical suffering or deprivation: the gifts of love and sexual pleasure: and the charms and delights of social life. Apart, in other words, from need and passion, the profounder ways in which we impinge upon one another are two in number, and both are indirect in their workings. One way is through the constant restraint that we place upon our urge to control, to manipulate, to change, others. This is, it must be recognized, no purely negative process because it requires us to be continuously aware of and to accept what others are really like, so that their awareness of our awareness and acceptance, both of them and of their singularity, becomes a source of strength to them. The other way is through the part that we, or rather our internalized counterparts, come to play in the inner worlds of others: a part that may be encouraging or sustaining, or that may be frightening and humiliating. There is a remarkable asymmetry in our preparedness to admit this process, for though it is obvious to each of us how large a part, either benign or malign, others play in our inner world, we are reluctant to credit ourselves with a corresponding significance in the inner worlds of others. But if we take introjection seriously, then we are bound to give weight to this way in which we help or can help one another.

It is, then, within this larger picture of personal interaction that the value of friendship as I think of it emerges. The Ancients asked the question whether the value of a friend lies in what he does or in what he is. The account of friendship that I propose indicates that the question should not really be posed this way. For what a friend does for us he does mostly through being what he is.

10. In the course of the last three lectures I have found things to say about love and friendship. I now want to consider them together.

Love and friendship stand contrasted. They differ in the feelings, emotions, and beliefs that they draw upon, and they also differ in their characteristic histories.

Sometimes the contrast between love and friendship may turn to conflict. There are different forms that the conflict can take, and different reasons for it. I may love someone whom neither I nor anyone else can like; or I may be unable to like anyone whom I love. I may be loved by someone who in fact does not like me; or I may be unable to feel liked by anyone who loves me. Any one of these situations is very painful, and, when one occurs, the reconciliation of love and friendship seems the most important objective in life.

Love and friendship differ in their origins. Love, as we have seen, does not presuppose an attitude on the part of the lover towards his beloved. It is a response — a response, not the response — to a felt relation: initially to the relation of total dependence, and then to whatever relation we come to substitute for it. By contrast, friendship must require an attitude. Being a response to the singularity of others, it is possible only with those whose singularity we are able to respond to appropriately. There are various ways in which this might be impossible for us. In some cases we cannot see what the person is really like. In some cases we can, but we are not able to respect what we see. And in some cases the effort that understanding the person would ask of us is too much. These, then, are the limits of friendship, and these limits are in effect fixed by our attitudes. Hence we choose our friends, and we choose them for what we take them to be, which, if it is a case of true friendship, must approximate to how they actually are. Friendship cannot be based on deceit, lies, or even on excess of error.

But once we have chosen our friends, then friendship in certain ways assimilates itself to love. The pressure of friendship itself brings it about that the very attitudes that initially selected our friends for us drop out of the picture. We accept our friends, once they are our friends, for what they are or what they make of themselves. If they change, this will make no difference if the friendship is well established. We get an indication of the way in which friendship sheds that dependence upon attitude in which it originates when one of our friends tells us that he cannot accept another. We are surprised. But to empathise with the rejection, indeed to argue against it, we need to put ourselves back into that frame of mind in which we formed the friendship: we need to revive the attitudes that encouraged it. And this, often enough, is what we cannot do, it is something that friendship itself impedes.

By contrast, love, once it is established, starts to generate attitudes towards the beloved which it did not require in order to arise. We have already seen one example of this in Lecture VII with the ascription of value to what we love, and another case, as we saw in the last lecture, is provided by lover's concern. But both these are happy examples, and it is by no means the case that love invariably attracts to itself benign attitudes. Part of the explanation for this lies in the history that love, love as such, characteristically has in our lives. For, unlike friendship, love does not have a history of accumulation, it has a history of substitution. We add one friend to another, but we tend to substitute one lover for another. And this means that love is permanently susceptible to the making of comparisons, the experience of disappointment, the desire to alter, and the insensitivity to differences. We assimilate, either in the mind or in reality, someone whom we now love to someone whom we once loved: we forget what the person whom we now love is like, or we try to change her. And, in refashioning present love upon past love, we forget, as likely as not, what the person whom we once loved was like. Add to this fact that love seems to us of immense importance, and it is not surprising that love should further recruit to itself attitudes that are designed to forestall or to depreciate loss: possessiveness, envy, idealization, and indifference. But to these attitudes love is itself the only antidote.

11. At the core of friendship, as I have characterized it, is acceptance. The friend accepts someone as another person and as the very person that he is. What acceptance involves is the overcoming of confusion, the abatement of intolerance, and the relinquishment of certain controlling attitudes. In the extreme situation that we have been considering, a friend accepts another in the hope that he may thereby come to accept himself. And in ordinary circumstances something of the same sort occurs, though not by design or

intention: being accepted makes it easier for a person to accept himself.

It is clear that this represents an enlargement of the notion of acceptance that figured in Lecture VIII. For there acceptance was largely epistemic, and it was focused principally upon facts. Acceptance, understood in a broader way, impinges heavily upon two of life's great misfortunes, in that its absence precipitates, and the renewed capacity to exhibit it can alleviate, both madness and the loss of friendship: and the question arises whether it also relates to the third, the misfortune of death. Are we in a better position to see what it is to accept death?

I return to Proust for the last time. In his reflections upon his grandmother's death the Narrator isolates the peculiar increment of information that any one of us would acquire if, already believing that he was mortal, he now learnt the time of his death: that it will be at a certain hour on a certain day, every moment of which he has already allotted to some task he has to do. Could it be that this extra detail, this fragment of chronology, which, after all, gives us no more than a more particular version of a belief we already have, is what is required to induce the acceptance of death? Or is it not more likely, the Narrator reflects, that someone who is so haunted by the strangeness, by the *singularité particulière*, of death that he rejects it will find in the very banality of fact that now attaches to death another reason to reject it? The knowledge that death will come to him after, say, a good lunch and a drive through certain familiar streets of the city in which he has always lived will allow him to feel that death is only an ordinary, unremarkable happening in life, which is the one thing that death isn't. Acceptance of a new fact about something that is itself not yet accepted can simply fuel a further exercise of rejection.

Acceptance of the death of a friend or a lover involves at once the acceptance of death and the acceptance of the death of that particular person. The acceptance of the death of a particular person is the acceptance of a fact. It is therefore primarily cognitive, with an affective aura. However the acceptance of death itself is more pervasive: there is no fact on which it is focused, and it therefore involves acceptance in that enlarged sense which the other two misfortunes of life have brought forward. But the acceptance of our own death is not like the acceptance of the death of a friend or lover. When we die, when each one of us dies, a particular person dies, but what is hard to accept about our own death is not the death of that particular person. Within the acceptance of our own death the acceptance of death itself spreads its wings wide: it is a major component.

The thought that death is a misfortune, or the fear of death, never ceases to attract to itself many other thoughts, many other fears, many anxieties, many disappointments. Freud talked in this connection of the fear of castration, exaggerating its role. But at the core of the fear of death is, I have suggested, an appetite and a belief which are in conflict. The appetite is the thirst, the insatiable thirst, for phenomenology, and the belief is a belief about one essential feature of natural specieshood. What the acceptance of death, and by extension a person's acceptance of his own death, must consist in is the harmonisation of the appetite and the belief. In other words, what must take place is the transformation of all desires and all emotions so that there is nothing left to prevent a person from experiencing phenomenology as something inherently, essentially terminable. He enters into his mental states not just as a person but as a mortal person. Some of the Ancients proposed that we should live each moment of our life as though it were our last. To accept death requires that we should live each moment of our life as though it could be our last, or as though the possibility of death was implicit in living. Such a transformation of our dispositions is not calculated to subtract from death the sense of it as a misfortune. Death is a misfortune. It is calculated only to make us feel that the very thing that makes death a misfortune — in effect, living, living as a person — is not dissociable from death.

But does not such a transformation as I talk of, or as the acceptance of death calls for, simply generate an illusion? For is it veridical for us to experience phenomenology as inherently terminable? Of course death does cut short life, but is not death a misfortune just because it is arbitrary, and could not phenomenology in principle go on indefinitely? At this stage I shall simply say that to argue like this is simply to resuscitate the pure concept of living, upon whose viability I cast doubt at the beginning of this lecture.

The transformation that I envisage is not cognitive. So in characterizing it I have not suggested that any of our beliefs needed to be modified by it: though it is certainly the case that our philosophical beliefs must become accountable to it. Nevertheless, much of what I have said in these lectures has been in error unless it is the case that this transformation, in order to be effective, or enduring, must be understood, even as it occurs.

I cite again the passage from Kierkegaard's *Journal* with which I began these lectures and to which I returned halfway through:

It is perfectly true, as philosophers say, that life must be understood backwards. But they forget the other proposition, that it must be lived forwards.

But what Kierkegaard, the Kierkegaard of this *Journal* entry, overlooked is that, for a person, not only is understanding the life he leads intrinsic to leading it, but for much of the time leading his life is, or is mostly, understanding it.

# Name Index

# Subject Index